THE STORY OF SCOTLAND

THE STORY OF
SCOTLAND

Nigel Tranter

Routledge & Kegan Paul
London

First published in 1987 by
Routledge & Kegan Paul Ltd
11 New Fetter Lane, London EC4P 4EE

Published in the USA by
Routledge & Kegan Paul Inc.
in association with Methuen Inc.
29 West 35th Street, New York, NY 10001

Set in Linotron Ehrhardt, 11 on 12pt
by Input Typesetting Ltd, London
and printed in Great Britain
by Billings, Worcester

British Library Cataloguing in Publication Data

Tranter, Nigel
    The story of Scotland.
    1. Scotland—History
    I. Title
    941.1   DA760
    ISBN 0–7102–1035–3

CONTENTS

v

PREFACE

Let there be no mistake about this – I am not setting out to write a history-book. For one thing, I am not a qualified historian – only a story-teller with an interest in history. For another, all too often history-books are dull, dull – and that in my eyes is a crime. How anyone can make history dull and boring is beyond my conception, especially Scotland's history, for history is in fact the most dramatic, colourful and exciting subject under the sun, the very essence of mankind's greatness and weakness, efforts and failures, heroics and cowardices, ambitions, knaveries and follies – indeed everything which story-telling is based upon, the very raw materials of drama, tragedy, comedy, farce. Yet generation after generation of academic historians *have* somehow managed to make history dull for millions of folk, in book and classroom, almost impossible as this may seem, by producing catalogues of dates, births, deaths and marriages, wars, treaties, alliances, movements and so on. All these, to be sure, do make up the skeleton, as it were, of history; but the flesh consists of the stories of men and women like you and me, their trials, temptations, triumphs, treacheries, even tendernesses. If I did not know better – for I have to read endless history-books, woe is me – I would defy anyone to make all that dull.

So this is a story-book, but about real people, folk who lived and died, loved and hated, fought and suffered, laughed and wept, and in doing it all grew into a nation, a great nation which, though small in numbers as nations go, is accepted the world over as amongst the foremost in character and achievement, yes, and folly! The Scots are a very odd people and always have been, a sort of animated contradiction in terms, capable of higher heights and lower depths than most, courageous, adventurous, intemperate, disputatious, romantic – however much they may disclaim it – sentimental, religious in the widest sense, and much more. All of which ensures that their history has to be the reverse of dull, much of it scarcely believable in fact.

I shall try to be as accurate as I know how in my story-telling. But strict accuracy in history is seldom achieved, even by the most learned and prosaic historians. For, if you consider for a moment, all the history-books have to go back and back, quoting this authority and that for their statements, each of which have quoted other authorities further back still, until you get to the original source material. And then you are apt to find that this, the very first account, can be so very suspect. Why? First of all, it very frequently was written by the winners because they had killed the losers; and second it was all too often not even first-hand writing, for so many of the folk who actually *made* the history could not write, and had to go to monks and priests, who could, to get it down. And the said monkish chroniclers all too seldom ventured outside their cloisters and monasteries, so that their accounts of events, especially battles, campaigns, secret deals and plots, and so on, are frequently wildly at odds with reality, as anyone going over ancient battlefields can vouch. And yet they have been quoted as gospel down the ages, as source material, for almost equally cloistered history writers and students. The novelist's first preoccupation, after making his reader want to know what happened next, is the suspension of disbelief – an absolute essential in story-telling. And, believe me, that can be the very hardest of tasks in rewriting so-called received history.

So what follows is, shall we say, an attempt to put the story into history, on a very superficial scale, missing out so much unfortunately – for a nation's story is only to be hinted at in the compass of one very modest volume, especially such an ancient and lively nation as Scotland. It will be to my grief, and probably my well-deserved shame, if, after all this, readers in the end find it dull, likewise. I suppose that I have almost asked for it?

Nigel Tranter
Aberlady

Chapter 1

MISTY ORIGINS

If you are not interested in misty origins, you can skip this.
Yet – you might find something that rings a bell.

Where to begin in trying to tell the long story of Scotland?
In most stories, it is no bad idea to start at the beginning.
But when the beginning is so far back in uncharted time,
and more misty than the Isle of Skye, that is not so easy.
Especially as it is not even Scotland we are really talking
about, for beginnings, but Alba, the Pictish kingdom, Scotland, as such, not being so-called until the ninth century.
And the Picts of Alba claimed to have the most ancient
origins and line of kings in all Christendom, going back
1070 years according to one authority, precisely 1360 years
according to another – not from today, mark you, but from
before that ninth century. Indeed they give the genealogy of
their kings, going backwards from one Cruithne to the Flood
– Cruithne being their own name for their nation, as well as
this king, the Gaelic word *cruithne* meaning wheat-grower,
which is highly significant, implying a settled civilisation of
agriculturalists in an age of hunters, raiders and nomads.
Anyway, this King Cruithne, period somewhat vague, was
mac or son of Cinge, mac Luthtai, mac Parthalan, mac
Agnoinn and so on right back to Japheth mac Noah! So you
see my difficulty?

Who, then, were these Picts of Alba, from whom we have
all descended? They were a Celtic people, for certain, eman-
ating like the rest from that cradle of races, the Euphrates
valley – or the Garden of Eden, if you can believe King
James VI and I – and working their way, in waves of

emigration round the northern Mediterranean shores, into Spain, where they left the Basques, France where they deposited the Bretons, to Ireland, and from there to Cornwall, Wales and Alba, all the Celtic lands. This journey, of course, took untold centuries – but the Celts have long memories, and vivid imaginations. Just when they reached Alba is hard to say, but probably about five hundred years before Christ. Who were there before them we do not know: prehistoric nomads in small numbers, who seem to have stuck to the coasts and lived in caves mainly, leaving only faint traces in bones, pottery and stone implements. Presumably the Picts absorbed them.

Now these Picts, our ancestors, were a fascinating people. (I continue to call them that, although of course we should really say Cruithne; but most folk think of them as Picts – when they think of them at all.) And we all ought to think of them a great deal more than we do, for they, not the Scots, are the stem from which most of us sprang. It was the Romans who gave them the name of Picts, which comes from the Latin *pictor*, a painter, or *picturatus*, painted. There is some dispute as to just what the Romans meant by this name. Some hold that it referred to the Cruithne custom of communicating by means of pictures or symbols, having little or no *written* language, save Oqhams, of which comparatively few examples have survived – and certainly their carved symbol-stones, of which hundreds survive, mysterious and fascinating, lend credence to this theory. Another school of thought believes that the term Pict indicates their ability to weave multi-coloured cloth, that is tartans, which for some reason the non-Celtic peoples never seem to have mastered. Perhaps both apply. The ridiculous canard, propagated by sundry southern scholars, that the Picts were so called because they painted their bodies blue instead of wearing clothes, is too silly to waste time on – although that is what *I* was taught at school. The Pictish race would not have lasted long in Alba's climate if this had been their habit! All the carvings and symbol-stones show them as wearing a variety of clothing, kilts, tunics, priestly robes, even stoles, armour of sorts and so on.

Mention of priests and armour indicates that they were a

religiously-minded folk, but also warriors. They must have been fighting men to have survived their long emigrations intact and to have retained their essential character and not be swallowed up by the peoples they moved amongst. Also to have carried with them their wheat-growing propensities, which is rather wonderful when you come to think of it, for this settled-folk philosophy could so very easily have been lost and the Cruithne become just one more restless, raiding tribe like the Vikings, the Angles, Saxons and Jutes, the Goths, and the Vandals, *et al*. But no, they were *settlers*, and they found their long-looked-for land at last, in Alba, the northern third of the British Isles, and went no further – not for centuries, at any rate, until the New World beckoned their descendants.

This craving for a homeland, so pronounced in the Scots ever since, was part and parcel of the religious character of the Picts – for rovers, raiders, voyagers and nomads seldom have much time for religious thoughts or observances. The Picts, of course, were not Christian when they came, but sun-worshippers, like other Celts. But this sun-worship was a highly advanced system and no crude superstition. Indeed they worshipped the Unknown God as represented by the sun, the giver of light, warmth, health and fertility to the earth. Their stone circles are an enduring monument to their faith, monumental in more than the material sense, for dedicated scholars and mathematicians who have studied those circles – of which there are still literally thousands surviving entire or in part – declare that they are not just set down haphazard on spots convenient of access or in a commanding position, but in fact are all most carefully and scientifically sited for astronomical purposes and geometrically linked with other circles near and far in a most extraordinary fashion, involving a remarkable knowledge of geography, surveying, mensuration and sheer calculation, implying a highly educated technical expertise, connected with the solstices, seasonal variations and timings, calendars and the like, all in the cause of astrological-cum-astronomical knowledge lost to us. Our Pictish forebears were no slouches in the matter of applied technology, even though they did not have the advantage of written text-books, apparently.

The other surviving evidence of both religious and intellectual advancement are the afore-mentioned symbol-stones,
the standing stones as distinct from the stone circles, which
dot our land and which we all take for granted, in farmers'
fields, where they are apt to represent a nuisance and tend
to get dragged away by tractors, on hillsides and moorland
and ridges, even in the grounds of Stirling University. How
we should cherish these sign-posts to our past.

Not all standing stones bore symbols, of course. Most,
probably, are all that remains of stone circles; some are just
rough, isolated monoliths marking the grave of a chief, or
other feature – although by their size, weight and height they
often pose a real problem as to how they were brought there
and erected. Some, of softer stone, may have lost their carved
or incised symbols, weather-worn. But there are many
hundreds with symbols remaining, and more always being
discovered. I well remember the excitement of my late wife
and myself when we found one, not hitherto recorded, in a
remote stone circle on Speyside.

What are these symbols? Well, they remain a mystery to
this day – which is rather extraordinary considering that we
can put a man on the moon and photograph the planets from
orbiting spacecraft, yet cannot decipher our own ancestors'
means of communication. There are many different symbols,
some obviously representational, like animals and birds and
fish, probably the emblems of chiefly or priestly houses, like
coats-of-arms – the boar symbol, for instance, represents the
emblem of the High Kings of Alba, and remained that of
the later Kings of Scots until as late as about 1200, when
William the Lyon changed it to the Lion Rampant whence
he got the by-name of the Lyon. Had he not done so, our
chief herald, the Lyon King of Arms, might have borne a
less dignified-sounding title!

As well as these obvious representations in carved stone
there are the difficult but all the more fascinating ones,
abstract designs repeated time and again all over the land
and clearly of deep significance – but of what? There are
basically a dozen of these, although there are slight modifica-
tions of some. To tell you the names given them by modern
archaeologists will not convey much, probably – the double-

disc-and-Z-rod; the crescent-and-V-rod; the rectangle-and-Z-rod; the flower-pot; the Celtic beast; the mirror-and-comb; and others.

No symbol-stone carries them all, of course. They come in differing combinations, sometimes indeed only one, obviously carrying what the Picts considered to be vital messages. Of them all, only one, the mirror-and-comb, has been allotted a meaning by general consent – and that is that it represents woman, women still being interested in mirrors and combs, even the most liberated. For the rest, your guess is as good as mine. The Celtic beast, sometimes rather stupidly called the Elephant, although its curling lapet or trunk comes from the back of the head, not the front, is highly interesting and decorative. It occurs from the Northern Isles to Galloway, so must have some very general application. Were these religious, dynastic, chiefly or shall we say professional signs? Did they mark graves, battles, holy places, gathering-places, settlements, craft-workshops, or what? Surely here is a branch of knowledge itching to be studied intensively by our Scottish universities? Happily this is now being appreciated.

The symbol-stones, which are the most intriguing pointers to our Pictish ancestors, change character suddenly and most notably, from the seventh century onwards. This, of course, is accounted for by the impact of Christianity. Ninian, a Galloway Pict of royal lineage, born about the mid-fourth century, had brought the Gospel back from a visit to Rome and St Martin of Tours, founding Candida Casa, or the church of Whithorn, in 397. But despite his missionary efforts amongst the southern Picts and people of Strathclyde, sadly he achieved little lasting success, and by a century or so later it was almost as though he had never been. Then, in 563 came Columba and his Brethren, from Ireland, and a great new chapter began.

But before we get to Columba and Iona, it is necessary to say something about another important development for Alba. This was the arrival of the Scots. In the last decade of the fifth century Fergus MacErc and his five brothers came from Dalriata in Ireland and took over the Pictish area of Ergadia, which we now call Argyll, setting up a small kingdom there which they named Dalriada, after their homeland in

Ireland. These were the sons of Erc, son of Eochaid Muin-remar, one of the sub-kings of Ireland, and presumably they found it expediant to emigrate, the Irish always having been a lively and quarrelsome lot. This band of Irish called themselves Scots, allegedly being descended from one Scota, a Pharaoh's daughter who had eloped with a Celtic princeling – and traditionally brought with her to Ireland Jacob's famous pillow of stone, which became the renowned *Lia Faill* or Stone of Destiny, a difficult piece of baggage to encumber themselves with on an elopement! A pinch of salt is probably required here. But at any rate, Fergus MacErc, his brothers and their party called themselves Scots, and seem to have managed to take over the Argyll area without major difficulty; at least there are no records of battles at this stage. No doubt they intermarried with the Picts, who were after all their fellow-Celts. So they set up this sub-kingdom of Dalriada, in Alba, and their successors remained there, apparently happily enough, for nearly four centuries.

It is probably sensible here to explain the kingship situation in the Celtic polity. Without in any way approximating to our modern ideas of democracy, the Celtic ruling structure was never the divine-right, dictatorial hegemony of one monarch. There was a High King elected by the lesser sub-kings, from the ruling house, not necessarily the eldest son of the previous incumbent of the throne, but the most suitable member of the royal family for the task by matrilineal succession, sometimes indeed only a cousin. Obviously this was a much better system than the usual hereditary succession, since weaklings, mental-deficients and other oddities could be by-passed. Also, since the High King was appointed by the *ri*, or lesser kings, in theory he could also be displaced by them, a safeguard against despotic rule.

The Picts used this system, the High King of the Cruithne, or Alba, being appointed by the sub-kings of seven great provinces. These were known as *mormaors*, a composite Gaelic word meaning great-officers. They retained this title of mormaor long after the Pictish polity had become the Scots, indeed right down to the 'Normanisation' period. MacBeth was Mormaor of Ross and Moray before he became King. The seven provinces or sub-kingdoms of Alba over which the mormaors ruled were Fife, Strathearn, Angus, Mar, Moray, Ross and Caithness. Later the mormaors became the Seven Earls of Scotland, still with the privilege of electing the Kings of Scots. Later still three other provinces or Celtic earldoms were added – Buchan (part of Mar), Monteith and Lennox (parts of Strathearn). It will be noted that these are all north of the Forth and Clyde. Alba proper never extended south of that line, although there were Pictish kingdoms there too, the Southern Picts having their capital at Traprain in East Lothian – the name Lothian derives from King Loth of the Southern Picts – and the Galloway Picts being an independent lot, occupying much of south-west Scotland. They later became absorbed, although very uncomfortably and rebelliously, in the Celtic kingdom of Strathclyde – which itself extended well down into what is now England, indeed to the River Ribble, where it more or less merged with the Celtic Welsh.

But for the moment we are concerned with Alba, out of which Scotland grew. The Scots, a comparatively tiny group of immigrants, really only a local aristocracy amongst a Pictish people, were confined to Dalriada, or Argyll, apparently generally on good and intermarrying terms with their Pictish neighbours in the rest of Alba. Then, in 563, came Columba.

Columba was an extraordinary man by any standards. Born in 521, he was of the same Irish royal house as the MacErcs who had founded Dalriada, and was of middle years when he came to Iona. Actually he was also related to the High Kings of Tara, and himself was in line to be offered the throne, indeed was so offered it, twice. His grandmother was a daughter of Lorn MacErc, one of Fergus's brothers. This family background is important in his story. We are not here concerned with his career in Ireland; suffice it to say that he had a prince's education, albeit a Christian one, for his great-grandfather, King of Donegal, had been converted. He grew into a tall and handsome man, fair-haired and well-built, a notable horseman, fond of sports and with a fine singing voice. But he had, it seems, a hot temper. Rejecting the princely life, although not all the privileges thereof, he became a monk – but it must be remembered that the Celtic Church monks were very different from the Romish ones,

7

nowise cut off from the people they lived amongst. He still moved in the Irish aristocracy, but therein sought to put Christian principles into action. He was offered a bishopric but refused it. Nevertheless, as a tireless missionary he was instrumental in founding a number of monasteries in Ireland.

Then he became involved in war, a war between the Christian and the pagan Irish kingdoms. There are a number of stories as to Columba's role in this, into which we will not venture here, since many contradict each other. But involved he was, in a battle in which many died – and whatever part he played, his conscience troubled him thereafter. And not only his conscience, for it seems to have become expedient that he should get out of Ireland, and fairly fast. So is destiny contrived.

Since go he must, it was not unnatural that Columba should look to Alba, where were his Dalriadic kinsfolk. The Mull of Kintyre, in south Argyll, is after all a bare dozen miles from the Antrim coast, well within sight. However, such sight was in fact unwelcome, for whether it was at the dictate of his powerful conscience or of whoever warned him to get out of Ireland, one of the conditions was that he was to go until he could no longer see his native land. So he and his twelve companions set sail in May 563.

These twelve, who became known as the Brethren of St Columba, after the apostolic example, were young Celtic monks and priests from the Abbey of Clonard, where Columba had done much of his training under the great St Finnian, and who looked upon the prince as their leader and had already aided him in the establishment of many Irish monasteries. They included men whose names are familiar to us all in Scotland through the churches which they founded – Brendan's Kilbrennan or Kilbrandon; Earnan's Killearnan; Madoc's Kilmadock; Kenneth's Kilchenzie; Ciaran's Kilchiaron, on Islay; and so on – Kil of course meaning cell or church. Comgal gave his name to Cowal, the southern region of Argyll. Drosten and Moluag are renowned in many areas.

It was not a very long voyage, as to distance, but it took a considerable time. For practically every island in the southern Inner Hebrides, and parts of the contiguous mainland also, has its tradition of Columba landing there, climbing its hills and still being able to see Ireland, and so moving on. But at last, moving northwards all the time, the voyagers came to Iona and, glory be, from this jewel of an island set in a sapphire sea, Ireland was out of sight.

Small wonder that Columba fell in love with Iona and settled there, even with a thousand other isles to choose from, for when the sun shines – and this was May, probably the loveliest month of the year on the Hebridean seaboard – Iona is as near to Heaven as you will find on this round earth, a small gem of heart-breaking beauty, of green machairs and rose-red cliffs, gleaming white cockle shell sands shimmering through aquamarine water with multi-hued seaweeds, rocky coves and small but striking hills, its pastures a riot of wild flowers, to the east and north the blue mountains of the great neighbouring island of Mull and to the west and south the isle-dotted sea of the Hebrides. In winter storms and grey skies it can be otherwise, admittedly – but this was May, with the cuckoos calling hauntingly, the gorse blazing golden and the bluebells dancing in the breeze. So what was to become Scotland's equivalent of Westminster Abbey was chosen.

There was more than beauty and the no-sight-of-Ireland to recommend Iona – a lovely name in itself, although perhaps its original simple name of I, *the* island of them all, is best. The Sound of Mull was nearby, the most effective and strategic waterway of all that seaboard, leading into the intricately cut-up coastline of the north Argyll and Lochaber mainland and the inner isles; it was part of the MacErcs' Dalriada; and it already had a Christian background, for here St Oran, an earlier Irish missionary, had made his base to preach to the Dalriadic Scots, and here he had died fourteen years before Columba came, and was buried, his tomb being called the Reelig Oran, the reliquary or grave of Oran – as still it is. Oran could not know that he was going to have such resounding neighbours to lie beside his earthly remains, for the Reelig Oran, in time to come, was to be the burial-place of forty-eight Kings of Scots, Dalriadic or Pictish, four Kings of Ireland, eight Kings or Princes of Norway, one King of France and one of Northumbria.

So here Columba and his Brethren settled down to build

their abbey and cashel, as the Celtic monasteries were called, a very simple and unambitious establishment by Romish standards, consisting of a rath, or earthen rampart and stockade, within which was the cille or kil or church, itself quite a humble edifice of wood and turf, more used to shelter the sacred vessels, font and communion elements and bells than to worship in – for much of the Celtic Church worship was done outdoors. Also, of course, they built the turf and stone beehive cells of the monks' living-quarters and a larger hutment for eating in, from a great flat stone as table – which is still there. No soaring cathedrals, cloisters, refectories, dormitories and the like for the Columban clergy; these things were man-made, and they preferred God's own creation to worship in.

They set up a self-supporting community, gathering helpers locally, until there were about 150 of them – and were then ready to do what they had come for, driven on by that conscience of Columba's, which was not to institute any establishment, however admirable, but to go and convert Alba to Christianity.

I am spending perhaps overmuch of my available space on Columba; but he was, by any reckoning, one of the truly great, and a person who had the most major influence on Scotland's story, to rank with, if not above, MacBeth, Margaret, David the First, Wallace, Bruce, James the Fourth, John Knox and the others.

He died in 597, so he had thirty-four years for his mighty task, and succeeded almost beyond any other missionary effort since Christ's own first apostles, for his influence extended far beyond Alba, and his Columban Church was to endure as Scotland's Kirk for 500 years. In his efforts he was much helped, undoubtedly, by his royal blood and authoritative nature, which enabled him to approach easily, argue with and convince and convert kings, chiefs and great ones. But also he had the common touch and a most realistic attitude towards religion and worship. Unlike the Celtic nobles, he insisted on working always with his own hands, building, ploughing, milling, humping sacks of grain, digging holy wells, carpentering like his Master – all of which endeared him to the ordinary folk. He was a great believer in the if you can't beat them, join them school of advocacy, recognising that the druidical sun-worship religion prevailing had a lot of good in it, not condemning it wholesale but using it to integrate into Christian worship. For instance he accepted the stone circles as the traditional open-air Pictish places of worship and, adopting them, placed his churches *within* the circles – and today, in Aberdeenshire, you will still find old parish churches and kirkyards within ancient circles of standing-stones. Indeed, the Scots word Kirk, for church, is held by some to derive from the word for circle. He used the pagan festivals, particularly at the New Year and Midsummer, when folk were accustomed to be in holiday mood, as Christian feast-days. And so on. The Picts, to be sure, like their descendants ever since, were an essentially religious-minded and metaphysically-conscious people, so he had good material to work on.

Stories and legends of Columba are legion, of course, many of them added to and embroidered with miracles and unlikely happenings as the ages passed – which would not have pleased the saint, for he was essentially a very practical man. All know how he journeyed, with Comgal and Kenneth, to Inverness, over 100 miles, in 565, and converted Brude mac Maelchon, High King of the Picts, a major victory in Christ's cause. Columba became Brude's *amn chara*, soul-friend and remained so for twenty years, an enormous help in his task. In 574 he ordained Aidan as King of Dalriada at Iona, almost certainly on the Stone of Destiny, which the Scots had brought to Argyll allegedly but which may well have been Columba's own portable altar and font. He turned his attention to the Southern Picts also, in Lothian, and like all the Celtic missionaries, with a fondness for islands, seems to have made his base on the isle of Inchcolm, still called after him, in the Firth of Forth.

Islands inevitably feature largely in the stories about Columba, especially the more picturesque tales. For instance, there is the one about Lismore, that highly attractive isle off the Appin coast of the Firth of Lorn – its name means the Great Garden – which Columba and his disciple and friend St Moluag both were ambitious to claim for Christ. Approaching it in their curraghs, it became a race between

them, and when it looked as though Columba's boat was
going to touch the shore first, Moluag picked up an axe,
chopped off his little finger and hurled this ashore, shouting
that *his* flesh and blood was thus first ashore on Lismore.
Here St Moluag's shrine developed and eventually became
the seat of the Bishopric of Argyll.

Then there is the tale about Tiree, that low-lying island
which Columba made the granary for Iona and its growing
population, and of which he approved sufficiently to bless it
to the effect that no evil thing, snake, frog, toad or weasel
should ever abide there – and none do, to this day, it is
claimed.

In 597, then, the spirited Columba went to his rest, and
no doubt to cause all sorts of upheavals and improvements
in Paradise, leaving Alba firmly Christian and his surviving
disciples and their successors carrying on the good work from
Iona – a work which is still going on, the Iona Community an
active force in the Church in Scotland, and the isle itself,
with its Abbey and shrines and magnificent Celtic high-
crosses, a magnet for pilgrims, tourists and ordinary visitors
from all over the world. Surely few who have been there can
ever come away unenriched.

Alba and Dalriada of the Scots continued to co-exist side-
by-side with only occasional friction – although we read of
one of the Scots kings being slain by the Picts. In fact
there were times when *Pictish* kings reigned at Dunadd, the
Dalriadic capital; but there was never real war between the
two so unevenly-divided peoples. Records are very misty
indeed for the period after Columba's death, the king-lists
vague and contradictory. Until 843, that is, nearly 250 years.
Then Kenneth MacAlpin, King of Dalriada, became High
King of the Picts also, and a new and significant dispensation
began.

There are a lot of mysteries about this great event, just
how it came about, even exactly who Kenneth was. He was
Alpin's son, yes, and appears to have been King of the Scots
for two years before he ascended the Pictish throne. But who
was Alpin? There are doubts whether *he* was ever King of
Dalriada – some versions of the king-lists do not mention
him at all, and others are thought possibly to have inserted

him afterwards, to legitimise Kenneth's later position. But we do know that Kenneth was a great and successful warrior – and this is probably the key to it all. You see, this was the period of the terrible Viking invasions, at least their beginnings, and both Dalriada and Alba were suffering. We know that two of the Pictish kings, cousins, were killed by the Norsemen in 839, and were succeeded in quick succession by Constantine and then Oengus, more cousins. The fact that Kenneth came and took over only four years later makes it look as though these two died also, probably at Norse hands. Kenneth, it is usually asserted, had earlier married Constantine's daughter and heiress, and presumably this was more or less the end of the ancient Pictish royal line. Kenneth had been successful in driving the Viking invaders from the Dalriadic coasts; what more natural and suitable than that this able general, married to the Pictish heiress – and remember that the Picts had a strong matrilineal tradition – should be appointed to take over the vacant throne of Alba, in order to drive out the Norse there also?

It is usually asserted in the history-books that Kenneth MacAlpin *conquered* the Picts. This is manifestly absurd, for the Dalriadic Scots did not represent 5 per cent of the Pictish population of Alba, and their army would never be in a position to take over their host-country. Moreover Dalriada, at this time, was in a weakened state, with internal dissensions, feuding amongst members of the royal house, and Norse invasion. Kenneth did have to fight some minor battles against Pictish chiefs, who presumably disapproved of him, but clearly the Pictish people as a whole accepted him – after all, he had sons, half-Pictish, grandsons of Constantine, to follow on. And Dalriada had been a sub-kingdom of Alba for four centuries. And to become the High King he must have had the support of the seven great Pictish mormaors.

What is a great mystery, however, is why thereafter the Picts started to call themselves Scots rather than Cruithne, and their kingdom Scotland instead of Alba. This probably happened only gradually; but happen it did, strange indeed considering that the Picts represented 95 per cent of the population and the mormaors remained the ruling council. All seems to have gone on as before, however, the Norse were held at bay and Kenneth reigned for sixteen years, to be succeeded at his death in 858 by his brother Donald, for four years, and then by his son, another Constantine.

This change of names and style, from High King of the Cruithne to High King of Scots, and from Alba to Scotland, was an extraordinary matter by any standards. Yet it does not seem to have worried the professional historians; I have never seen it even referred to in their books. But it certainly intrigues me. From now on it is *Scotland's* story.

Chapter 2

ALBA INTO SCOTIA

Two hundred years is a long time, even in a nation's story. Yet the two centuries from Kenneth MacAlpin's reign onwards fall to be very sketchily described indeed, so scanty are the recorded details. Not that little was happening, mind you – on the contrary, too much was happening, most of it bloody, as is witnessed to by the great number of kings who succeeded each other during that period, most of whom were lucky to reign for four or five years, some for only one or two, indicating battle, murder and sudden death as normal conditions prevailing.

There were three main sources of trouble. First and foremost the continuing Norse invasions and raids, coming now not only from Scandinavia but from Orkney, Shetland, Iceland and the Viking colonies established on the east side of Ireland. These Norsemen were devils, savage killers glorying in war, slaying their way endlessly round northern Europe, uninterested in settlement, only in bloodshed, booty, rapine and women. Hosting, they termed it, and every spring the longships set out on their voyages of conquest, but not conquest for any reason other than blood-lust and loot, the scourge of the North. What was the reason behind this continual savagery of the Norsemen and Danes at this period is hard to say. But obviously they considered it to be their due role in life, a sort of crusade of death. Yet they were not trying to build an empire, nor spread a way of living, nor a faith, only enjoying themselves and pursuing their hosting with a crazy enthusiasm, the world's finest seamen and toughest warriors, making heroic songs and sagas out of their endless killings, apparently conscienceless, devising ever more elaborate and imaginative methods of destruction. Their imagination is exemplified by their habit of dealing with the slain, after one of their attacks, cutting off the heads, washing the blood from the faces, combing and even plaiting the hair and beards, and then hanging up the heads by the hair in neat rows on walls and stockades. What they did to the women is not for description here; and children received no mercy. It was, of course, a barbarous age – but the Norsemen were beyond all. They terrorised Scotland for centuries.

That was one source of continual warfare. Another was the English, or at least the petty kingdoms which then made up what is now England. These were also suffering from the Danes, but at this time began the process, which was to continue down the centuries, of turning their attentions northwards in attempted conquest, particularly towards Lothian, a fair and fertile land and ripe for being taken over, the Southern Picts being less numerous and warlike than those of Alba. And this of course provoked retaliation from the Scots. If all this was not enough, the Scots were all too ready to fight amongst themselves, a characteristic which prevails to the present day, if no longer usually to the effusion of blood!

So the scanty records of these two centuries tell us little save of wars, battles, assassinations – and the names of kings, sixteen of them until, with Malcolm II, the Destroyer, we reach more detailed history. Here they are – mere names, yes: Donald, Kenneth's brother; Constantine II; Aed; Eochaid; Giric; Donald II; Constantine III; Malcolm; Indulf; Dubh or Duffus; Culen; Kenneth II; Constantine IV; Gryme; Kenneth III; Giric II; Malcolm II. Names, yes – but interesting at least in that they are almost all Pictish, be it noted, rather than Dalriadic Scots names. Yet they and their mainly short reigns can mean little to us, for lack of information – save that many of them killed their predecessors.

Only a few tales and stories have survived to put, as it were, flesh upon these royal bones of the tenth and eleventh centuries. We hear that one of them, a Constantine I think it was, after having slain a Norse chief, in good retaliatory fashion cut off the Viking's head and hung it at his saddle-bow. However, the Norseman laughed last, in that he had a projecting tusk of a tooth, and this, the head bouncing with the horse's trotting, dug into the King's bare knee – presumably he was wearing a kilt of sorts – and, puncturing the skin, set up blood-poisoning from which the monarch died. There surely is a moral here, somewhere?

Then there was the case of Dubh or Duffus, who was assassinated in 967 at his own castle of Forres, and his body taken and hidden under the bridge at Kinloss. Everyone was much upset, mainly apparently because the sun did not rise until the body was found. Astronomers tell us that there was an eclipse of the sun that month of that year.

Again, in 994, Kenneth III died dramatically at Fettercairn in The Mearns. Apparently he had had occasion to kill Malcolm, son of the Mormaor of Angus, for good reasons or ill, and the young man's mother, the beautiful Finella, noted as a witch, thirsted for vengeance. She had a brass statue made in the likeness of the King, which held in one hand a golden apple studded with gems. She then lured Kenneth to her house at Fettercairn to view this wonder. There she told him that it was made in his honour, and that he would further honour her, his humble servant, if he would graciously accept the precious apple. When the King reached out to take it, a hidden mechanism was released which shot out poisoned arrows which killed Kenneth. The lady, needless to say, came to a grisly end thereafter.

These tales have to serve us in lieu of more factual history. But some substantial information has come down to us, typically via the Church – which of course could produce writers to tell us. We learn that Iona had to be abandoned, after continued savage raids and massacres by the Norsemen. Most of the precious treasures which had accumulated there, relics, vessels of gold, manuscript gospels and the like, were removed to Ireland, to Kells and Derry, for safe-keeping – an interesting indication that the Irish Church was still looked upon as the Mother-Church – and the functioning head-quarters of the Columban faith moved inland to Dunkeld in Atholl and then to Scone, well away from the wretched Vikings. The Stone of Destiny went from Dunadd likewise.

Possibly for the same reason, or merely that it was more central for the government of the kingdom, Kenneth MacAlpin moved his capital southwards from Inverness to Forteviot in Fortrenn, the area around Perth – which was holy as well as convenient, for this was where the land triumphed over the sea, in other words where the River Tay's fresh water overcame the tidal salt-water of that great estuary, significant to our forefathers, especially in view of the Norse menace which came by sea. So Scotland gained a more practical centre – although clearly the Forres and Moray Firth area remained very important for the rulers, no doubt largely because this was the heartland of Moray, by far the most important of the mormaordoms, then much larger than today's county.

Thus we come down to less misty times. We know more about Malcolm Forranach, the Destroyer, for three main reasons: he won the Battle of Carham, in 1018, whereby he gained Lothian from the Northumbrians who had over-run and annexed it; second, it so happened that he reigned at the same time as the renowned King Canute; third, because of his successor, Shakespeare's 'venerable Duncan'.

Malcolm II was a very tough character indeed, who had slashed his way to the throne by killing others nearer to it, hence his by-name of the Destroyer. And he managed to hold on to that throne for twenty-nine years, 1005 to 1034, phenomenal for those days. And the Battle of Carham maintains his reputation. But oddly, the other two items for which he is best-known were scarcely either heroic or tough. King Canute, or Knud as he was really named, the Dane who had taken over the English petty kingdoms, was an able character of bounding ambition. He had started to call himself Emperor of the Anglo Saxons and Danes, and was looking around for new domains to add to his empire. Scotland seemed an obvious candidate, and Canute marched north with a great army. Malcolm and the Scots waited for him at that most blessed barrier, Scotland's moat, behind which so many other defenders were to wait down the ages, the Forth at Stirling. This was the first point where the long Forth estuary might be bridged, and with all the soft and flooded marshlands of the upper Carse of Forth westwards, right to the Highland fastnesses at Aberfoyle, impassable for armies. Any invasion of Alba, Scotland north of Forth, had to cross at Stirling; and behind the narrow bridge was a mile of bog and flooded land, spanned by a single narrow causeway, which could be easily defended. These features are still there, and though the Carse is now drained, the village at the north end of the causeway from Stirling Bridge is still called Causewayhead; and the far western end of the Carse is still a vast waterlogged waste, the Flanders Moss, now designated a nature-reserve.

So Malcolm waited there for Canute – and this is one of the first occasions when the young MacBeth, Malcom's grandson, appears to play a part on the national scene when, as Mormaor of Moray and Ross, he brought the armed strength of those two provinces to his grandsire's aid.

Well, the scene was set for a great battle, the Scots outnumbered but in a strong defensive position. But only a minor skirmish developed, with Canute trying out the defences, losing a number of men, and recognising the realities of the situation. However warlike and ambitious, he was a shrewd general and perceived that although he probably could defeat the Scots eventually, especially if he took time to gather boats, and ferried his armies across the Forth further eastwards, it would be at great cost in men and would take much time. And Malcolm recognised this too, being likewise shrewd. So they agreed to parley, however undramatic for seasoned warriors that might seem. Talking, Canute wanted Malcolm to accept him as overlord – a mere form of words, he declared, that was all, which would not affect Malcolm's position at all, etcetera. The King of Scots refused; but when Canute pointed out that he already had over-run and held Lothian, the Merse, Teviotdale and the rest, won by Malcolm only sixteen years before at Carham, Malcolm faced the undoubted fact that he could not oust Canute from these; and he agreed to pay fealty and tribute of one serf, one cow, one horse, and one bushel of meal for those parts only, certainly not for his ancient inheritance, Scotland proper north of Forth, old Alba. So the fatal oath of fealty was taken, something which meant little or nothing to Malcolm and his mormaors, but which was to echo down Scotland's story nevertheless for six centuries, as precedent for English kings' claims to paramountcy over Scotland, even though it even then only applied to Lothian, the Merse and Teviotdale, the first germ of an enduring plague.

Malcolm's other claim to fame, which he would scarcely be anxious to have broadcast either, was that he had produced no sons, only two daughters. And there were no brothers, cousins and kinsmen near the throne – he had seen to that, most bloodily. So his possible heirs were three grandsons. Bethoc, the elder daughter, had married Crinan, Mormaor of Atholl and Abbot of Dunkeld, hereditary Primate of the Columban Church. Something falls to be be said about this last. The Celtic Church did not insist upon celibacy in its priests, abbots and bishops, and gradually hereditary lines of upper clergy developed, rather like the Levites of the Children of Israel. This situation was strengthened by the need to defend the churches and monasteries against the invading Norse, so that it paid to have warrior bishops and abbots and their clansmen. When Iona eventually had to be abandoned, and the move was made to central Dunkeld in Atholl, the Mormaors of Atholl found themselves protectors of the Church's headquarters. Indeed Dunkeld had been chosen because it *was* the seat of the Mormaor. As well as that, as its name implies, it was the dun or seat of the Keledi – the Friends of God, a name which has become corrupted to Culdees. This was a powerful sect of ever-growing influence within the Celtic Church, starting as a reforming group, similar to the Benedictines and Franciscans in the Romish Church, strong on doctrine, a sort of Church within a Church. So Crinan of Atholl inherited the protection of the Columban faith, and a dominant position amongst the Keledi. This had its importance in what followed. He and Bethoc had a son, Duncan.

The other daughter of Malcolm, Donada, married the Earl Sigurd the Stout, of Orkney, no doubt a diplomatic union in an attempt to keep at least the Orkney Vikings at arm's length. This couple had a son also, who became one of the most famous Vikings of all time, Thorfinn Raven-Feeder, Earl of Orkney, of whom the sagas endlessly sing. He was Malcolm's grandson also, and he made him Earl of Caithness – which Orkney more or less already controlled – at the age of five, the first earl in the Scottish polity but of course also a mormaor. His father, Earl Sigurd, was killed at the famous Battle of Clontarf, in Ireland, and the boy Thorfinn succeeded as Earl of Orkney and Caithness. His mother, Donada, still a young woman, married again, this time Finlay, Mormaor of Moray and Ross, the most powerful noble in Scotland. They produced MacBeth mac Finlay, another grandson for the King.

So these were the possible heirs to the Scots throne – although Thorfinn could probably be ruled out, for the Scots would be loth indeed to accept a Viking as their monarch. But the other two were wholly Scots and sons of mormaors. For some reason, Malcolm favoured Duncan. Why is not clear, for Duncan mac Crinan was a nasty piece of work by any reckoning and moreover was presumably a haemophiliac or 'bleeder', for his by-name was Ilgarach or Bad-Blooded. He was the elder princess's son, of course. But MacBeth had an advantage too, for he was married to Gruoch, who was higher in the Scots royal line than any of them, even Malcolm himself. She was the daughter of Bodhe, who had died young and granddaughter of Kenneth III, whom Malcolm had slain in his scramble for the throne, as he had killed her brother, the former a son of King Dubh or Duffus, responsible for that eclipse of the sun. So Gruoch had a tragic background but a most royal one. Incidentally, MacBeth's name is not always understood. That was his *Christian* name, even though starting with a mac – *Mac-Beatha*, Son of Life, the *beatha* being the same as in *uisge-beatha*, of whisky, water-of-life.

Well, when Malcolm died at a great age, Duncan succeeded as King of Scots, not MacBeth – and, as his grandfather ought to have known, made a very bad king from the start. He led a great, inadvisable and disastrous expedition into England, challenging Canute. Repulsed, he turned his attentions northwards and demanded of his cousin, the Earl Thorfinn, that he paid him tribute and tax for his mortuaths of Caithness and Sutherland, and when the Raven-Feeder told him in no uncertain terms what he could do about it, Duncan marched north, allegedly to teach Thorfinn a lesson, but more essentially to attack MacBeth in Moray, *en route*, for he and his other cousin had never been friends and he presumably saw him as a menace.

There is not the least evidence that MacBeth was contemplating any rising against Duncan; but when the latter came marching through his territories with fire and sword, he could not stand idly by. Moreover Thorfinn was his half-brother and ally. Thorfinn had a toehold on Moray soil, at Burghead, near Forres, or Torfness as it was then called, where his fleet of longships could base. Duncan made for Torfness and Thorfinn and MacBeth waited for him, although not together, the latter loth actually to attack the crowned King of Scots who had sat on the Stone of Destiny. Not so Thorfinn, who roundly repulsed Duncan's army.

But Duncan had an ally too, one Echmarcach, King of Dublin, an enemy of Thorfinn's, whom he had summoned to his aid. He came, belatedly, also burning and slaying, from the west. This was too much for MacBeth. Duncan and Echmarcach were about to join forces at the River Lossie, near Elgin, MacBeth's Moray force in between. To prevent a junction, MacBeth attacked Duncan's retiring force, and true to the notions of the age, personally fought his way to Duncan's own position. There the two cousins fought it out, sword to sword. Both were wounded, but Duncan the more seriously. And he was a 'bleeder'. He was taken to Bothgowan, a blacksmith's forge near Elgin, and there he died. His army disintegrated thereafter, and Echmarcach retired whence he had come.

This, then, was the 'murder of the venerable Duncan' about which Will Shakespeare wrote, and translated into brilliant drama, to the delight of misled audiences ever since the seventeenth century – Duncan was in fact only twenty-seven years old. Shakespeare took it, of course, partly from Hollinshed, an English chronicler, but mainly at the behest and almost the dictation of King James VI and I, who was anxious to 'improve the image of the Scots in London', his own included, where he was known as the Scotch Monkey. James seemed to think that a popular play was the way to do it, and a comedy being unthinkable in the circumstances, a tragedy was indicated. Since he descended, however remotely, from Duncan rather than MacBeth, the latter

became the villain. Also, the objective was to institute an
entirely mythical Stewart link with the ancient Celtic
monarchy, so Banquo was invented. Lastly he was anxious
to score off his queen, Anne of Denmark, with whom he
could not get on; so the female in the play had to be a fiend
in human form – Lady MacBeth. Why the inoffensive Queen
Gruoch should be demoted for all time to be Lady MacBeth,
Shakespeare and James alone know. She seems to have been
a fine and much-wronged woman, and certainly had nothing
to do with Duncan's death in action.

Duncan had married a daughter of the Earl of Northumbria and produced two sons, Maelmuir and Donald Ban. But
before that he had fathered a son on a woman only known
to history as 'the miller of Forteviot's daughter'; and though
illegitimate, he was named Malcolm after his great-
grandfather.

In the choice of the next monarch, these two legitimate
princes were passed over by the mormaors, as children and
therefore useless at leading a beleagured nation, and
MacBeth was appointed King, Thorfinn apparently not
desiring to be considered for the throne, preferring the
Viking's roving life anyway. But he remained his brother's
ally throughout.

So MacBeth's reign began, and a most notable reign it
proved to be. He seems to have been the first King of Scots
to perceive that he had other responsibilities than warfare
and the defence of the kingdom. He was an able fighter,
certainly, but his reign is renowned not for its battles so
much as for his institution of the rule of law, after a regular
system, something scarcely considered hitherto. The Laws
of MacBeth, with the machinery he set up to carry them out,
represent the first really civilising influence on a govern-
mental scale which Scotland had experienced, other than that
of the Church. MacBeth indeed supported the Columban
Church and it supported him. He reigned for seventeen
years, ably backed by his wife, who had a notably important
influence, not only as the closest representative of the more
ancient royal line, but as the mother of the next king-to-be.
Something of MacBeth's quality is shown forth in this matter,
for Gruoch, as a girl, had been married before she wed

MacBeth, to one Gillacomgain, who had actually slain Finlay, MacBeth's father, and made himself Mormaor of Moray in his place. By Gillacomgain Gruoch had a son, Lulach. Gillacomgain himself was soon killed off by Malcolm the Destroyer. Thereafter MacBeth wed the widow with the infant son. Now MacBeth produced three sons of his own by Gruoch, but all along appears to have recognised that Lulach had the better right to the throne, as Gruoch's eldest son. So he had all the arrangements made that, when he died, he should be succeeded by his step-son not by any of his own sons. There can have been few examples of this sort in history – especially as Lulach was a strange, withdrawn character and difficult.

But however good and selfless MacBeth's intentions, there were other influences at work. Duncan's two legitimate sons seem to have been quite content to live quietly in their mother's county of Northumbria; not so the bastard Malcolm – who had a very big head for his body and was nicknamed Canmore, *ceann-mhor*, or Big Head. He grew up with a very different nature, tough, ruthless, ambitious, like his great-grandfather and namesake. Despite his illegitimacy, he was determined that he should have the Scots throne; and the new Earl of Northumbria, Siward the Dane, a cousin of Canute, recognised that he could use Malcolm as catspaw to gain Scotland for himself.

So the latter part of MacBeth's reign was plagued with trouble from England. There were constant battles, notably the great one fought at the confluence of the River Earn with Tay, in 1054, at which Earl Siward's own son was killed, and which left MacBeth not defeated but direly weakened. And we all know what happened after that. Malcolm Big Head, with English support again, invaded north of Tay whilst MacBeth and the Scots were still licking their wounds, and this time the invader showed a genius for one aspect of war, the first occasion we read of where camouflage played an important part in warfare. Making his way to his grandfather Crinan's mortuath of Atholl, always somewhat hostile to MacBeth and his Moray line, Malcolm conceived the idea of advancing his army secretly southwards to MacBeth's seat of Dunsinane by means of his troops all carrying birch branches and moving very slowly, so that they would not be apparent to the look-outs until they were in a position to launch a sudden and unexpected assault. This was the famous occasion when Birnam Wood came to Dunsinane.

In his weakened state, and taken by surprise, MacBeth was in no condition to win this battle. But it was not utter disaster and he escaped from the field and fled northwards with a few of his friends, aiming for Moray where he could raise another army from his own folk. But it was not to be. Pursued hotly by Malcolm, and wounded, he was overtaken at Lumphannan in Aberdeenshire, so near home and aid, and was cut down actually by the MacDuff Earl of Fife, one of his own mormaors, with Malcolm Canmore standing by watching.

So ended the best reign in early Scots histroy. Lulach the stepson mounted the throne in succession, but really only in name, and six months later he also was hunted down and slain by Malcolm Canmore, and a new chapter began. Thorfinn, Earl of Orkney, had died a few years before — otherwise history might indeed have been very different.

Chapter 3

MARGARET AND
THE WILL OF GOD

The reign of Malcolm III was an extraordinary one also, significant and most formative for Scotland; but that was not on account of Canmore himself, who was something of a boor, bloodthirsty and without statesmanlike qualities. His one delight was in raiding, pillage, slaughter – and considering that he had been brought up in Northumbria, it is rather odd that this was his favourite stamping-ground for rapine and wholesale savagery, without apparently any specific ambition to annexe Northumbria itself. Perhaps as child and youth he had suffered for his illegitimacy at the Northumbrian court, and felt the need to settle old scores?

At any rate, it was on one of these Northumbrian raids, in 1070, that he met his fate – just as, on another, many years later, he was to meet his end. He had reached Wearmouth, now a suburb of Sunderland, when a great storm blew into the haven there some sea-battered ships, taking shelter. And on one of them was Edward Atheling, the true heir to the English throne, grandson of the Saxon King Edmund Ironside and grand-nephew of Edward the Confessor, with his Hungarian mother and two sisters, Margaret and Christina. It should perhaps be explained that this was four years after the Norman conquest of England, with William the Conqueror consolidating his hold. Edward the Atheling, from exile in Hungary where his mother was a daughter of the saintly King Stephen, had made a bid to rouse the Saxons and eject the Conqueror, but this had failed. Fleeing, from the Humber estuary, for Hungary again, the storm had caught the ships, and the fugitives ran into the mouth of the Wear. And ran into the hands of Malcolm Canmore also.

What might have happened to the Atheling, his mother and the other sister, had it not been for Margaret, is a matter for debate. But the rough and brutal Malcolm fell headlong for the beautiful and talented Margaret, an extraordinary situation. And the story of Scotland was to undergo one of its most profound changes of direction.

It falls to be pointed out here that Malcolm was already married. His queen was none other than the daughter of the now dead Thorfinn Raven-Feeder, named Ingebiorg; and no doubt Malcolm had married her to try to ensure non-interference in his affairs by the Orkney Vikings – as his great-aunt Donada had been married to Earl Sigurd seventy years before. By Ingebiorg, Malcolm had two sons, Duncan and Donald. However, this does not in any way seem to have inhibited his appetite for Margaret Atheling.

Now Margaret was a strong, complex and interesting character, as well as beautiful – all that Malcolm was not – and notably religious. They were a very religious family: her mother the Princess Agatha was pious to a fault, her sister Christina became an abbess, and Margaret herself always carried about with her a fragment of Christ's true cross – or so it was believed to be – given her by her grandfather King and Saint Stephen of Hungary; this became known, in time, as the Black Rood of Scotland, and from it Holyrood takes its name.

Malcolm's advances did not get much encouragement from the young woman, but her clear-eyed strength of character seems to have prevented him from merely taking what he desired, as was his use and wont. In the end, once the storm had subsided, he sent all the Athelings up to Scotland, to his capital of Dunfermline, in the patched-up ship, semi-prisoners. Incidentally, the Hungarian captain of the vessel was one Maurice, from whom the Drummonds are descended. Malcolm went on with his Northumbrian terror.

Queen Ingebiorg received the refugees at Dunfermline and looked after them until the King returned. Just what happened than is not recorded, but the next we hear is that Ingebiorg and her two sons were banished from Dunfermline to the royal castle of Kincardine – the same whence Kenneth III had been lured to his death by Finella. Shortly afterwards, although still a young woman, the Queen died 'not without suspicion of poison', and next year Malcolm married Margaret.

Now it is only fair to say that Margaret probably was entirely innocent of any collusion in the matter of Ingebiorg. She did not *want* to marry Malcolm – indeed his manners and character must have been obnoxious to her. But she and her family were entirely in his power, and she believed it to be her Christian duty. You see, she was convinced that God had sent her to Scotland. After all, when they set sail from the Humber, Scotland was the last place the Athelings intended to reach. Yet here she was, and in a position to become Queen of this strange northern realm. Why had God sent her here? Surely to reform this land's heretical Columban Church and bring it into the true fold of Rome – it could be nothing else. So Margaret conceived this to be her appointed life's work – and for that young woman, this was sufficient to drive her through all opposition and hell itself.

Theirs was an extraordinary marriage. She did not manage to change Malcolm, and he remained the bloodthirsty robber-king to the end; but he also remained passionately attached to his beautiful and so able wife. He let her do more or less what she wanted – so long as she did not interfere with his warlike pleasures. They had six sons in quick succession – and not one of them bore a Celtic and traditional name, all were Saxon, which is surely highly significant – Edward, Ethelred, Edmund, Edgar, Alexander and David. The two older princes by Ingebiorg were banished to the remote Highlands.

Very quickly Scotland began to feel the impact of Margaret Atheling. She civilised the semi-barbarous court of Malcolm. She encouraged trade and manufacture and the arts. She sought to improve the conditions of the poor and serfs. She imported craftsmen – also, of course, Romish clergy. She became greatly beloved by the common folk, even if eyed distinctly warily by the military aristocracy.

But above all, she focussed her attentions upon the Celtic

Church, determined to change its entire direction, worship and image. It is astonishing that any one woman could contemplate such a task – but little was beyond Saxon Margaret and her sublime faith that God had sent her. She built Dunfermline Abbey, beside the palace-castle, the first major stone church in Scotland – and installed Romish priests therein, from England. She actually restored Iona's burnt abbey, even if in very different fashion from heretofore, in stone. She set about trying to convert the Columban clergy – and found the Keledi hard nuts to crack. But she personally debated with them in public, unheard-of behaviour for a woman, on what she considered the errors of their faith – and she was eloquent, informed and sincere, never doubting the rightness of her own point of view. A pity that Columba was not there to argue with her – that would have been a duel of wits, faith and determination indeed. But Columba's successors, after 500 years, were of feebler frame.

It is interesting for us, from today's stance, to consider what were Margaret's main objections to Columban Christianity, apart from the fact that it did not recognise the overlordship of the Pope in matters spiritual. There were three main heresies, in her eyes. First and foremost, that the Celtic Church celebrated Easter on the wrong date. This may sound almost incredible to our ears as a basis for damning a whole Church, especially when the reasons for the Romish argument are considered – but from the Popes down this was held to be vital, at that period. The contention was this – that the period of Lent, the preparation for Good Friday and Easter, should represent Christ's forty days in the wilderness overcoming His temptations. This, of course, was accepted by the Columbans, and they made *their* Easter Sunday forty days after the beginning of Lent. But the Romans declared that this was a miscalculation. For the forty-day period necessarily included five or six Sundays. And Sundays, they held, could not be fast days. So that it was forty *fast* days which should precede the Feast of Easter – in other words, forty-six days altogether, when Sundays were included. I do not think that the Vatican went so far as to suggest that Christ Himself had broken his fast each seventh day, in the wilderness; but His Church, in considering Sunday as a feast-day, could not include Sundays in the fasting period of Lent. So forty-six days it was, and there was a week out in the celebrations of Easter between the Celtic Church and the rest of Christendom.

Your opinion on this is as good as mine – but that is neither here nor there. Such was Margaret's principal stumbling-block.

There were others, of course. The dispensing of holy communion in two kinds to the ordinary worshippers was another grievance. The Columbans gave their flock bread and wine, but the Romans gave only the bread, the celebrant and priests alone sipping the wine. Just what was, and is, the argument behind this one-element dispensing I have never fully discovered, despite asking Roman Catholic priests. If it was that wine could be expensive, then that was surely a matter for individual congregations and celebrants? If the wine represents the blood of Christ, why should the ordinary worshipper be denied it, when possibly in more need of it than the priests? Still, that was the system in which Margaret had been brought up, and she saw the other as a mistake. Then she objected to open-air worship and turf-roofed hovels for churches, believing that great stone cathedrals and abbeys represented man's most worshipful gestures towards his Creator. I am sure that she considered the stone-circle business as utterly deplorable. She believed in a suitable hierarchy in Christ's Church, from the Pope downwards, cardinals, archbishops, bishops, abbots, priors and so on; and that they should wear beautiful vestments, to the glory of God, not the rough homespun habits, often tattered and travel-worn, of the Columban clergy of all ranks – not that there were many ranks amongst these. Even their tonsures were wrong, the Romans shaving the crowns of their heads, the Celtic monks the forehead.

If all this is looked at from a present-day Reformed standpoint, I think there is little doubt as to whose side most of us would be on. Indeed, if Margaret had never been, and the Columban Church had been allowed to continue, it might even be fair to suggest that the great Reformation of the sixteenth century might never have had to take place. Of course the Columban Church would have had its decadences

– but then so did the Roman one, and underwent many internal reformations from time to time, and this would no doubt have happened in Scotland too, especially in the much more 'democratic' native Church.

Be all that as it may, in this struggle Margaret won hands down. She knew what she wanted, was persuasive, never aggressively arrogant – and of course she was powerful, as most influential queen of a monarch who could not have cared less about such matters. If I have gone on at some length on this matter of the Church, it is because of the profound effect this change had on the entire Scottish polity.

Margaret did, however, suffer one major reverse and a very personal one. For purely political advantage Malcolm appointed their fourth son, Ethelred, to be Abbot of Dunkeld, and as such Primate of the Columban Church, as had been Crinan his great-grandfather, at an early age. What Margaret thought of this we do not know, but she certainly lived to regret it. For young Ethelred, up in Atholl amongst the Keledi, became converted to their way of thinking, so much so that he became a priest in the Celtic Church himself; and then, of all things, married without his parents' approval – as of course Columban clergy might. And not only married but wed a daughter of the late King Lulach – which could have created all sorts of complications. The developments are interesting, in that he consequently became something of an outcast in the family, if not a black sheep, and was disinherited from possible succession to the throne on the grounds that he was now a priest, although only a Celtic one. He seems to have adopted the Highland way of life, and recognising that the Saxon name Ethelred was unacceptable in the Highlands, changed it to Eth, which was near enough to Aed and pronounced almost the same way. His children took the style of MacEth, and this in due course became corrupted to Mackay. Later, he was given the earldom of Fife, but never seems to have acted as though he was the senior earl or mormaor of the kingdom.

There was another black sheep in the family, Edmund, the second son, but he was simply a poor type, as can happen in any family – although he did end up in a monastery, presumably put there to get him out of the way – a Romish monastery, at St Andrews. The other four sons continued to please their mother, if not their father, especially Edward the eldest and David the youngest.

Apart from Margaret's side of things, Malcolm III's reign was not notable for great happenings. In 1078 he won a battle at Monymusk in Aberdeenshire against the men of Moray who supported MacBeth's sons and Lulach's son Malsnechtan; but apart from this, the main event of the reign was hardly a triumph. The Norman William the Conqueror, now firmly on the English throne, decided to do what Canute had done before him and have a try at taking over Scotland, in 1072. He was met by almost the same circumstances but, having taken the precaution of bringing a fleet with him, was able to by-pass the Forth crossing and reached the Tay. However, perceiving the likely costs of a great battle in the Scots heartland, and with matters boiling up in England behind him, he again decided to do what Canute had done – parley, and gain an oath of fealty from Malcolm, as Lord Paramount. Malcolm, who never kept oaths anyway, saw this as the easy way out, and came to Abernethy, on the south side of Tay, and said the required form of words; the feudal idea meant little or nothing to the patriarchal Scots anyway. William required a hostage as token of good behaviour – meaning no more invasions of England – and Malcolm gave him his unwanted eldest son (by Ingebiorg), Duncan. So the Conqueror went away with the unfortunate young prince, and thereafter claimed Scotland to be a sub-kingdom of England. It made no difference to Malcolm, needless to say, who continued with his raiding into Northumbria; but it was one more nail in Scotland's constitutional coffin.

How much Malcolm cared for his oath of fealty is demonstrated by his end. In one of his forays into northern England he managed to get himself killed at Alnmouth, in 1093. He was, perhaps, no great loss; but he had with him his eldest son, Edward, and he was severely wounded and in fact died on his way home, near Jedburgh.

So, suddenly, all was changed, and the weakest third son, Edgar, found himself on Scotland's throne, Edmund being safely out of the road in the monastery, and Ethelred also ruled out. It was, probably, a pity that the old Pictish custom of the mormaors choosing the best and ablest of the royal house to reign had lapsed, and primogeniture had taken its place meantime.

The news of her husband's and son's deaths found Margaret in low water indeed, at Edinburgh. For some years she had been changing, becoming less sure of herself. Although she continued with her ministrations to the poor and her good works generally – for instance the setting up of a free ferry across the Forth for pilgrims to visit her Dunfermline Abbey and the new Romish shrine at St Andrews, a hitherto unknown amenity which got called the Queensferry – she was drawing in upon herself. She was getting older, of course – she was now forty-seven – but it was much more than that. She was starving herself, deliberately, took on continual penances and night-long praying, even made a solitary hermitage for herself on an islet in Forfar Loch to which she was ever more inclined to retire. Instead of any more magnificent abbeys and churches, she built the stark and tiny chapel in Edinburgh Castle, still known as St Margaret's Chapel and a magnet for visitors who wonder at its stern, restricted lines and brief dimensions for so great a queen. The only explanation of it all seems to me to be that Margaret had suffered a crisis of conscience and confidence, rightly or wrongly. Doubts at last had caught up with her. Whether it was the realisation that she had been mistaken in putting down the Columban Church; or whether it was that she might have some responsibility in the death of Queen Ingebiorg and the shameful exclusion of her sons; or her failure with two of her own sons; or even her inability to reform her husband – who knows? But latterly she had become a distressed and unhappy woman.

She was ill at Edinburgh Castle – no doubt partly as a result of her self-inflicted privations – when the news of the disaster at Alnmouth reached her. Thereafter she seems to have, as it were, turned her face to the wall and let herself die, chastening herself to the end, proclaiming herself a sinner and praying for God's mercy – a strange finish for a woman who had in fact changed the face of Scotland and done it in entire goodwill.

No one who has considered Margaret Atheling in any

depth can fail to admire her, and wonder, and wonder
again . . . ?

Chapter 4

THE MARGARETSONS AND THEIR NORMAN CONQUEST

Chaos followed the unexpected deaths of Malcolm, Edward and Margaret. Edgar was presumably next in line, but was a strange young man, utterly unready for the throne, moody and difficult. William Rufus, who had succeeded to the English throne as William II on the death of the Conqueror his father in 1087, still held Duncan, Malcolm's elder son by Ingebiorg, as hostage, and looked like imposing him on Scotland as a puppet-king in Malcolm's place. So the Scots mormaors, or earls as they were now styled, chose the late Malcolm's legitimate brother, Donald Ban or the Fair, as king.

But barely was Donald crowned, in 1094, than William Rufus sent up the captive Duncan, with a great English army, and defeated the unfortunate Donald, who escaped and went into hiding. Duncan was now enthroned more or less by English force, as Duncan II; but he, poor soul, did not last long, for he was murdered at Mondynes, in The Mearns, near Kincardine Castle, that fatal spot for the royal line, less than a year later, and Donald Ban got back the throne.

In all this turmoil the three Margaretsons had fled to England with their two sisters, and after three years more of Donald, William Rufus repeated the performance and sent up Edgar with an English army, to grasp the crown. Again Donald was defeated – he seems to have been not much of a general – and this time was captured. Edgar promptly put out his uncle's eyes and sent him to be a scullion in the royal kitchens.

So that was Edgar mac Malcolm, Margaret's third son.

He reigned, with English support, for ten years, and ten grim years for Scotland they were. Apart from his savage treatment of his uncle, he seems to have been quite unfitted to wear the crown, lacking in drive and leadership and the ability to get on with his fellows. He did not have good health, and seems to have suffered from depression. Completely under English domination, with his two brothers and sisters in Rufus's hands, he bowed also to the Norsemen, yielding up to them, not only by failing to defend them but by actual treaty, the Hebrides and the West Highland seaboard, even abandoning Iona to the Vikings. This was going to cost Scotland dear.

Edgar never married, indeed appeared to have no interest in women, and as far as we can tell precious little interest in anything else either. He did not even take religion very seriously, despite his upbringing, and founded only one monastery, the modest Coldingham Priory in Berwickshire. Although still a comparatively young man, he seems to have become something of a recluse. For Scotland's sake, it was probably as well that he died early, in 1107, a misfit as monarch if ever there was one.

It was now Alexander's turn, the fifth son. He was more fortunate, in that William Rufus had been killed in mysterious circumstances whilst hunting in the New Forest, and had been succeeded by his brother Henry, who was a very different and better character. Henry had married Alexander's and David's elder sister, Matilda, so these two were now brothers-in-law of the King of England. Alexander did not have to have an English army to gain him his throne but seems to have succeeded without trouble.

He, too, was a very different character from the previous monarch, impetuous, hot-blooded, fond of women and of enjoying himself, but not noted for good judgment. He inherited much trouble, of course, from the wretched reigns preceding his own, but at least he was not always facing English threats and demands, and he was able to take a more independent line, for Henry I was a less aggressive neighbour as well as brother-in-law. Indeed Alexander wed Henry's bastard daughter, who, however, was said 'to lack both modesty and beauty'. This marriage was not a success and produced no offspring; but at least this double linking of the royal houses gave Scotland a period of peace. But of course, it did still more to increase the English influence in Scotland's affairs, however peacefully. Alexander does not seem to have done much fighting. Indeed the most major warfare in which he apparently engaged was when he obeyed Henry's request to bring an army south-westwards to aid in a punitive expedition against the Welsh, who were rising against their Norman overlords. David also took part in this expedition and seems to have played a nobler part than did most of the invaders, saving a monastery and certain monks from outrage, and thereafter giving them succour and a permanent home.

Alexander does not appear to have had any very strong family feelings. At least he did not seek to bring his brother home from exile in the south, and in fact denied him the lands in south Scotland which Edgar had left David in his will. Oddly, it was King Henry who sent David north, at length, not actually to Scotland, but to be his governor and viceroy in Cumbria, making him Earl thereof, and giving him a company of young Norman nobles to aid him in his task.

It is probably appropriate to enlarge here upon the subject of Cumbria, Galloway and the old Strathclyde. As mentioned earlier, there was a separate British kingdom of Strathclyde, stretching from Dumbarton, or Alcluyd, right down the west side of what is now Scotland and England almost to Lancaster, whereafter started the Welsh principality. In time this kingdom broke up, and was taken over by the Kings of Scots. But, it never was satisfactorily integrated into the Scots realm. Galloway always remained semi-independent and traditionally awkward; and the Cumbrians paid only lip-service to the Scots crown. So, inevitably, when the Norman conquerors began looking around for fresh conquests, Cumbria was an obvious target, and they moved in, the Scots not doing anything much about it. Nevertheless, the Cumbrians, having been used to running their own affairs pretty much as they liked, did not take kindly to Norman overlordship. There was constant trouble – and of course they used the Scots connection and the innate Galloway unruliness to aid them. So the shrewd Henry of England saw that sending a Scots prince up there as his representative, his own brother-in-law, might be an excellent idea, especially as David mac Malcolm was proving to be an able and reliable character.

David, then, arrived in Carlisle, so near to his native land, around 1112, after almost twenty years of exile, and with his young Norman assistants and friends, brilliant soldiers if somewhat heavy-handed, he made a great success of it, managing even to keep the Gallowegians in order too, with the blessing of his brother Alexander who had never been able to manage them himself. Indeed, Alexander, who on the whole preferred hunting and roistering and wenching to keeping his realm in order, saw his younger brother, on his doorstep, as a godsend after all, and made him governor of the difficult area of Scotland south of the Forth also, the very area which Edgar had in fact left to him. This at the same time as he was Henry's viceroy in Cumbria – an extraordinary situation.

So David was learning the arts of government over a great and diverse area, for two kings simultaneously, and doing it notably well. It should be mentioned that he had married a young widow whilst in the south, one of the greatest English heiresses of the day, another Matilda, Countess of Huntingdon in her own right and Countess of Northampton by marriage. The Huntingdon earldom owned manors in eleven different English counties and produced enormous revenues – and since it was very much a love-match Matilda was glad to let David handle her vast rentals, which was something new for a member of the Scots royal house.

Alexander's reign, although not shameful like Edward's, was scarcely a resounding one and calls for little comment. The most dramatic event was, in fact, an accident – an accident to the King himself. In 1123, Alexander was out fishing from a small boat in the Firth of Forth – or the Scotwater as it was then called – in itself saying something about King Alexander I, when a sudden storm blew up and capsised the boat. The four occupants were swept away, and no more was heard of the King for days, although one of the bodies was washed up near Culross. However, Alexander was not drowned but was cast upon the island of Inchcolm, more dead than alive, inhabited only by a Columban hermit, living only upon shellfish and the milk of one cow and occupying the cell which Columba himself may have once used. This monk found the half-drowned monarch, took him to his cell and nursed him back to life. Nobody knew about this, of course, for the hermit's links with the mainland were scanty indeed, but eventually signal-fires brought out fisherfolk, and the King was conveyed back to his Dunfermline palace – where David had already been summoned from Carlisle to succeed him since Alexander had no legitimate offspring. So David returned to his Cumbrian and Borderland duties and Alexander ordered an abbey to be built on Inchcolm in gratitude for his rescue. But, being his mother's son, he made it a Roman Catholic one, for the Augustinian Order, which might indicate a certain insensitivity. What happened to his saviour, the Columban hermit, is not recorded.

However, although restored to his throne, Alexander seems to have been not fully restored to health after his ordeal, for he lived only another year and died after a reign of seventeen years. So David, the youngest of the six sons of Malcolm and Margaret, ascended the Scots throne, unlikely as this would have seemed at one time.

Now Scotland at last had an able, vigorous, resourceful, responsible – and rich – King, one of the best monarchs she ever had. To do any sort of justice to David I would take a volume in itself, not the few words I can spare here. He was, of course, more his mother's son than any of them, and notably religiously-minded – but in a very practical way. He was full of ideas – and had the means to carry them out. As it happened, both of these means came from England: there were Matilda's huge revenues; and there were David's Norman friends. With them he transformed Scotland. Some, I suppose, might say that the nation might have been better without them both; that is a matter for debate – but not here.

Something must be said about these young Norman importees of David's, both those who had been working with him in Cumbria and a lot more whom he brought up from the south during his long reign of twenty-nine years. Admittedly they were an alien, tough and probably arrogant influence in our Celtic land, most of them the younger sons of English Norman nobles. But they proved themselves here, as in England, Wales and Ireland too, as notably good at merging with the native ruling class, in a generation or two becoming usually amongst the most 'nationalistic' members of their adopted countries. It must be remembered who and what they were. As their name implies, they were the descendents of Norsemen, those who had invaded and conquered northern France not so long before. William the Conqueror was directly descended from the Viking Rolf the Ganger – so called, not because he led a gang but because he seemed to walk, when on a horse, so long were his legs; ganging being walking, whence come the words gangrel and gangway. And Rolf's brother conquered Orkney and become its first Earl, with Thorfinn Raven-Feeder *his* direct descendant. So, although they spoke French, these Normans were not Frenchmen and had no abiding city in France, not deep roots anywhere else – and so were glad to put down roots wherever they could gain lands and power. They were only a little removed from the Vikings at this stage, but had developed the art of land-warfare to a remarkable degree, as the Vikings themselves never did, perfecting cavalry tactics in a fashion unknown hitherto and evolving archery as a weapon to great effect, where it had previously been used only for hunting. These two, heavy cavalry, the equivalent of our modern tanks, and archery, that of our machine-guns, revolutionised warfare and made the Normans the most effective military men in the world. So their adherence to David's crown in large numbers made an enormous difference to Scotland. When one considers the names of some of them, one perceives the impact – Bruce, Stewart, Lindsay, Fraser, Comyn or Cumming, Melville, Gordon, Montgomery, Chisholm, Balliol or Baillie, and the rest. Scots of the Scots, you might say – but all Norman families, and all imported by David I. They made rather a point of marrying Celtic heiresses, gaining large lands and putting down those roots.

Their impact, however, had its drawback, for David and still more for the ordinary folk of Scotland. For these Normans had no tradition, not only of any common origin with the people but of caring in any way for the population. I do not say that the native Celtic chiefs and landholders were always gentle and considerate lords to their folk; but theirs at least was a patriarchal society and the chiefs lived close to their clansfolk and depended upon them for support. The Normans knew and cared nothing for this; they were feudalists, with an entirely different outlook, much less personal, where land and power mattered much more than people. Save in the remoter Highlands, Scotland lost much by this change in attitude, which gradually spread over the entire country.

Another change the Normans brought with them was in housing – they brought the stone castle. Hitherto such were almost unknown in Scotland. The Picts had had their duns or residential forts, usually erected on strong defensive sites, but consisting only of ramparts and ditches of earth and turf, surrounding a timber stockade within which were the simple hutments and houses. From these developed the larger hall-houses of the chiefs and greater men, again built of timber and clay, with turf or thatched roofs, still within stockades to form courtyards and very often still on the sites of the Pictish duns. The Norman stone castles were something new, proud, dominant, oppressive, symptomatic of their owners' attitude to the folk amongst whom they came to live. The chiefs had depended upon their clansfolk living close around them, for security; the Normans saw people differently and found their security in massive stone towers, arrow-slit windows, moats and drawbridges. So, however romantic the ruins of their castles today, they represent a price Scotland had to pay for her new military strengths.

David perceived all this, of course, and sought to counter the ill effects as best he could. He was as great an innovater and reformer as was his mother, with the means to put his ideas into practice. He had learned a lot in the long years in England, what to avoid as well as what to copy and develop; and he devised many improvements of his own. He found the throne and its central authority deplorably weak, and the power of the great lords and chiefs much too great – and getting greater with the advent of the Norman mailed fist. So he concocted a mighty and ambitious design, to counter local tyrants, strengthen the crown and make MacBeth's laws – which had largely fallen into abeyance – practical again. The idea was to divide up the nation and land into small units, under local law-enforcement officers, or magistrates, thousands of these necessarily, instead of the few great mortuaths or provinces of the earls and the thanedoms of the lesser lords. The problem was, of course, where was he to get the thousands of magistrates? He required an educated man-power.

David also desired to strengthen and systemise the Romish Church, which had now succeeded the Columban one but was still without any national structure. And he perceived that these two requirements could, at least at first, go hand-in-hand. The Church was good at education, indeed had almost the only educated people in the land. So he devised the parish system – which in fact still subsists here today. The entire land was to be divided up into parishes, each with its own local church building and priest, and the parishes grouped into dioceses, under bishops. These parishes would be civil entities as well as religious, and on the civil side be grouped together to form shires and sheriffdoms, sheriff being merely a corruption of shire-reeve or judge. This is still the form, and we have to thank David I for it. An enormous task he took on.

There was still the mighty problem of manning these parishes, both with priestly incumbents and with magistrates. The first must come first. There were no universities at this stage. Where was the educated man-power to come from? Monastries and abbeys seemed to be the only answer – so David started on the greatest abbey-building campaign ever contemplated by one man. He would build and endow liter-ally dozens of these places – not only for the glory of God, although that was very much in his mind too, but as power-houses to produce men of education who could be priests and magistrates.

In this tremendous conception David started from scratch. But he had Matilda's great revenues from her English manors, her support and his own driving faith. Selkirk Abbey was the first, although after twenty years it moved down-Tweed to Kelso. Then Jedburgh, Melrose and Dryburgh followed, all close to David's own favourite seat, Roxburgh Castle, where Tweed and Teviot join. The first actual parishes established were hereabouts also, the very first of all at Edenholm or Ednam as it is now called, just north of Kelso. Learning by trial and error he went on and on, spreading further and further afield, and making his lords and lieutenants do their bit at endowing abbeys and monasteries also, even the very doubtful Normans. Kilwinning in Cunninghame, Newbattle in Lothian, Dundrennan and Lincluden in Galloway, St Andrews in Fife, Restenneth in Angus, Kinloss and Urquhart in Moray, Rosemarkie and Fearn in Ross, and so on, all up and down the land he went, building, building. This almost feverish activity has been categorised by many writers as indicating a crazy piety and one of his own royal successors, James I, labelled him ruefully as 'a sair sanct for the crown'. But David was no crazed pietist. He was an intensely practical man as well as a devoted Christian, and these abbeys and priories transformed the face of Scotland, for not only did they produce the educated man-power required but they went in for agriculture, stock-rearing and even manufacture and coal-mining in a big way, greatly increasing the Church's wealth admittedly but also the nation's, and giving a most notable example to the secular landowners as to how to get the most out of their lands. This, at least, was something the Celtic Church never seems to have concerned itself with.

David involved himself in all this in a most personal fashion, designing and often using his own hands in the labour of building his abbeys, as well as paying for the work and visiting the new parishes. How personal was his connection with the founding of his abbeys is illustrated by the following story. He was hunting one day in the forested land which then lay beneath Arthur's Seat, the great hill which rises to the east of Edinburgh, when, in the chase, he and his chaplain got separated from the other hunters. A large stag, wounded by one of the others, suddenly dashed out of the woodland and in its pain and panic charged the King's horse, which reared and bolted, unseating its rider. David fell, half-stunned, and the stag lowered its head to rush in and gore him with its antlers. The young chaplain riding behind leapt from his own horse to hurry to the King's aid. He was not present as a huntsman but only as an attendant on the monarch, and had no weapon to use against the maddened beast. But he had something else – Queen Margaret's famous Black Rood, the fragment of Christ's cross contained in a silver casket hanging on a chain, which he wore round his neck and which went everywhere with David, a reminder of his faith, his duty and his mother. Whipping this off, the chaplain swung it in front of the stag's lowered head and, possibly with the sun glinting on the silver, the animal drew back, turned away and made off, and the fallen monarch was saved. In gratitude, David vowed that an abbey for Edinburgh would be built on that very spot, and the chaplain would be its first abbot. It would be named the Abbey of the Holy Rood. And it was so. Its ruins are still standing, and attached to them is the famous royal palace of Holyroodhouse.

Despite his strength in Norman knights – or possibly partly because of it – David did not do a great deal of actual battling. He did not have to. But strangely, for that religiously-minded man, the one great battle linked with his name had a very religious slant to it – and he was on the wrong side.

It happened in 1138. Henry I of England was dead, and had in theory been succeeded on the throne by his daughter, the Empress Maud, David's niece. But the crown had been usurped, in her absence on the Continent, by a nephew of Henry's, Stephen of Blois, and there was civil war in England. This involved David, in turn, for he had promised to support his niece. Stephen was at York and the King of Scots took an army down there to challenge the usurper, believing that Maud's English supporters would join him. These did not, in fact, and the two armies met at Northallerton, between York and Durham – although Stephen himself stayed behind and left, of all people, the aged Archbishop of York to lead his forces. And the Archbishop had his own way of conducting battles. He consecrated communion bread and wine, then had these sacred symbols hoisted on top of a tall mast, which he ordered to be carried before his host – and sent word of what he had done to the advancing Scots. The English took up a strong defensive position on a hill on Cowton Moor and awaited the Scots attack. Needless to say, the extraordinary situation of seeming to fight against the consecrated Body and Blood of Christ had a major effect on David and his people – as was the intention. However much they told each other that this was utterly shameful as a device and not to be taken seriously, nevertheless the thing was there, sapping morale, worrying, causing dissention. The Scots attack was in consequence less successful than usual, and was repulsed with heavy casualties. Without actually being defeated, for the English never left their defensive position, David felt compelled to withdraw from the field, an unhappy man indeed. This became known as the Battle of the Standard, and was surely one of the most astonishing contests in the age-long series between the two nations. It was indecisive, but had a great effect on David mac Malcolm, who never forgave himself for the casualties suffered.

The last years of David's long reign were sad ones. Queen Matilda died in 1152, in May, and the very next month their only child, the Prince Henry, died also, two crushing blows. Henry had never been strong. He had been present at the Battle of the Standard, and had in fact made a grievous mistake there, in his wing of the battle. He left three young sons by by the Countess Ada of Northumberland, and these grandsons, Malcolm, William and David, now became the King's heirs.

David continued with his good works and constructive schemes right to the end; but never really got over the deaths of his wife and son. He himself died the following year.

Scotland had lost one of her greatest sons, after twenty-nine years on her throne. He left a different nation behind him.

Chapter 5

ENGLISH LEOPARD AND SCOTS LION-CUBS

As so often happens with great men, David was succeeded by what might be termed nonentities. Kings who came to the throne as children did usually have a difficult time of it, and their realms with them – as Scotland had reason to discover all too often, regencies seldom being very successful. The eldest of the three grandsons became King Malcolm IV, generally known as Malcolm the Maiden. Although this Maiden by-name refers to the fact that he never married, there was more to it than that. After all, his grand-uncle Edgar had never married either, but he was not dubbed the Maiden. Young Malcolm, I fear, was just not of the stuff of kings, weakly in body and in character, of a seemingly petulant nature and unreliable. There is not a great deal of any real note to say about his reign and Scotland's fate during it, save that this period coincided with the rise of the first Lord of the Isles, the great Somerled, from whom the MacDonalds, MacDougalls and other major clans descend, and who almost single-handed drove out the Norsemen from the West Highland seaboard and most of the Hebrides which they had occupied since Edgar's day, and established his own sub-kingdom there, a remarkable feat. He got no help from King Malcolm.

With a weak hand at the helm, the great nobles, the Normans especially, soon began to reassert themselves as against the power of the crown, and some of David's good work was undone. Also the English King Henry II, Maud's son, who succeeded the usurping Stephen in 1154, saw the opportunity to impress his will on Scotland – although he was in truth more interested in doing so on France – and Malcolm was not the one to oppose him vigorously. The revenues of the earldom of Huntingdon proved now to be something of a fatal flaw in the fabric of the Scots royal house, for desire to retain these so useful funds militated against any strong line being taken with the English pretensions; and of course the Scots kings had to pay fealty to the English monarchs for an English earldom – which always made a weak gesture. Malcolm became Henry's formal vassal in 1157 and gave up all Scots claims to Cumbria and Northumbria in order to keep Huntingdon. He went off on the English wars in France as one of King Henry's staff, and accepted knighthood at Henry's hands.

All this greatly worried the Scots lords and there followed the Revolt of the Seven Earls, an extraordinary situation with all the former mormaors, or lesser kings, turning against the occupant of the throne. In earlier times this would have spelt the end of Malcolm, but the Norman element preferred a weak king to a strong Celtic influence, and fought Malcolm's battle for him. The Celtic earls were not very competent militarily either, and the revolt fell through.

But this lesson did not strengthen Malcolm's tremulous hand. He made further concessions to Henry and it was whilst so doing that he fell seriously ill at Doncaster in 1164. He recovered sufficiently to return to Scotland, but died soon afterwards, in 1165, mourned by few.

He was followed by his brother William, the only one so-named in Scotland's long story. It would be nice to declare that he was a major improvement on Malcolm, especially as he has achieved a sort of spurious glamour by being by-named William the Lyon. However he acquired this style not through any especially lion-hearted character but merely because he it was who first substituted the Lion Rampant as the royal emblem instead of the Boar, which had served since Pictish times.

He *was* a better king than his brother, however, even though scarcely a paladin, and his reign had quite a major effect on Scotland, partly because it lasted for so long – no less than forty-nine years. But it was not distinguished by any great events, and William appears to have been the sort of man to whom things happened rather than one who made them happen. He was handicapped throughout, of course, by being wholly under Henry II's thumb, quite as much so as Malcolm had been, he too becoming Henry's formal vassal in 1174. He did as Henry told him, so that the Plantagenet all but ruled Scotland through William, shameful as this was to Scots pride. William had a lot of trouble with rebellions in Galloway and Ross – the former through sheer 'ungovernableness' and the latter because of the dynastic ambitions of descendants of the older Celtic royal line – and Henry actually came up in person to put down the Galloway rebels for his vassal William. He also dictated William's marriage – at the belated age of forty-three – to Ermingarde de Beaumont, daughter of an Anglo-Norman viscount. He sent the King of Scots here and there on this errand and that, and summoned him south at will. It is just as well, undoubtedly, that Henry was on the whole a comparatively moderate character, and seems to have quite liked William, for had he been like many of his predecessors and successors, Scotland would have lost her independence there and then – or had to fight desperately to preserve it.

In William's favour it has to be said that he did try to support his grandfather David's law-enforcement ideas and is recorded as holding assizes from time to time in various parts. He also founded Arbroath Abbey and got some of his lords to endow Lindores, Inchaffray, Beauly and others. He continued the policy of introducing Normans. But nothing will make his long reign sound momentous, dramatic or good for Scotland.

Perhaps the most dramatic event, indeed, was wholly bad for his realm – at least his great-grandmother Margaret would have so declared. For the peaceable William somehow managed to get into a quarrel with the Pope and was actually excommunicated, and all Scotland put under interdict, something so out-of-character as to be barely credible. But he, and Scotland, survived.

Eventually this unlionlike Lyon died, in his seventy-fourth year, a great age for those days, and his son Alexander II reigned in his stead. One final word about William – he left a great tribe of illegitimate sons and daughters, who were to prove something of an embarrassment to the next monarch.

Because of his father's so-late marriage, Alexander was only sixteen when he mounted the throne. Nevertheless, despite his lack of years, he had been helping William to rule – if that is the word – for some time previously, for he was an able and vigorous youth – half-Norman of course, or more than half, since his father's mother had also been the Norman Countess Ada. The Celtic blood was getting very thin in Scotland's royal family. But at any rate, Alexander was an improvement on his predecessors.

He was advantaged, to be sure, by the fact that he had to deal with King John of England. Not that he made a pleasant character to deal with, one of the most treacherous and deplorable of English monarchs, youngest son of Henry II; but in that his tyrannies and follies so enraged his own barons that they would not fight for, indeed would fight against, him – and so gave Alexander of Scotland the opportunity to break loose. This he sought to do, young as he was, making many armed excursions into England – this also to emphasise his claim to Northumberland. John retaliated, of course, even erecting a castle at Tweedmouth as base, and twice carrying fire and sword deep into Scotland, burning Berwick, Dunbar and Haddington on both occasions. This ding-dong warfare must have been very unpleasant for the Border shires, however enthusiastic the kings.

However, John's villainies in his own realm caught up with him. He was forced by his nobles to sign a great limitation of his powers, the Magna Carta, in 1215, and died suddenly the following year, leaving a seven-year-old son, Henry III.

So Scotland had a breathing-space and Alexander took advantage of it to try to solve his many problems in Galloway, the Highland west and the north, where the Celtic element was in constant revolt, probably as much against Norman behaviour as against the High King himself. This is no place for any catalogue of campaigns and expeditions. Suffice it to say that Alexander's vigorous nature was kept fully engaged. By 1230 he could claim to have pacified the north, and by 1235 Galloway – only temporarily, however.

On the English front, it is worth recording that the year

King John died, Alexander made one more of his moves over into Northumberland and actually got the Northumbrian barons to pay him oaths of fealty – indication that, despite the weak renunciations of previous reigns, Scotland still considered that Northumberland was a Scots fief – and presumably the Northumbrians accepted it. In 1217, when one of these refused homage, Alexander promptly marched south and besieged his castle of Mitford, and was not interfered with in so doing.

But when Henry III grew up, of course, there was a different story to tell, and he duly began to bring pressure to bear on Alexander – as usual, largely through Huntingdon and its wealthy manors. To retain these, the King of Scots had to swallow his pride and go down to England and do homage to Henry as an English earl. Part of the price he had to pay for these fatal riches was to have to marry Henry's sister Joanna, in 1221. This was scarcely a successful match in any way and, the lady producing no offspring, the problem of the succession began to loom large. The heir was Alexander's uncle, David, titular Earl of Huntingdon, the younger brother of Malcolm and William. But he had only one son, who died young, and three daughters. When the uncle himself died, in 1219, and Queen Joanna remained childless, the situation became serious, with the only heirs being the far-out progeny of these three daughters. One had married Alan, Lord of Galloway, another Robert de Bruce of Annandale, and the third an English baron, Henry de Hastings.

In the circumstances, with Galloway always in revolt, and also with its lord and the eldest sister producing only a girl, the famous Devorgilla, this line was contra-indicated. And an English succession, through Hastings, was not to be considered. There remained Bruce, Lord of Annandale, a Norman admittedly, whose wife had produced another Robert Bruce – this the best available choice. So in 1238 Robert de Bruce achieved recognition as heir-presumptive to Alexander, an agreement which was to bulk large in Scotland's story hereafter.

However, not yet. For the same year Queen Joanna died and Alexander, still only forty, was free to marry again. He did so without delay, and presumably it was a love-match this time, for the lady was not dynastically important, and French at that – Mary de Coucy, daughter of a French baron.

This romance may have been joy and relief to Alexander but it seems grievously to have offended Henry III, who clearly thought that *he* should have the choosing of any wife for the King of Scots. He showed his displeasure in two ways. First, he refused to countenance any longer that an English earldom should be held by a Scot – and since he could not just take Huntingdon away without compensation, cunningly paid the moneys not to Alexander but to the three daughters of the late titular Earl. When this was not well received by Alexander – who showed *his* displeasure by parading through Northumberland again in strength – Henry marched north with a large army, suggesting that Alexander's French marriage indicated a possible allegiance with the France of Louis IX and a threat against himself, far-fetched as this was.

So it looked like being back to the old fisticuffs. But wiser counsel prevailed, and possibly the birth of a son to the new Queen helped to put Alexander into a more co-operative frame of mind. At any rate, he went to Newcastle to meet Henry and made peace with him. Just what were the terms agreed on is not wholly clear, especially on the subject of vassalage, now that Huntingdon was gone. Probably Alexander agreed to relinquish, temporarily at least, his claims to Northumberland, and disclaimed any ideas of a special alliance with France. And we know that he agreed to a contract for the new-born prince, another Alexander, one day to marry a daughter of Henry.

Anyway, the Plantagenet turned and marched south. It was not to be war, after all. But Scotland's rulers had lost Huntingdon and its revenues, for good or ill. There are two opinions as to whether all the wealth which David I had married a century before was a blessing or a curse to Scotland. It had been a continuing weakness, towards England, causing the Scots monarchs to make constant submission to their English counterparts in order to retain it, making them undoubted vassals as far as that earldom was concerned and so giving some excuse for the latter to claim that they were superiors to the Kings of Scots. On the other hand without that wealth, David would not have been able to build all those abbeys and so educate the men he needed to convert Scotland into a country approximately under the rule of law. It poses a difficult question.

Arising out of this meeting of the monarchs at Newcastle, there was an attempt to define the line of the actual borders between the two realms, always vague – and an indication, now, that Alexander had agreed to consider Northumberland as being in England. It is to be feared that this effort did not achieve any marked success, for the demarcation of the borderline remained as debatable as ever and continued so for centuries, as the term Debatable Land implies. But it did produce one rather amusing side-issue. The Border folk had the odd custom, amongst many such, of deciding on disputed ownership of land by what was called judicial duel or combat, the disputants fighting it out in arms, singly or in equal groupings, the winners being accepted as lawful owners. Even Holy Church had to abide by this unusual form of litigation for its land along the Border, and had to hire champions. On this occasion the Pope made vehement protest, but Alexander was unable to do anything about it – Borderers being Borderers – and the offended Pope Honorius III thereupon excommunicated the King of Scots once more and placed Scotland under interdict. It so happened that Henry and England were themselves already in this sad state, for other offences, so that the two kingdoms were at least in harmony on the subject of the Vatican.

Preoccupation with the English threat had the usual concomitant, in that the Celtic north took the opportunity to rebel once more. And on this occasion the matter was complicated by the descendants of Somerled of the Isles fighting amongst themselves, and of King Hakon of Norway perceiving the chance to take back the Hebrides, in the confusion. All this, in 1249, took the fifty-year-old Alexander up into the north-west in armed strength, and on the Isle of Kerrera, off Oban, he took fever and died.

Once again Scotland was left with a child monarch, with all its attendant problems – Alexander III, aged nine.

And now there developed one of those power-struggles – or indeed a series of them – such as were to rack the nation down the centuries, not for the throne itself but for who should control the throne during the minority of the King. There were no suitable and legitimate uncles or cousins, in this instance, and it became a battle between the great lords. The old Seven Earls authority had all but died away, leaving the Norman lords to vie with each other – and tough characters these were, the Bruces, Comyns, Stewarts, Lindsays and the rest. The Comyns were undoubtedly the most powerful, even though Bruce still held the position of heir-presumptive, and the Stewarts of course were High Stewards of the kingdom. But the Comyns, by skilful marriages with heiresses, had managed to gain the three former Celtic earldoms of Buchan, Angus and Menteith. Also they held the great lordships of Lochaber and Badenoch and had been given much land in Galloway to help control that province. These, with the other aggressive Norman families, had grabbed all the high offices of state, Justiciar, Marischal, Constable and so on, as well as the Stewardship, and they competed amongst themselves to manage the young King as regents. So, in this tug-of-war, Alexander had a difficult and trying youth – which he was not to forget.

There were two of these competing lords who were rather different. One was Alan Durward, Earl of Atholl, a Celtic noble who had married one of the late King's bastard daughters and so could style himself a brother-in-law of the young monarch. He was Hereditary Door-Ward of the kingdom, that is keeper of the royal castles and palaces, whence came his name of Durward. He held a powerful and strategic position, and he was an aggressive character, rivalling any Norman. His power suffered an eclipse, however, when it was discovered that he was petitioning the Pope to have his wife's birth legitimised, which would make their son lawful next heir to the throne – something nobody would stand for. The other different lord was Sir David de Lindsay, Lord of Luffness in East Lothian, who, although not one of the most powerful nobles, seems to have been most able and responsible. He was one of the previous King's Justiciars, and at a late stage, as Alexander grew towards full age, appears to have gained the regency by merit rather than with the mailed fist. I am particularly interested in Lindsay, for he lies buried in a ruined chapel less that 200 yards from my home at Aberlady. When Alexander reached full age and began to rule on his own, Sir David went on a Crusade. And, dying in the Holy Land in 1264, of fever not of wounds, like so many of the crusaders, he told a Scots monk called Lauder who was nursing him, having been dispossessed from the monastery on Mount Carmel by the Saracens, that if he embalmed his dead body and took it back to Scotland, his heir would reward him by giving him land at Luffness to found a new monastery, and aid him in the task. This was done; the first Carmelite house in Scotland was established near Aberlady, and Sir David's recumbent effigy still reposes in its ruined chapel, in armour with shield covering him. Many of the stones from the monastery are built into the walling of my house.

While still only a boy, Alexander was married off, at York, to Henry's daughter Margaret, a pale and rather pathetic figure. She remained with her father until her husband was of an age to cope with a wife.

When Alexander eventually reached man's estate, he had had enough of being trammelled, manoeuvred and dictated to, for his was a strong and forceful nature. He took the rule into his own hands in no uncertain fashion and took a strong line with his nobles, Alan Durward in especial being given his marching orders. He too went off on Crusade, although apparently less willingly than Lindsay. The King did not have things all his own way, of course, but he was nobody's puppet now, certainly not Henry's, his father-in-law. There was constant bickering between them. Henry III was a curious, devious man and unreliable – but at least it never came to war between them. He tried to get Alexander to do homage to him, for more than the various lands still held in England, but this was refused. Poor Margaret, his daughter, must have had a difficult life between them. She was not the one to satisfy her forceful husband in any way – but she did bear him two sons and a daughter, sadly none of them strong, however.

The most resounding event of this reign was the famous Battle of Largs, in 1263, when King Hakon of Norway, ambitious for more than the Hebrides, decided to try conclusions with Alexander. With a large fleet of longships, carrying a great army from Orkney and Shetland as well as Norway, he came sailing down the west coast of Scotland. Advisedly, Alexander let him come, without seeking to stop him, until he reached the Clyde estuary, on the wise principle that in any fighting in the Highlands and isles, Hakon would have the advantage and the Scots strength, especially in their Norman cavalry, would be hard to bring to bear. Hakon came, based himself on Arran, and from there sought to invade the Ayrshire coast. Alexander could not prevent this, for he had no fleet – anyway he wanted the Norsemen to land, where of course they had no horses to pit against the Norman knights. The weather was against Hakon – why he had waited for the wild weather of October and November is not clear – and storms delayed the attack, and then high seas made landings difficult. The Scots, in the end, won hands down, as Thomas the Rhymer had prophesied, and Hakon as well as being defeated died on his way back to Norway. At long last, after four centuries, the Norse menace to Scotland was lifted, this time for good.

I mentioned Thomas the Rhymer, Sir Thomas Learmonth of Ercildoune, in Lauderdale, now Earlston. He was a fascinating character, probably Scotland's first major poet, who had an influence on the nation, and beyond, far in advance of what might have been expected for a small Borders knight, a mere vassal of the Earl of Dunbar and March. It was his prophesies rather than his poetry which made him so famous, for they had an extraordinary habit of coming true – and to some extent have continued to do so in later centuries. Alexander thought a lot of him, especially after Largs – sufficient for him, much later, to change the venue of his second wedding, at the last moment, because Thomas, in a dream, saw the roof of Kelso Abbey falling in upon the congregation. So the wedding was transferred to Jedburgh Abbey instead. Kelso's roof did indeed fall in, in time – but not until the eighteenth century, and upon a Protestant congregation, part of the abbey then being used as a parish church. Indeed, Thomas foretold the King's tragic death shortly afterwards.

Two lowering shadows, hinted at by True Thomas, darkened the latter part of Alexander's reign – the deaths in his family, and thereafter the recurrent trouble of the succession; and Edward Plantagenet, his brother-in-law. Henry III died in 1272, and Edward his son, then known as the First Knight of Christendom – although he massacred whole cities, men, women and children, whilst leading a Crusade – came hastening back from his crusading to take over the English throne. Very quickly England, Wales, Ireland, France and Scotland too, realised that there was a new dispensation, and a dire one. For Edward Longshanks as he was called – he seems to have been a throw-back to his distant ancestor Rolf the Ganger, and quite as ruthless – was strong, strong, and fiercely ambitious, and as able and cunning as he was savage. Christendom was in for trouble with its First Knight. And his sister was Queen in Scotland and the heirs to the Scots throne were his nephews.

Alexander was wary, as well he might be, knowing his brother-in-law. He evaded a peremptory demand for homage save that for the usual English estates, but sought otherwise not to provoke Edward. And for the moment that determined character turned his attentions on France, Wales and Ireland. Scotland could wait.

The waiting was not a happy time. Queen Margaret died in 1275. David, the younger son, died in 1281, and that same year the daughter, Princess Margaret, went overseas to marry King Eric of Norway, and died the following year giving birth to still another Margaret. The King's elder son, Alexander, Prince of Scotland, was himself very delicate, and his father, inevitably concerned for the succession, decided that he must be married and produce an heir quickly. He chose for his son the daughter of the Count of Flanders – who would make a useful ally, able to threaten Edward's southern flank if need be, a forerunner of the Auld Alliance – and the wedding took place hurriedly, the bridegroom scarcely in a fit state for marriage although the bride was lusty enough.

Alas, it did not work. The prince died soon afterwards, without begetting a child, and King Alexander was left with only a baby grand-daughter in Norway as sole heir, the Maid of Norway as she was known.

And of course, Edward was angry about the marriage, one more nail in Scotland's coffin. He decided to marry his own young son, Edward, to the Maid of Norway, and gain Scotland that way.

But Alexander was still a vigorous man in his early forties. He could marry again. But he might not have long, and there must be no mistake this time. The woman chosen must be fertile, able to bear children – that was the essence of it all. He did not consult Edward, but sought another alliance, which could at need serve as threat and deterrent to his brother-in-law, and his choice fell upon the beautiful Yolande de Dreux, Duchess of Brittany, a young widow already with children. They found each other mutually delightful and were wed, at Jedburgh Abbey as already mentioned – but although they avoided any Kelso Abbey roof-falling, True Thomas, at the wedding-feast, saw a dire vision of skeletons dancing amongst the happy throng. Consternation reigned.

Within five months Alexander was dead, riding over a cliff at Kinghorn in Fife one stormy night when hastening back, against advice, to his attractive Yolande. Thomas the Rhymer's forebodings were fulfilled. Scotland waited for a while to see if Yolande was pregnant; but she was not. The nation's heir was a little girl in Norway.

The child was sent for, and her young father, King Eric, seems to have made no difficulties. But the fatal sequence was not yet complete. The Maid of Norway's ship crossed the Norse Sea, but at Orkney the child, Queen in name for four years, died.

The dreaded situation had come about. Scotland had no clear heir to the throne – and Edward Longshanks's dread shadow loomed large.

Chapter 6

THE HAMMERING OF THE SCOTS

It is ironical, to say the least, that it should be Bruce of Annandale, the grandfather of the hero-king-to-be, who precipitated Edward of England's direct assumption of over-lordship in Scotland. It came about thus.

In 1286 a Great Council of State was held at Scone a month after Alexander's death, to approve the Maid of Norway's accession to the throne. Meantime six Guardians of the Realm were appointed and it was the nomination of these which caused the trouble, for Bruce was not included, whereas his enemies, the Comyns, gained two of the seats. It is notable that all the Guardians were Normans, save for the MacDuff, Earl of Fife.

Outraged, Bruce and his supporters signed a bond, at Turnberry Castle in Ayrshire, declaring the Bruce right to the throne. Turnberry was the seat of the Celtic earldom of Carrick. Robert Bruce's son, another Robert, had married Marjory, Countess of Carrick in her own right, and acted Earl in her name. Their son, who was to be the famed hero, would succeed to the earldom in due course.

When the Maid of Norway died, other competitors for the crown arose, mostly descendants of the three daughters of David, Earl of Huntingdon, the foremost contender being John Balliol, son of Devorgilla of Galloway who had married an Anglo-Norman baron – and Balliol was related to the Comyns. Old Bruce – he was now in his eighties – saw what was likely to happen, and took to arms. Civil war ensued. When the Balliol-Comyn faction appeared likely to gain the upper hand, Bruce appealed to Edward to decide the issue.

Edward had presumably been waiting for just some such situation. He moved up to Norham Castle on the English side of Tweed and summoned the Scots magnates to come and accept him as overlord, and competent to decide on the succession. Incidentally, he also arranged for English armed forces to be standing by and a fleet to blockade Scotland if need be. Edward left nothing to chance.

The Scots demurred about the overlordship situation but accepted Edward as arbiter over the succession, since some such arbiter there must be, if it was not to be decided by sheer naked steel. Perhaps this, in fact, would have been better in the end; but it is easy to be wise after the event. Edward made the choice for them.

By this time thirteen candidates had come forward for the Scots crown; but basically the choice was between Bruce and Balliol, and Edward chose the weaker vessel, John Balliol, an English baron, who could be relied upon to do as he was told. He was, to be sure, the son of the eldest of the three famous sisters.

Despite rumblings of protest, Scotland had to abide by this decision – for one thing, Edward had insisted on all major castles in Scotland being handed over to his grim lieutenant, Bishop Anthony Beck of Durham, before he would give any judgment, and English garrisons now dominated the land. John Balliol was crowned – and proved a weakling from the start, as was only to be expected. The Scots called him Toom Tabard, which means empty coat, a mere English puppet. And Edward rubbed his, and the Scots', noses in the dirt with a vengeance so that there would be no doubts as to who was master now, ordering King John about like any lackey, summoning him to London on the most trivial excuses, hectoring him in front of all.

Eventually even the worm turned. After four years of this John Balliol protested, basically over being summoned, with his army, for overseas service in England's foreign wars. Edward promptly marched north, in full and terrible strength, with the most efficient and feared fighting machine in Christendom.

Deliberately he paused at Berwick-on-Tweed, then Scotland's greatest seaport, and with a savagery hitherto unequalled in this land he sacked the town and butchered men, women and children, to the number of 17,000 it is said. Today there are only 13,000 folk in Berwick, but it was then the largest single town in Scotland. Edward even ordered the bodies to be left lying in the streets, so that the stink of them would warn all rebellious Scots as to who was master. Then he moved on into the country, with his mighty host, beating a small Scots army at Dunbar. Mail fist pounding, Edward Plantagenet was in his element.

At Stracathro in Angus he caught up with King John and, riding into the church there on his great war-horse, he humiliated Balliol almost beyond description, tossing the Scots crown to his soldiers to play with and announcing that there was now no king in Scotland save himself. All the Scots lords, chiefs, bishops and land-holders would come south to stinking Berwick and there sign a great document acknowledging him as their only true soveriegn lord and swearing fealty to him and him alone – on pain of the direst penalties and forfeiture of all lands.

And they came to unhappy Berwick and signed what became known as the Ragman Roll, the capitulation of the beggarly Scots – where the word rigmarole comes from, meaning a nonsense and worthless screed, the Scots' later attitude to it. The Scots aristocracy has ever since been condemned for this weak and pusillanimous reaction. But while it was certainly no heroic behaviour, it must be realised what the pressures were. Edward's army held the land, its castles occupied, its people terror-stricken by innumerable acts of savagery. Berwick, a city of the rotting dead, had been carefully chosen for the signing. Also, the feudal system, on which all land-holding now depended and with it the entire structure of government, required a lord-superior at the apex of the pyramid of homage and fealty. Without such there was chaos, and all the Norman-built edifice of state broke down. Now there was no king or lord-superior other than Edward – Balliol being banished to France. So the Scots nobility and their sons and heirs, the lesser lairds and chieftains, the bishops, abbots and priors, all came and signed the Ragman Roll and did homage to their conqueror.

Scotland has reached some dire depths in her long story,

but surely none so deep as this. But, as was to happen time and again in the future, the Scots people rose out of the ashes of shame – and led by one man, William Wallace.

It would be difficult to over-sing the praises of this young man. He was of Celtic race – the name Wallace is only a corruption of Welsh, meaning not that his family came from Wales but that they were of Cymric or Strathclyde stock, as distinct from the northern or Gaelic Celts. He was the son of a Renfrewshire laird, Sir Malcolm Wallace of Elderslie, a vassal of the High Steward. Appalled by what was happening to his country, desolated by the weakness he saw all around him, and enraged by the sheer brutal ferocity of the occupying forces, he all but single-handed raised the standard of revolt.

One could almost say that the patriot William Wallace was the *inventor* of patriotism as far as Scotland was concerned. It needs to be pointed out that the conception of a nation and nationhood was almost non-existent at that time. The Picts had been such a nation, but it was a long time since the Pictish nation had faded away. The arrival of the Scots military aristocracy, the infusion of Norse blood, then of Anglo-Saxon, and finally above all the Norman take-over, all had tended to destroy the idea of a united Scots nation. Also the population was divided into a rigid class structure. The predominant Norman ruling caste were much more in tune with their English-Norman opposite numbers than with the remnants of the Celtic rulers – and a great many of them also owned estates in England. The Church was a world unto itself. And the common people had little or nothing in common with their rulers.

Into this dire and defeated disunity came Wallace with the burning idea of one nation, a nation to be welded together, in the fires of warfare, for freedom. It was an astonishing vision for a young man in his twenties and of no lofty background. The Scots people have all but worshipped William Wallace ever since – and he deserved it all.

At first his task seemed hopeless, crazy. He had to start in a very small way, with mere pin-pricks against the occupying power, and taking enormous risks. But gradually he aroused others, his own kind of people, small men, not the great ones, who saw him as a rabble-rouser, indeed a menace to a precarious and difficult order with which they were trying to come to terms. He quickly recognised that he would not get much support from the Norman aristocracy nor the Anglo-Saxon element either, so he looked to the Celtic folk – who, after all, still represented the majority of the population, even though with the least influence. Significantly it was in the north, from Moray, that he gained his first really powerful assistant, in Sir Andrew Moray, of part-Celt, part-Flemish ancestry.

In time these two managed to relight the torch of hope in Scotland – and turned that torch into a great conflagration indeed when they won the extraordinary victory of Stirling Bridge against the English might, using the same strategic advantages exploited by Malcolm the Destroyer and MacBeth, of the narrow Forth crossing and the causeway through the marshland beyond, to impede and bog down the enormous weight of heavy cavalry and armoured knights. The almost unbelievable had happened, and Edward's military machine had been defeated – if only temporarily, and in that monarch's absence – and the Scots could lift up their heads again. Sadly, Andrew Moray was mortally wounded in the battle.

Wallace now called an assembly and council of the Scots magnates, at Selkirk, then in the depths of the Ettrick Forest and considered safe from English interference, for, of course, the English still occupied the land and garrisoned the castles. It was reasonably well attended, even by the Normans, who could no longer deny that Wallace was a force to be reckoned with, however much they might look down on him as an upstart.

And now Robert the Bruce, the young Earl of Carrick, comes upon the scene. He had been something of a playboy hitherto, born very much with that silver spoon in his mouth, and as it happened, made much of by Edward, for political reasons no doubt, as a possible aspirant for the Scots crown, who might be useful one day. His grandfather was dead, and his father, now Lord of Annandale, was a feebler type who did Edward's bidding. His son Robert had succeeded his mother as Earl of Carrick. Edward was even said to have paid Bruce's gambling debts; and he encouraged his marriage to his own god-daughter, Elizabeth de Burgh, daughter of Edward's old companion-in-arms, de Burgh, Earl of Ulster. But the young man was half-Celtic, and with the seeds of greatness in him; and Wallace's magnificent example spoke eloquently to him. He had signed the Ragman Roll, with the rest; but he had begun to rebel, in a small way, before Stirling Bridge. He was not at that great battle, being involved in holding his own territories in Ayrshire and the south-west; but he came to Selkirk and put himself wholly behind Wallace. Indeed it is almost certain that he it was who knighted the patriot. Before Stirling Bridge Wallace was merely William; but after it he became *Sir* William. Recorded history is strangely silent on who knighted him; but English chroniclers declared scornfully that this rebel and ruffian had actually been knighted by one of the great Scots earls. Now, at this time, there were only two Scots earls prepared to come out in favour of the national cause – and one of them, the Celtic Earl of Lennox, actually changed sides from the English to the Scottish when he saw the way the Battle of Stirling Bridge was going. Wallace's opinion of such behaviour can be imagined, and he would surely never agree to accept knighthood, which meant so much in those days and elevated the recipient into a totally different status, from any such turn-coat. Carrick was the only other earl available. He himself had been knighted by Edward – and in theory any other knight can make a knight, and only a knight can do so, although it was normally only great nobles and army commanders, other than monarchs, who did so. Anyway, Bruce supported Wallace, who was elected Guardian of Scotland by the council at Selkirk.

But, of course, Edward's fury had to be reckoned with, none doubted. He came north in wrath, and, as ever, Edward's wrath was shattering. Wallace, Bruce and the rest knew better than to risk any major confrontation against the might of England, and reverted to guerilla tactics, ambushes and the like. But, after a time, Wallace was cornered at Falkirk, in July 1298, and forced to do battle. He was deserted by his Norman cavalry, who rode off in offence, and the hero only escaped by the skin of his teeth, into the wastes of the Tor Wood, with Bruce's help. Edward resumed his control of Scotland, with renewed malevolence. It was at this time that he returned to Scone Abbey, from which he had thought he had taken the Stone of Destiny, two years before, along with Queen Margaret's famous Black Rood. Now he pulled the abbey apart almost stone by stone; most clearly he realised that he had been duped, and that the Stone he had taken to London was only a lump of Scone sandstone, whilst the real *Lia Faill* remained in Scotland. Needless to say he did not find it.

Now, of course, Edward's every effort was to lay hands on the rebel Wallace, whom he branded as a traitor to himself. And in time bribery and threats won the day. Wallace was betrayed just north of Glasgow, at a place called Robberstone, now Robroyston, and brought before the Sheriff of Dumbarton at Dumbarton Castle, Sir John Stewart of Menteith – who handed him over to the English. 'The False Menteith's' name has been execrated ever since; but his offence was secondary to that of the man Ralph de Halliburton, who actually betrayed and captured Wallace, and of whom, oddly, few people seem to have heard.

What Edward Plantagenet did to William Wallace thereafter is, of course, beyond all telling. He was tried, in London, as a traitor to the King of England, and condemned to be hanged, cut down whilst still conscious, disembowelled and his entrails burned before his eyes, and then decapitated and dismembered, by order of the First Knight in Christendom. There were to be no more Scots rebels.

Bruce meantime was playing a difficult part. With Wallace's Guardianship over, he and John Comyn the Red, Lord of Badenoch, were appointed Joint-Guardians – but very much in hiding, of course. This Comyn was a brother-in-law of King John Balliol and himself a far-out competitor for the throne, a hot-tempered and violent man but a good fighter. He and Bruce were hereditary enemies, of course, and just could not get on together. It was a sorry period, high hopes dashed, and with the Scots quarreling amongst themselves the English resumed power everywhere.

The news of Wallace's terrible end had a great effect on Bruce, and forced on him the recognition that there could be no half-measures with Edward, that it must be all or nothing. He had been to some extent trading on the fact that Edward had some sort of fondness for him and most probably had never quite given up the idea of using him as a puppet one day – for the Plantagenet was growing old and he had little respect for his own son, who would become Edward II. But after Wallace, Bruce recognised reality, and that the part he was playing would not do, as well as being unworthy of Wallace's sacrifice. He decided to make the supreme effort. But he still had to deal with the Red Comyn and the massive Norman support that character enjoyed.

So he made a compact with Comyn. Let them agree to share the Scots crown – one to have the title of King, the other to have the royal lands, for nothing was more sure than that whoever chose the kingship would immediately have to become a fugitive from Edward, whereas the ownership of the great crown lands, so long as homage was done for them to Edward, would carry no great risks and gain major wealth. Bruce knew his Comyn – who chose the latter, promptly.

But he had underestimated Comyn – if that is a fair description of it. For the Lord of Badenoch covered his hoped-for acquisition of the royal lands by going to Edward and letting him know that Bruce intended to assume the crown. The Plantagenet reaction can be imagined.

However, Bruce learned of this act of treachery and went to challenge Comyn with it. He found his enemy in an odd location, the church of the Minorite Friars at Dumfries. There and then, before the altar, he charged Comyn with the betrayal, was laughed at – and thereupon, in an outburst of anger, drew his dirk and stabbed the other. Comyn fell, bleeding.

Appalled, then, by what he had done, Bruce rushed out of the church and cried out to his companions waiting outside that he feared that he had slain the Comyn.

'Feared?' Kirkpatrick of Closeburn, one of his vassals demanded. 'Never fear – I will go and mak siccar!' Kirkpatrick ran into the church, dagger in hand, and finished off the dying man. The motto of the Kirkpatricks ever since has been 'I mak Siccar' or 'I make Sure'.

And now Bruce was faced, not only with a stricken

conscience but with a dire political situation. Probably few of his supporters would abandon him for what he had done; but Holy Church would, murder – personal wielding of the murder weapon, that is – being automatically punished by excommunication. Edward could order the massacre of thousands and pay no penalty; but to slay a man with one's own hands, not in battle, and before an altar of all places, would inevitably demand excommunication. And once a man was excommunicated, personally, all priests and clergy of the Romish Church were expressly forbidden to administer to him the sacraments and blessings of the Church. To be crowned King of Scots required the ministrations of the Primate of the Scottish Church, and the Abbot of Scone, at his coronation.

Bruce's act of fury, then, forced his bloodstained hand indeed. He reckoned that if he was to be king, he had only six weeks to effect it. It would take three weeks for the news to reach Rome and the Pope, and three weeks for the order of excommunication to come back to Scotland. Thereafter no coronation ceremony could be held. Also, of course, Edward's reaction to the situation would be swift.

So it was all haste. The coronation must be hurried on. Fortunately Bishop Lamberton of St Andrews, the Primate, was a supporter of Bruce, as was the Abbot of Scone, patriots both, who agreed to arrange all before the excommunication order came through. It would inevitably be a somewhat scrappy coronation, but lawful enough and sufficient.

On 25 March 1306, at the traditional Moot-hill of Scone Abbey, Bruce was crowned King Robert of Scots, the first of that name. Almost certainly he was crowned seated on the true Stone of Destiny, for he was most concerned that all should be done in fullest traditional fashion – for nothing was more certain than that Edward would declare that the coronation was invalid and a mockery, without his permission. We know that Edward had been duped over the Stone, so that the real one was still in Scotland, very different, as described by the ancient chroniclers, from the lump of hewn sandstone under the Coronation Chair in London. And there is a strong tradition that on his death-bed twenty-three years later Bruce gave the Stone into the safe-keeping of Angus Og, Lord of the Isles, his friend, to be held secure in the Hebrides – where presumably it still remains.

There was another traditional ceremony connected with the Stone. Whilst the new monarch was seated upon it, before all, the crown should be placed on his head by the senior of the *ri*, or lesser kings, mormaors, now the MacDuff Earl of Fife. But at this time the Earl was a minor, and in the power of Edward. So Bruce called upon his sister, as representing the house of MacDuff, the Hereditary Crowners – who, as it happened was the wife of the Comyn Earl of Buchan, a cousin of the slain Red Comyn. When the lady did not turn up on coronation-day, Bruce cannot have been very surprised. But when she did arrive, next day, having been held up, he actually went through the crowning ceremony a second time, so that she could officiate – surely the only time in history that a King of Scots was crowned twice.

Now Scotland had a monarch again. But it was really only in name, for Bruce had very little military support, with the Comyns, still the most powerful family in the land, against him, and many of the Norman lords taking their tune from them. Also, of course, the land held by occupying English troops and garrisons. All this was underlined only a month or two later, when Edward's army, under Aymer de Valence, Earl of Pembroke, oddly another brother-in-law of the Red Comyn, caught up with Bruce's company at Methven in Perthshire, not far from Scone, and defeated the scratch force in a night attack. Bruce was not yet the brilliant guerilla leader that he was to become.

Thus swiftly the new king of Scots became a hunted fugitive. He fled westwards into the fastnesses of Argyll, sending his wife, the new Queen Elizabeth, and his daughter Marjory, in his younger brother Nigel's care, to the north of Scotland, probably heading for Orkney and thence to Norway, where Bruce's sister was married to the Norwegian king – but the party was betrayed by the Earl of Ross and handed over to Edward. He hanged, disembowelled and beheaded Nigel Bruce, locked up his god-daughter Elizabeth, and committed the child Marjory to a cage in the Tower of London, with orders that no one was to speak with her – although later this ordeal by silence was revoked and she was sent to a nunnery. The Countess of Buchan paid for her coronation act by being hung in an open cage of timber and iron on the outer walls of Berwick Castle, for all to gaze on; whilst Bruce's sister Mary was similarly treated at Roxburgh Castle. That these ladies survived their ordeals is remarkable.

Bruce himself, lurking in Argyll with a small group of close associates, was soon in difficulties. For the Lord of Argyll, Lame John MacDougall of Lorn, was a cousin of the Red Comyn, and was happy enough to hunt down the excommunicated fugitive, especially as Edward appointed him his Admiral of the Western Sea.

There was nowhere safe now for Bruce in his own kingdom, and he had to flee the country. There are various suggestions as to where he went, first of all to Rathlin Island off the Irish coast and then perhaps to Ireland itself, or to Orkney, or even to Norway and his sister. But in fact he seems to have landed up much nearer home, in Moidart, at Castle Tioram, the seat of the Clan Ranald descendants of Somerled the Mighty, where the head of the line was a woman, Christina Macruarie of Garmoran. Christina took pity on the unfortunate monarch, succouring him to excellent effect, until he was in a state to resume his struggle. She remained his friend to the end, thereafter.

During his period in the west Highlands, Bruce was not idle. He sent messengers and scouts far and wide, up and down the land, gaining news, appealing for support and promising action. He learned the grim details of what had happened to those who had already supported him, and been caught, and the reign of terror which now held Scotland. Fourteen of his adherents had been hanged in one day at Newcastle. He recognised the size of his task.

Nevertheless, in the winter storms of 1307, Bruce made his way south to Arran, and in early February made his secret night-time descent upon the Scots mainland, at his own Turnberry in Ayrshire. With local help, he surprised the English garrison of his castle there and retook it. The King of Scots was back.

Here is no place to try to recount the activities of the years which followed, as the young monarch – he was still only thirty-two – fought his extraordinary battle against the might of England, the hostility of much of his own nobility and the state of depression of his people. He had to follow very much in the footsteps of Wallace – with Wallace's fate ahead of him if he failed. And more often he seemed like failing than winning, inevitably, in the unequal struggle. But he learned, learned much about human nature and his own and others' weaknesses, learned to use the land to fight for him – and Scotland, with its hills and passes, its rivers and bogs, its lochs and forests and estuaries, was a magnificent land to use for guerilla tactics. He gathered an ever-growing following, bringing hope to his folk with each little success. He avoided pitched battles, and he exploited every flaw in the massive façade of the occupying power. But sometimes his reverses were shattering and he seemed to be hurled back to where he had started, and worse, in that each defeat eroded something of the fragile faith he had conjured up in the Scots people. There is no reason to doubt the tradition which has made the spider a favourite insect with many Scots, contrary to the norm, in that one night, dejected, exhausted and hiding alone in a cave somewhere in the Galloway hills, all but ready to give up, Bruce watched a spider, by the light of his small fire, hanging from the cave-roof on its thread, seek time and again to swing itself like a pendulum so as to reach and cling to the lateral walling. And how at last it achieved its goal. If a spider could fail and fail but go on trying, so could Robert Bruce, he decided – and went on, determination renewed.

He was given one great encouragement – the death of Edward. The Hammer of the Scots was on his way north again, in July of the year 1307, to further wreak his hate on Scotland, when he fell ill at Lanercost Abbey in Cumbria. When he realised that he was dying, he ordered a litter to be made and himself carried upon it to the Solway bank at Burgh-on-Sands where he could look across the great estuary and curse Scotland with his last breaths. Or not quite the last, for he reserved that for his somewhat lack-lustre son. He ordered that unenthusiastic young man, before all his lords, to take his dead body and boil it in a great cauldron until all the flesh was off the bones. Then these bones were to be carried onwards into Scotland by the new King Edward, and never to leave his side until that accursed land was wholly prostrate at England's feet – and his son to swear by all that was holy so to do. The son swore and the father passed on his way, assuredly, to judgment. And Edward II promptly ordered the army to turn around and march back whence it had come. He buried his father's body in Westminster Abbey, amidst great pomp.

So Bruce gained a slight breathing-space. But even though the new King of England was no warrior like his father, he was easily dominated, because of his weakness, by the older Edward's tough Norman lords and veteran commanders, who had a vested interest in continuing the oppression of Scotland. The struggle went on.

For seven long years Bruce fought for his throne and kingdom, a dire and unrelenting warfare, epic by any standards. He gradually gathered round him a group of devoted and most able lieutenants and associates – Sir James Douglas, probably his closest friend although much younger; Sir Thomas Randolph his nephew, whom he created Earl of Moray; Sir Gilbert Hay of Erroll whom he made Great Constable; Walter the High Steward; Sir Neil Campbell of Lochawe; Sir Alexander Fraser, who married his sister; Sir William Irvine, his Armour-Bearer; and so on, a noble roll of honour; and, of course, his brother Edward.

Edward Bruce was something of a problem and trial to Robert. He was brave, bold – too bold – and a brilliant captain of light cavalry. But he had ambitions far beyond that. He was unruly, hot-tempered and lacked judgment. Many a difficulty he landed his brother in, although he also was effective in warfare. For instance, the notorious Herschip of Buchan when the Comyn earldom was severly ravaged after the Battle of Inverurie, and for which Bruce has been criticised, was largely Edward's work.

But his greatest embarrassment, oddly enough, led to his brother's greatest triumph. In 1313 he was alotted the task of trying to reduce the mighty castle of Stirling, held by an English garrison, and a serious handicap to the national cause, naturally, since it dominated the strategic crossing of Forth. But Edward Bruce, with typical impatience, could not face the wearisome prospect of sitting down and besieging the fortress possibly for weeks, to starve it out. So, of all things, he concluded a bargain with the castle's governor. He offered him a year, either for the English to beat the Scots forces and relieve Stirling – or to surrender it at the end of that period; a piece of outdated chivalric nonsense. And, of course, the obvious result was that the enemy perceived that this renowned stronghold must not be lost. It must be relieved, beyond all question. Even the non-martial Edward II in London saw that. This could not be left to the occupying forces in Scotland. He gathered together the mightiest army mustered for many a day, and marched north.

So Bruce the King was faced either with letting Stirling be relieved and his hard-built-up credit suffer a major blow – or else to face this huge English army in pitched battle, something he had been deliberately avoiding all these seven years. There was really no choice, thanks to Edward Bruce's rash act. It was battle, or terrible set-back, probably both.

Bruce made his plans with great care, once again determined to make the land fight for him. King Edward must converge on Stirling, however his armies might approach – and the Scots were afraid of being outflanked. So the decisive struggle must be near Stirling itself. The Forth would hem the invaders in on the north. The great and dense forest of the Tor Wood could hide the Scots forces almost to the last. And just south-east of Stirling was the narrow coastal plain, all cut up with streams, pools and ditches, where the mouths of the Bannock Burn found their multiple way to the meanders of Forth and salt water – a wet bogland. There, then. If the English could be lured into that waterlogged area, their heavy armour sunk in the swamps and their archers isolated on the few dry islands in the bog, their dread might could probably be largely negated.

And this was what was done on 24 June 1314, at the Battle of Bannockburn, the greatest victory in all Scotland's history. It took a deal of doing and was touch-and-go many times. Mistakes were made on both sides, in the confusion and slaister of mud; and the English fought bravely enough, however frustrated and trammelled by the situation into which they had been coaxed – and of course they had a vast preponderance in numbers, arms and military equipment. Fortunately, Angus Og of the Isles made a last-moment arrival on the scene, with some thousands of Islesmen, putting new heart into the Scots; and even the non-fighting folk, the baggage-carriers, servants and priests, flung themselves in at a strategic moment. And Bruce's superb generalship, learned in those long years of struggle, never faltered. Whereas King Edward fled the field when he saw defeat looming.

This tremendous battle has been described many times. Suffice it here to say that the story of Scotland took a profound turn that day, and the nation was never quite the same thereafter. Whatever happened in the future, the Scots had had Bannockburn.

Chapter 7

OUT OF THE ASHES
TO DUST AGAIN

It is a very common fallacy to accept the Battle of Bannockburn not only as the climax of Bruce's mighty struggle, almost
of his career, but as though it was the achievement of
Scotland's goal and enduring independence. Nothing could
be farther from the truth. Bannockburn made the goals possible, but Bruce's herculean task was far from over; it was
only the first phase completed.

A very little consideration will demonstrate the truth of
this. Scotland won that battle against all odds. The country
lay desolate, stricken, after eighteen years of savage warfare
and occupation, much of it derelict indeed, because of the
scorched-earth policies of both sides; the people cowed,
dejected, divided. This was the land of which Bruce found
himself a monarch in 1314 – an appalling prospect. Somehow
he had to turn this broken realm into a united, law-abiding
and prospering nation, a challenge to daunt any man.

Remember that the English menace was still there. It had
not faded with Edward II's defeat in the one battle, however
great – and was not to fade for another three centuries.
Indeed, even to gain a temporary peace-treaty, such as Bruce
so direly needed for his internal realm-building, took another
fourteen years, Edward refusing, as he put it, to sit down
and talk with one of his rebels.

This situation makes it all the more extraordinary that
Bruce, only a few weeks after Bannockburn, should actually
have gone on a progress into Tynedale in Northumberland
– a progress, mark you, not an invasion nor armed raid.
Looked at baldly, this just does not seem to make sense, with

Scotland in chaos, everywhere the King turned a nation requiring strong remedial action, rule and governance. Yet the hero-monarch sets out on a mere prolonged jaunt down over the Border, a sort of social promenade, taking with him not only his trusted leaders but also his newly-restored Queen and daughter, his sister and the Countess of Buchan, delivered from their cages, and other ladies – for it must be emphasised that the great numbers of lofty English prisoners captured at Bannockburn had enabled Bruce to do a most notable ransom-exchange, and get all his hostages who had not been executed, back from England.

Why this odd excursion, so seemingly time-wasting and superficial? The question puzzled me for a long time; yet little attention appears to have been paid to it by the historians. Oddly enough, I gained the clue to the mystery in an obscure book, not about Scotland at all, but on the Irish campaigns of Edward Bruce, by one Olive Armstrong, in a mere aside in which the author says: 'Edward Bruce claimed as much right to the kingdom of Ireland as Robert Bruce had to the Lordship and Liberty of Tynedale in Northumberland.' With the significant addendum: 'See Northumberland Assize Rolls, 1278.'

So I went seeking the Northumberland Assize Rolls, the local law-court records of that far-distant age. These dusty manuscripts are not in Scotland, of course, but kept at London's Somerset House. I set my London publishers on the job, and eventually they sent me photostat copies of the only two records for 1278 referring to Tynedale. These were in medieval script and unreadable by myself. But a helper at Edinburgh's Register House interpreted them for me – and the mystery was solved. One of the scripts was little to the point, but the other was very much so. Here it is:

> Beatrix of Quitefeld appeals in the county Thomas of Wytewel of Newcastle, for sending Alan Lewedyman, John of Aberutstoun, Brun Aleyn, Roger the parson of Quitefeld, Richard Faceben and Peter the groom of Roger, to rob her house at Quytefeld, of goods to the value of 100 marks. She comes and withdraws.
> Therefore is sent to gaol, and her pledges, Robert of

Mitford and Haulin of Newcastle, in amercement. Thomas is acquitted. The jurors attest that the trespass alleged was done in Tynedale, in the kingdom of Scotland, out of the kingdom of England, and the truth cannot be inquired into here. (Assize Roll (Northumberland) 7 Edw. 1.)

You see, the last sentence, written eighteen years before Edward I attacked Scotland, is the answer. Tynedale was legally in the Kingdom of Scotland, according to Edward's own law-officers. All Northumberland, of course, had often been claimed by Scotland during various reigns. But in 1139 King Stephen had actually signed over all Northumbria to David I and although Henry II regained it in 1157, the Tynedale section was expressly granted back to William the Lyon two years later. This had never been revoked, so that in 1314 it was still lawfully part of Scotland; and Bruce's progress therein was made to take oaths of fealty as monarch from all the Tynedale landowners – which fealty he duly received under the feudal system. This was done there and then for the very good reason of bringing pressure to bear on King Edward, by showing him that the Scots were prepared to force issues, so soon after Bannockburn, and to make him contract a peace-treaty, which was so urgently required. It was not successful, in that Edward did not do so; but that was undoubtedly the reason for this extraordinary progress, and no doubt served Scotland well in other ways.

It is an interesting thought that since there seems to have been no official revocation of this enactment of Henry II since then, Tynedale could still be claimed to be part of Scotland.

Reference made to Edward Bruce's Irish adventure leads us to another unusual and distracting excursion on Robert's part, two years later, when the King had to cross the Irish Sea to the rescue of his headstrong brother, in the winter of 1316–17. It was much against Bruce's wishes, but brotherly love and the recognition that an English preoccupation with Ireland could help Scotland's cause convinced the King to go. His brother had gone over, the year before, and managed to unite many of the Ulster kinglets and chiefs to try to drive

the English out of the Dublin and southern Irish areas; and
these had enthroned him as King of All Ireland, something
of an empty title, in May 1316. However, Edward Bruce had
not changed his character in assuming a throne, and his rash
behaviour and ill-planned campaign soon got him into serious
trouble, so his brother had to go to bale him out.

It was not a successful venture, with Robert having to
conduct a rescue and face-saving retiral rather than any
victorious invasion. He masterminded a long and difficult
retreat all the way from Limerick in the south-west back to
Dundalk, the Scots-Ulster base in the north, plagued all the
way by bad weather, hunger and even pestilence, as well as
the English and hostile southern Irish. Indeed this little-
known and seldom described episode in Bruce's career was
one of the most exacting and trying of his life, demanding
of his greatest powers and strength of will, however lacking
in glory.

At Dundalk Bruce learned of an English invasion of Fife,
and various other events which demanded his presence back
in Scotland – which had been left in the care of the Good
Sir James Douglas. He returned across the Irish Sea, leaving
his brother to rule in Ulster. A year later, the hapless Edward
Bruce suffered a great defeat, and fell in the battle. The
sorry Irish venture was over.

In the years that followed, consolidation at home and raids
into England were the order of the day, the latter of course
to try to force King Edward to make peace. It was during
this period that James Douglas, who led so many of the raids,
gained his dread reputation in England, whereby even the
children were hushed to sleep of a night by the crooned
refrain:

> 'Hush you, hush you, do not fret you,
> The Black Douglas will not get you.'

Bruce himself was to win a great victory as far south as
Yorkshire in 1322, keeping up the pressure. Then Edward
II was deposed, in 1327 and his son Edward III mounted
the throne. Promptly the Scots attacked again, and at last, in
1328, the longed-for peace-treaty was concluded. Typically,
it has become the habit in the south to refer to this as the

Treaty of Northampton; but it was only the preliminaries of
the vital compact which were settled there. The treaty was
finalised and signed in Edinburgh, and was so named. An
interesting feature of it was the English offer to return what
they called the Stone of Scone, kept at Westminster. It is
significant that the Scots did not want it, something which
ought to have made succeeding generations realise that this
was not the true Stone of Destiny but a mere fake. That the
Westminster Stone is still revered is rather astonishing; but
of course, it has perhaps been hallowed by the subsequent
royal bottoms for 700 years!

It was now as though Bruce felt that, with this long fight
for the establishment of peace won, his life's work was over,
for he died the following year, aged fifty-five. It is noteworthy
that he had long believed himself to be a leper, the finger of
God upon him for his murder of the Red Comyn. Yet he
had to keep this dread fear secret, for in those days leprosy
was not only a living death but was so accounted by the
Church, as a sign of God's especial condemnation, so that a
victim was considered to be *legally* dead, his wife a widow
entitled to marry again, his heirs entitled to take over his
property, and he was even formally buried, in an empty coffin
at midnight, and then driven forth from the abodes of men
and forbidden to enter cities and towns and even churches.
Not only this, but he could no longer, of course, hold any
public office or position. So Bruce dare not let it be known
that he believed himself to be a leper, or he could no longer
have been King. This was a cross he had to bear alone, save
for a few of his closest associates. Actually, almost certainly
his trouble was not true leprosy, of the white or fatal sort, but
what was then called red leprosy, merely a sort of dermatitis.
Ironically it was not this which killed him, in the end, but
probably dropsy.

On his death-bed at Cardross, according to tradition, the
hero-king gathered round him his trusted friends and
committed to them certain charges. Three are especially
notable. To his nephew Thomas Randolph, Earl of Moray,
he gave charge of his five-year-old son David, to act as
Regent – a sore charge indeed, for he guessed that trouble
was inevitable. To Angus Og, Lord of the Isles, it is said

that he entrusted the true Stone of Destiny, to ensure its safety in the said troubles, telling him to take it away to his Hebridean seaboard and keep it secure there until it was safe to restore it to Scone and to one of his own descendants. Presumably it is somewhere up there still. Third he ordered the Good Sir James Douglas to have the heart cut out of his dead body and taken on crusade against the Infidel. Apparently Bruce had sworn a vow in his days of desperation that if God would but give him his kingdom eventually, he would show his gratitude by leading a Crusade. He had never been able to redeem that vow, so now this was the best that he could do. Douglas, of course, did as he was bidden and took the royal heart, in a silver casket, and headed for the Holy land, with others of the King's faithful lieutenants, including Lockhart, Sinclair and Borthwick. They got only as far as Spain, which the Saracens had invaded, and in a battle there, at Tebas de Ardales, with things going badly, Douglas took the casket on its chain from around his neck and led the Scots in a mounted charge into the thick of the fight, hurling the reliquary ahead of him and shouting, 'Lead on, Brave Heart, as thou was ever wont to do!' He was cut down by the Moors and fell over his friend and master's heart. Lockhart and Sinclair fell there also, defending the precious relic. But Borthwick survived to bring the heart back to Scotland, where it was buried at Melrose Abbey – the rest of Bruce's body, of course, having already been interred at Dunfermline Abbey. It is interesting that when, some years ago, the bones of the hero-king were dug up and re-interred in the latter abbey, the rib-cage was found to have been sawn open.

From that day onwards the Douglases added a crowned heart to their coat-of-arms. It is still their pride. The Lockharts did the same, but oddly, without the crown.

Despite all the long fight to win that peace-treaty with England, its worth was demonstrated all too soon, for with the death of Bruce and the accession of an infant King, the power-politics of the day swiftly moved into action. The English saw their opportunity, and encouraged Edward Balliol, son of the late King John of unhappy memory, Toom

Tabard, to return from France and claim his father's throne, giving him an English army to aid him.

So, from the start, young David II's reign was bedevilled. He only had Randolph, Earl of Moray, as Regent for three years, for that last of Bruce's paladins died at Musselburgh while preparing to resist Balliol, naming it 'the honest toun', meaning strongly loyal – which has been its proud by-name ever since. But thereafter there was disaster. Balliol landed at Kinghorn in Fife and marched for Perth. At Dupplin he was met by the disorganised Scots, lacking a leader other than the Earl of Mar, who was no soldier. He declared that they would drag the Englishmen by the tails which everyone knew they possessed inside their breeks – but omitted to take the English expertise in archery into account. The Scots lost the battle, and so soon after the child-king's accession, Balliol went through a coronation ceremony at Scone. But not on the true Stone of Destiny, of course – which was probably why Scotland never admitted that it had ever had a King Edward. Most of the nation could not accept this French-speaking Englishman as monarch anyway, and were loyal to Bruce's son. But once again an English army of occupation was there to enforce obedience, to some degree. Balliol promptly acknowledged himself to be Edward of England's liegeman.

It was a grim period, so soon after the triumphs of Bruce and the famous Declaration of Independence of 1320. If Douglas had not died in the Spanish incident things might have been different, for he was the youngest of Bruce's close leaders and a most able warrior. And most of the other lieutenants were now dead, or old men, twenty years on from Bannockburn.

But a new generation of fighters was arising, as always in Scotland's chequered story, and these became ever more effective; so that no more than three months after his so-called coronation Balliol was surprised and defeated at Annan and had to flee the country, allegedly with one foot booted and the other naked. The victors in this case were a son of Randolph and the brother of the Good Sir James Douglas.

But however heartening, that did not get rid of the English castle garrisons in Scotland, and the auld enemy lost no time in sending up reinforcements. Now three other names come prominently into focus to fight for Scotland's independence, amongst others – two men and a woman. The young men were Sir Alexander Ramsay of Dalwolsey, as Dalhousie was originally spelt, and Sir William Douglas, illegitimate son of the late Sir James, known as the Knight of Liddesdale and the Flower of Chivalry. Sadly Douglas was to prove a very withered flower of chivalry, however brave and able a soldier.

To start with the lady, as suitable; she was Black Agnes, Countess of Dunbar and March, and the daughter of the late Regent, Randolph, Earl of Moray, and therefore a kins-woman of Bruce. Her husband appears to have been less notable; but during his absence his wife, in Dunbar Castle, barred the way of one of the many punitive English armies marching north from the Border to try to restore Edward Balliol in 1338. So Black Agnes got herself besieged, deliber-ately – the object being to give time for the loyal forces to rally, gather and resist. Montague, Earl of Salisbury, the English commander, could not leave this hornet's nest behind him to cut his lines of communication.

Dunbar Castle, now only a couple of fangs of masonry, was all but impregnable before the days of artillery, built uniquely on separate stacks of rock, with linking, bridging corridors, at the mouth of Dunbar harbour, a very difficult place for a land-based force to take. So there was nothing for it but for the English to settle down to a siege.

For nineteen weeks, no less, Black Agnes defied the enemy. Attack as they would, and did, Salisbury's troops were repulsed.

> 'Came I early, came I late,
> I found Agnes at the gate!'

Salisbury realised that he would require aid by sea, and sent for an English fleet. When this came, it brought heavy siege-machinery, mangonels, great catapults for the hurling of stones, and covered battering-rams known as sows. With these in action, the Countess herself used mockingly to parade the walls and parapet-walks in sight of the enemy, dusting off the gashes and marks made by the missiles with her white kerchief – to the fury of the attackers. She even gave Salisbury a taste of his own medicine, calling down: 'Beware, Montagow (his surname) for farrow shalt thy sow!' and having large lumps of displaced masonry flung down upon the battering-rams and so crushing them and their operators.

After some weeks, the defenders ran out of food and might have been forced to surrender. It was then that Sir Alexander Ramsay, who had already distinguished himself in many forays against the occupying forces, came to the rescue. He could not seek to challenge the English fleet, but loading up a flotilla of fishing-boats from the Forth havens with food and drink, and approaching at dawn from behind the cover of the mighty Bass Rock, by seeming to be engaged in fishing he got his craft through the enemy lines and then made a dash for the Dunbar harbour before the large vessels could raise sail to intercept. He was able to land his precious cargo and bring fresh fighting-men to the garrison.

After a few more weeks, with winter setting in, the English gave up the siege in disgust and went home. But Ramsay was not finished. He managed to reverse the situation by leading a carefully-selected small force south-eastwards to attack, besiege and capture by a ruse the great royal castle of Roxburgh, where Tweed and Teviot joined, held by the English. This feat put him in control of all the East Borders, and the young King David, now returned from France and beginning to demonstrate his rash impulsiveness, which was to cost Scotland dear, appointed Ramsay to be Sheriff of Teviotdale as reward, although Ramsay did not want it, and advised against it, for the sheriffship had been held until then by Sir William Douglas of Liddesdale, that Flower of Chivalry, Ramsay's colleague and comrade-in-arms, who had himself tried to take Roxburgh and had failed.

This foolish royal appointment was to prove a grievous blow to Scotland, for Douglas was resentful. His clan looked upon the Middle March of the Borders as their own preserve. He himself was controlling the West March from his Liddesdale seat of Hermitage Castle, still a mighty landmark. Learning that Ramsay was holding a sheriff-court hearing in the parish kirk of Hawick, Douglas descended upon it in force and attacking his erstwhile friend carried him off to

Hermitage. There he entombed him in a vaulted cellar, without food or drink, and left him to die. His corpse, when brought out, was found to have the finger-tips gnawed to the bone.

So ended two of the brightest hopes for Scotland's cause, for after such behaviour Douglas's name was abhorred by patriotic Scots, and after a short-time he was ambushed by his own nephew, who became the first Earl of Douglas, and slain. What caused the so-called Flower of Chivalry to act so has puzzled many. The present writer has his own theory.

Edward Balliol, however, from his Northumberland bases, suffered a series of humiliating defeats, and suddenly the usurper had had enough. King Edward had to come storming up to urge him on, and in a dramatic scene at the recaptured Roxburgh the puppet monarch snatched off his crown, grabbed up a handful of earth and pebbles from the ground and thrust all into the Plantagenet's hand – symbolising his final renunciation of the Scots throne. Edward took this entirely literally, claiming that he had now been handed the crown by the reigning monarch and that therefore *he* was lawful King of Scots, not just Lord Paramount, the title his grandfather had assumed. Sending Balliol off back to England, he marched northwards over the Lammermuir Hills heading for Stirling and Scone, to go through his own Scots coronation ceremony in the traditional style. He got only as far as Haddington where, encountering resistance, he burned the famous nunnery, known as the Lamp of Lothian because of its scholarship and erudition, whilst his fleet sailed up Forth and his sailors landed to savage the sacred shrine of the Virgin Mary at Whitekirk – causing, as the Scots believed, a great storm to blow up from the north in retribution, which dispersed the fleet and sank many ships. Because of this, with armed resistance and the continuing grim weather – it was now February – Edward turned for home. This invasion came to be known in Scotland as the Burnt Candlemas.

That was the end of the usurping Balliol, as far as Scotland was concerned. He became merely Edward's pensioner, at £2,000 a year, a great sum for those days, and is reputed to have waxed adept at poaching deer from the English royal parks.

Fortunately for the northern kingdom, Edward Plantagenet thereafter got ever more deeply involved in his French ambitions – always a preoccupation with that family, which had its roots there – and indeed started calling himself King of France. He did not resume his march on Scone.

At home, young King David proved himself to be no worthy son of his great father, and by weakness, rashness and folly failed his kingdom and antagonised his nobility. Probably the major disaster, which was not so very long in following, was not wholly to be blamed on him, however. For the convenient policy of the Auld Alliance with France which required that one nation would go to the aid of the other when either was attacked by their mutual enemy of England, now demanded that the Scots assailed Edward's rear while he was fighting across the Channel. David was nothing loth, and now aged twenty-four, led the greatest army Scotland had assembled for many years south over Tweed into England, as required by the treaty, however reluctant his lords and chiefs. They were not opposed till, at Neville's Cross near Durham, due to crass mismanagement, the army was direly defeated. David himself was captured and was sent ignominiously a prisoner to London.

So started a long captivity. It is significant that midway through its eleven years, David was permitted by his brother-in-law – for he had been married, as a youth, to Edward's sister the Princess Joanna – to return briefly to Scotland, under parole, to try to arrange his ransom, but failed to do so; thus little did the Scots think of the great Bruce's son. He had to go back shamefacedly to durance vile.

It was 1357 before the hapless monarch finally got back to his kingdom to take up the reins of government. Almost better that he had not done so, for his was no hand to be on Scotland's difficult tiller for the remaining fifteen years of his reign. Oddly enough the period was not notable for war, at least not English war, although civil war was never far away. This was because Edward badly needed money for his French campaigns, and he had allowed David to return on condition that he paid a ransom of £60,000; and recognising that he would not be able to raise such an enormous sum in a hurry, gave him nine years to pay it in instalments, during which time there would be a truce between the two kingdoms.

So this unhappy part of the reign was bedevilled by something new for Scotland – money troubles. And probably the Scots, the nobility and gentry anyway, and no doubt the burghs too, would have preferred the normal war. For now it was all assessments, taxation, fines, forced contributions, levies, enough to wring tears from stones. And it was all not very successful at that, for the Scots had hitherto never been greatly concerned with money as such, however interested in land, wealth in cattle, sheep and crops, and of course power. The nation howled and wept its protest – and largely failed to pay. As the years went by, and Edward's French adventures cost more and more, and the Scots defaulted, the ransom demand went up to £100,000, an unheard-of figure. Presumably Edward had never heard that truthful Scots saying that you canna tak the breeks off a Hielantman.

Edward was angry at more than the financial failure, moreover. For David added to his offence by his ongoings with women. This was not so unusual – but when the Queen was Edward's sister the thing was more serious. And David was anything but discreet about it all – and worse, he was allegedly spending the hard-won ransom money on his ladies. One of the most costly, Katherine Mortimer, was actually stabbed to death on the road at Soutra Hill by the Earl of Atholl, so upset was he over his revenues being squandered; and Margaret Drummond, widow of Sir John Logie, was equally expensive – and ambitious into the bargain. The daughter of Black Agnes of Dunbar joined the queue. Queen Joanna departed for the south and her brother's protection.

There was more to all this than just scandal and extravagance, for David and Joanna were childless and the obvious and only heir to the throne was the former Regent, Robert the Steward, Bruce's grandson. When the Queen became ill in London and seemed apt to die, and Margaret Logie declared to all and sundry that she was going to marry the King if that happened – and she already had a son to prove that she was fertile – things looked ominous for the Steward and his clutch of determined and unruly sons. The allegations made about Lady Logie, her antecedents and her private life, do not bear repeating, and civil war was threatened again, this time with the Douglases backing the Stewarts, with whom they were much intermarried.

David sought to distract attention by the time-honoured device of uniting the nation in *foreign* war to stave off civil war – and at the same time to try to solve his money-troubles. He sent secret envoys to France, offering to invade England once more, truce or none, behind Edward, if the French would pay his ransom debt. The French were unenthusiastic.

Then in 1362 the Queen died and David promptly married Margaret Logie – or more probably the other way round. The Steward's indignant uprising went off at half-cock, and the new Queen – who seems to have been a woman of spirit, whatever else, and more of a man than David – roused a faction to defeat the Stewarts. Robert was forced to sign a most humiliating document promising lifelong support and obedience not only to the King but to his officers and appointees whomsoever they might be. Bitterness reigned.

But the new Queen-Consort's high handed ways were too much even for David Bruce, and before very long he was seeking a divorce. Whereupon the bold Margaret sailed off to Rome in person to browbeat the Pope into refusing it.

Perhaps, in the circumstances, it was as well that David died suddenly in 1371, aged forty-seven, after one of the most inglorious – and longest – reigns in Scotland's story. No doubt his people sighed with relief. Ransoms did not have to be paid for dead men.

Chapter 8

THE PRICE OF MISRULE

So the Stewarts had the throne at last. But thanks to David's prolonged occupancy, Robert II was elderly when he succeeded, in poor health, and had never, even at his best, been a very effective character. Moreover he was almost blind, having long had an affliction of the eyes – indeed his by-name was Old Bleary. But he had five sons, John, Robert, David, Alexander and Walter – and these were an altogether different kettle of fish. Robert had never been able to control them, and mounting the throne in no wise helped in the matter; the reverse rather, for they were now princes, and might do as they liked, and did.

It is almost certainly unfortunate for Scotland that John was the eldest and Robert the second son, for the latter was strong, determined, ruthless, and might have made the sort of king the country required; whereas John was studious, hesitant, gentle – but the heir. The land was to pay for this imbalance. A pity that the old Pictish choice of succession did not still prevail. Of the three other sons, David, Earl of Strathearn, seems to have been reasonably normal, probably the best of the family, but made little impact compared with the others. Walter the youngest, Earl of Atholl, was a wild, drunken reprobate. And Alexander, the fourth son, was of course the notorious Wolf of Badenoch. These were the hands into which poor Scotland was delivered on David's death, for their father was now little more than a figurehead.

Robert, Earl of Fife, quickly took over the government, after a fashion, for both his feeble sire and later feebler brother. The others were not interested in government;

ungovernable themselves, they looked upon Scotland as their personal playground for their own savage games. It so happened that King Edward of England died soon after Robert II's accession, and was succeeded by the ten-year old Richard II, so fortunately or otherwise the English menace was temporarily in abeyance.

The young Stewarts, of course, were not the only ones to take advantage of the weak hand at the helm. Much of the rest of the nobility took their cue from them, especially the great house of Douglas, and the land was in perpetual turmoil, with feud and rapine, raiding and private strife. When the protagonists were lofty and sufficiently powerful, this private war could all but turn national. The famous Battle of Otterburn, which in England is called Chevy Chase, and out of which ballads were made on both sides of the Border, is just an example of what went on.

In 1388 the second Earl of Douglas, married to one of the King's daughters, decided that his family feud with the Percy Earl of Northumberland demanded more than just the usual cross-Border raiding. It is indicative of his own power, and the lack of royal control, that he was able to muster what amounted to a major invasion, with an army of reputedly over 40,000, 5,000 of whom were 'lances', or mounted men – and including three of his princely brothers-in-law, Robert of Fife, David of Strathearn and Walter of Atholl. Alexander of Badenoch, who had made himself Earl of Buchan by marrying the Countess in her own right, was Lieutenant and Justiciar of the North, and did not concern himself with affairs south of Forth and Clyde.

This enormous host was really much too large for Douglas's purpose, so he divided it up, taking only some 3,000, but all knights and mounted men, and sending the rest off to the West March, under the royal brothers, to invade Cumberland by Carlisle, more or less as a private venture but also to distract the Percy's attention. The Earl of Northumberland was old, but he had two vigorous sons, the elder being Henry, known as Hotspur, one of England's most famed champions, and who was Douglas's *bête noir;* the other was the Lord Ralph Percy, who was at the time operating in Cumberland – hence this diversion.

So Douglas led his own hard-riding force down through the Cheviots, by Redesdale. He let the Percy, at Alnwick Castle, know that he was coming, too, as required by chivalric custom. But when he got to Alnwick, without being intercepted, he found that Hotspur was at Newcastle. So, nothing daunted, on the 3,000 went. They found the walled city of Newcastle shut up against them and, encircling it, challenged Hotspur, if he was within, to come out and face them, in single combat with Douglas if he so chose. But there was no response. The Scots, of course, could not sit down and besiege the city – all northern England would have come to its rescue. So after sundry mocking gestures and insults, Douglas ordered a retiral, but slowly, trailing his coat, as it were, in the hopes that Hotspur would come on after him, once he had gathered sufficient men.

And the Percy did, but not quite as Douglas planned. For he came after the Scots by night, and caught up with them in mid-Redesdale, at Otterburn, with the Scots encamped and asleep. Leading a brilliant forced march, Hotspur fell upon the invaders in the darkness.

However unsporting Douglas considered this to be when wakened by the clash, he rallied his host and disposed them as best he could, in that narrow valley in the dark. Whilst he was shouting his orders he was being buckled into his armour by John Bickerton of Luffness, his armour-bearer, in haste. Then he put himself at the head of his central array, seeking to get to grips with Percy himself. Horses were, on this occasion, left behind as useless, in the darkness and close country.

The fighting was fierce and confused, but the Scots were gradually getting the better of it. Then, at the height of the bloody struggle, the Earl of Douglas suddenly staggered and called out that he was struck, wounded, and fatally so, crying indeed that he was a dead man – which was strange, for although it was hand-to-hand fighting, his close supporters had seen no vital blow struck, and the Earl was encased in armour. But he was obviously stricken and sinking. With his dying breath he ordered his personal esquires to hold him up and carry him forward into the thick of the battle, while continuing to shout that dread war-cry of 'A Douglas! A

Douglas!' which had been the terror of the English north since the Good Sir James's day. This was done, the young men bearing upright the body of the now dead Earl, until the battle was over, Hotspur captured and the Northumbrians in flight. This was the famous battle won by a dead man.

Thereafter, the mystery was uncovered. Douglas was found to have been stabbed in the back, through a gap in his improperly laced-up armour. And the only man who could have known that this gap was there was his armour-bearer who had dressed him whilst the orders were being given – and who had now disappeared. Presumably John Bickerton had some personal grudge against his lord and had taken this opportunity to work it off. Needless to say the Douglases saw that he paid for his treachery, when they found him back at Luffness.

This, the theme of the Ballad of Otterburn, or Chevy Chase, was sung about for long years. Apart from the dramatics, the incident illustrates vividly the conditions prevailing in Scotland – and England too – towards the close of the fourteenth century.

If anarchy of this sort was rife in the south of the country it was certainly no better in the north. Alexander Stewart, Earl of Buchan, Justiciar of the North, treated that vast area as little more than an arena for his private and savage sport.

From his Badenoch seats of Ruthven and Loch-an-Eilean Castles he used to terrorise that entire province. A favourite sport with which he was apt to entertain his guests was to burn portions of the great Rothiemurchus Forest, to drive out not only deer, wild boar and wolves but any clansmen or caterans who were lurking therein, the sportsmen, waiting to windward, shooting or riding down indiscriminately the fleeing animals or men. This Justiciar of the North had his own notions as to the administration of justice. A preferred device was to fling suspects, or anyone else whom the Earl did not like, into the Water Pit, a semi-subterranean dungeon of his Moray castle of Lochindorb, built on an island in that loch. About three feet of icy water always part-filled that grim dark vault, so that anyone immured therein had to remain standing, or drown. If they survived a few days and nights of that, they were adjudged innocent.

Undoubtedly the Wolf's most notorious exploit arose out of his disagreement with Holy Church, or more specifically with the Bishop of Moray. He had never found his lawful wife to his taste – except in so far as she had brought him the great earldom of Buchan. He lived with a concubine of some note, called Mariota de Athyn, actually a Mackay from Strathnaver, by whom he had four sons. Whether out of desire to marry Mariota or otherwise, the Earl asked the Bishop to arrange a divorce, and was refused. Perhaps the Bishop was a friend of the Countess. And in fury the Wolf descended in force upon the Bishop's cathedral and town of Elgin, the great church one of the finest in the land, and burned it, and much of the city with it, including the Maison Dieu Hospice, the Greyfriars and Blackfriars monasteries, the main parish church and no fewer than eighteen clergy manses. Apparently no punishment was ever meted out to this royal brigand for this deed – or any other.

After all this, it is ironical to consider where the Wolf of Badenoch ended up – at least as far as his earthly career was concerned. If you visit the delightful and peaceful ruined cathedral of Dunkeld, seat of the bishopric to the south of Badenoch, you will find in the place of honour behind the high altar a magnificent tomb surmounted by a handsome recumbent effigy of a knight in shining armour, in a pious attitude of prayer, as douce and proper as you could wish, with a most laudatory inscription, even with a lion at his feet, the mark of a Crusader, all behind a most splendid modern oak screen, designed by Sir Robert Lorimer no less. Rest in peace, indeed. Such is fate.

Robert II, father of these heroes, died in 1390 and was succeeded by the eldest of his sons, the gentle John. But after John Balliol and England's wretched King John of Magna Carta fame, John was considered to be no happy name for a monarch, and he was crowned as Robert III. So there were now two Roberts in the family, and the younger one, who had been ruling for their father, now did the same for his brother – if ruling is the word; at least he made the decisions, and the King became more or less a recluse. As time went on, however, the real Robert had trouble with his nephew, the elder of the King's two sons, David, the first to be styled Duke of Rothesay – a title held today by the Prince of Wales, who incidentally is also the High Steward of Scotland. Because John Robert had made his son a duke, brother Robert of Fife and Menteith insisted that he should be made a duke too, something new for Scotland. So he changed his style to Duke of Albany, significantly the old Pictish name for the entire kingdom, whereas of course Rothesay was merely one of the royal castles.

David of Rothesay was a high-spirited youth, if not always noted for good judgment, and the rivalry between the heir to the throne and his uncle grew ever more intense. The King wrung his hands but could do little to impose his feebler will on these two, and the country became largely divided into two factions, for Rothesay and for Albany. A pity that they did not fight it out in the time-honoured judicial combat, which was such a feature of the age.

Such judicial combat indeed reached its apex, surely, in the last years of the fourteenth century, in an almost unbelievable affair, the famous contest on the North Inch of Perth. This took the form of an arranged battle to the death, held as an entertainment before the King and court and vast crowds, between two Highland clans long at feud and with differences to settle, the Clan Chattan Mackintoshes and the Cummings, descended from the Norman Comyns now thoroughly Scott-icised. There were to be thirty champions on each side, and they were backed by brothers-in-law of the King, the Cummings by the Earl of Moray, of whose earldom they were vassals, and the Mackintoshes by Sir David Lindsay of Glenesk, later the first Earl of Crawford. The Duke of Rothesay was to act as umpire. The Wolf of Badenoch was by this time dead, but his eldest bastard, Sir Alexander Stewart of Badenoch, was supporting the Mackintoshes, a Badenoch clan.

In an atmosphere of high holiday the scene was set. At the last moment the Mackintoshes were found to be a man short, and a brawny Perth blacksmith, Hal Gow of the Wynd, with Clan Chattan connections, was enlisted. At a blare of trumpets the sixty stalwarts set to, before everyone discarding all clothing save for the short kilt of philabeg. They were armed with sword and dirk, axe and crossbow – with only

three arrows allowed for each – their only protection the
leathern Higland targes or round shields. They fired off their
arrows as they approached each other, transfixing a few who
had not covered their vitals adequately with the targes. Then
throwing away the bows, they charged in with cold steel.
Cheered on and wagered over by all, noble and simple, they
hacked and stabbed and thrust and slew, with no rest, no
retiral and no quarter, to the martial music of the pipes.

It took quite a long time to reach a conclusion on that
blood-soaked water-meadow of the Tay, but at last there
remained eleven men of Clan Chattan, approximately on
their feet but all wounded, and only one of the Cummings,
still alive but gibbering inanities on the ground. The decision
was, shall we say, clear-cut. Presumably it was accepted by
the clans concerned, as well as by the audience.

That was Scotland under the early Stewarts, with no
English to fight. But in 1399 Richard II of England was
deposed, presumably as being insufficiently warlike, and
Bolingbroke his cousin mounted the throne as Henry IV. He
was made of different stuff, and the Scots once more had to
look to their defences. And now the two dukes of Rothesay
and Albany, who should have united the factions against the
common foe, did not, and the realm was endangered. So
much so that when King Henry invaded Scotland and
summoned them both to do homage to him at Edinburgh,
although neither would do so, Rothesay held Edinburgh
Castle against the English and Albany marshalled an army
on Calder Muir, only fifteen miles away, but did not advance
to his nephew's aid. It was as well that uprisings in Wales
called Henry away after only a three-day siege, and the threat
to Scotland was lifted meantime. But it presented a grim
prospect for the future.

During three years the trouble between these two Stewarts
worsened. Then Albany struck – although, as usual with
that crafty individual, he worked through others. David of
Rothesay was arrested on his way to St Andrews and taken
to Falkland, the royal hunting-seat in Fife, and there flung
into a cellar without food or drink. It took him eighteen days
to die. Two stories are told as to how he lasted so long: one
that grains of corn trickled through the floorboards of a

granary above; the other that a sympathetic serving-woman, a nursing mother, managed to squeeze milk from her breast through a straw poked through a crack in the masonry to the starving prince. True or not, these were insufficient to save him. He died before word of his imprisonment could be learned by his friends and a rescue mounted.

Now, although the ailing recluse who was Robert III refused to accept that his brother was responsible or to punish him, he did greatly fear for his eleven-year-old younger son James, the only person between Albany and the throne, when he should die. So secret moves were made to protect him. The Sinclair Earl of Orkney smuggled the boy out of Stirling Castle, in his uncle's absence, and got him to Dirleton Castle in East Lothian to wait, hidden, for a ship to come to take him to France and safety in that country, Scotland's traditional ally. But Albany got to hear of it and sent a large force to grab the prince. A battle was fought nearby, during which the boy was ferried out to the security of the Bass Rock, in the mouth of the Firth of Forth, where even Albany could not lay hands on him; and on that sheer, windswept stack amongst the boiling seas, the heir to Scotland and his guardians roosted for a month, until the vessel arrived to take him to France.

But meanwhile Albany had not been idle. He sent secret word to England to let Henry know that a French ship would be proceeding southwards with the Scots prince aboard and would be worth intercepting. So, off Flamborough Head in March 1406 English ships were waiting. The *Maryenknyght* was boarded and James was taken prisoner, to commence an eighteen-year captivity in the Tower of London.

When King Robert heard this news, he turned his sad face to the wall, and died. Albany assumed the official style of Regent of Scotland, complete ruler at last. When he wrote to Henry he called himself Governor of Scotland by the Grace of God, and referred to the people as his subjects.

The Stewarts, thus far, have scarcely shown up to advantage. However, an improvement was on the way. The Sir Alexander already mentioned, the Wolf's eldest son, was a very different man from his father, good-looking, strong, gallant. He has been blamed for being altogether too gallant in the matter of Isobel Countess of Mar, of whom he is alleged to have taken advantage – and very notable advantage, gaining the great earldom of Mar by her, as his father had gained Buchan. But this lady, countess in her own right, was a very experienced female indeed, considerably older than Alexander, and renowned at court for her ability to look after herself. Moreover she was married to Sir Malcolm Drummond the brother of the late Robert's Queen – to whom, however, she did not yield the title of earl. When Alexander fell for her, he may indeed have had his eye upon the earldom of Mar; but there was no reason why the lady should have granted it to him, any more than to her husband Drummond. It seems to have been a love-match from the start, and the young man moved into her main seat of Kildrummy Castle, Sir Malcolm spending most of his time on his own lands in Strathearn. Then Drummond was waylaid and slain – and by none other than one of Alexander's brothers – and there were no lack of fingers to point at the said Alexander Stewart. He promptly married the Countess Isobel and was indeed conceded the earldom by the lady.

Admittedly all this looks black. But there are factors to be taken into account. First, it was out of character for Alexander to be concerned in the murder, judging by the rest of his activities and career. He was, moreover, on bad terms with the brother who slew Drummond; indeed all three other brothers were very different men from Alexander, taking after their father whereas he very much seems to have resembled Mariota de Athyn. He always swore his innocence of any complicity – as in those grim days he had scarcely any need to do. And he proved a good Earl of Mar and a reliable influence in the realm, which was badly needed.

At any rate, most of Scotland had reason to be grateful to Alexander Stewart. For in 1411 a great crisis developed. Donald, Lord of the Isles, descendant of Bruce's Angus Og, quarrelled with Albany and decided that he was a disaster for Scotland and should be replaced as Regent – and possibly one day King – and by himself, Donald. You see, Donald's father had married, as his second wife, the Princess Margaret, Albany's sister, and Donald was the first-fruits of that union. So he was a grandson of Robert II and the cousin

of the captive King James – and cousin of Alexander of Mar.
When he translated his ideas into action, assembled a huge
Highland army at Inverness, and marched southwards to
unseat Albany, Mar was given the task of stopping him.

It was an enormous and daunting mandate and responsibility. The regency had no standing army, and at short notice
Mar had to scrape together men where he could, his own
vassals of Mar and Badenoch providing the bulk of his force.
By the time that he had gathered some sort of muster, Donald
was approaching Aberdeen. They could wait for no more
reinforcements.

Mar chose to wait for the Highland host on the long ridge
of Harlaw, near Inverurie, above the valley of the Urie – not
far from where, one hundred years before, Bruce had
defeated the Comyn Earl of Buchan. Now two of Bruce's
great-great-grandsons were to fight over the future of Bruce's
realm. Mar selected his ground skilfully for, much outnumbered, he was going to require the land to fight for him. His
were the opposite of Bruce's tactics, for he had a mainly
mounted force against dismounted islesmen and clansmen,
so he wanted terrain where cavalry could operate to best
advantage, yet not reveal their comparative weakness in
numbers. Harlaw's whaleback ridge, fairly level on top and
wide enough for a battle, had slopes dropping away on either
side to offer flanking hiding-folds and hollows for mounted
units, out of which they might appear suddenly and sweep
round behind the advancing Highlanders.

It proved to be a tremendous battle, one of the bloodiest
in even Scotland's so bloody story. But Mar had an instinct
for strategy, a sure eye for the all-over picture of the battle,
so vitally important in generalship, and the courage and
determination and cool head equally necessary. He won the
day, but at a fearful cost, for Donald was a notable leader
also, and more experienced – but in a different kind of
warfare – and no more lacking in fortitude and dash than
were his Highlanders. Perhaps had the battle been fought at
sea, or on the Highland mountains, where the Lord of the
Isles was used to campaigning, the result might have been
different than on the rolling Aberdeenshire grasslands. At
any rate, as darkness fell, it was Donald who withdrew what

was left of his great host, and morning saw them on their way back to their upland and island fastnesses. Mar was left on the ridge of Red Harlaw, to count his losses.

To scan that casualty-list is like reading a roll of honour of Scotland's North-East, Aberdeenshire's in especial. Seldom indeed can so many of knightly and lairdly status, as distinct from what they might call lesser men, have fallen in a battle – this because of the use Mar made of his mounted chivalry. Indeed much of his infantry, coming along by forced march behind, did not reach the scene until all was over. It was not often that provosts died in arms, but Provost Robert Davidson of Aberdeen did, and many of his most prominent citizens with him. Scrymgeour, the Hereditary Standard-Bearer of Scotland fell, as did the Sheriffs of Moray and Angus and the son of the Sheriff of Banff. Likewise Sir Andrew Leslie of Balquhain, Master of the Horse, and all six of his sons. Sir Alexander Irvine of Drum, successor of Bruce's armour-bearer, slew the famous Red Hector Maclean of the Battles in epic single combat, but died doing it. Few castles and halls of the north-east were not in mourning thereafter.

The question arises, of course – was it worth it? Was it all necessary? Well, that is arguable at this remove in time, and with hindsight. All we can say is that the vast majority of the Scots people believed it so then and thanked God for their delivery – and the Earl of Mar. If Mar had failed, the history of Scotland thereafter would have been very different, undoubtedly, for there was nobody else to stop Donald before he and his Highland host got to Stirling and Edinburgh. Would a reversion to Celtic rule have been so grievous a development? Especially with Albany at the helm? I for one do not pretend to know. But most of our ancestors had no doubts.

It is fair now, perhaps, also to consider Albany's own impact on the land, seen as it were from a distance. With rulers, moral judgments have to be tempered with realism, something not to be forgotten. As James VI was to say so often, kings cannot be judged like other man, for they have different priorities and responsibilities. Some of the most successful rulers have been moral failures, and some of the finest character the least successful. Albany was a ruthless, treacherous and direly ambitious man undoubtedly, but during his long, strong rule – he did not die until 1420, when he was over eighty – Scotland had more peace, of a sort, than during most reigns. Once he was in sole command, he kept the nobility in order, expert at playing one off against the other; by sleight of hand he ensured that English interference was at a minimum; and conditions were at least no worse for the common people than heretofore, probably better, for he was popular with the citizenry and went out of his way to remain so, and to put down the financial corruption which had gone on since the days of gathering David II's ransom – and they were not always having to pay for wars, foreign or internal, after Harlaw. We must leave the verdict to a higher power.

Chapter 9

ROMANCE AND REVENGE

Young James Stewart – the first of that name – was in his thirteenth year, then, when he started his long imprisonment in the Tower; and learned within a few weeks that he was King of Scots, his father dead. He grew up a studious, sensitive, wary youth, but with a strength of character forged in a hard school indeed. He was not physically ill-treated in England, and was allowed to gain a good education; but as well as the irksome monotony of his life as a captive, he had to suffer the constant humiliation of disrespectful treatment by his captors, the frustrations of an active and imaginative temperament restrained – for he early developed as a poet, thinker and musician, as well as an athlete, horseman and even wrestler – and the gnawing knowledge that his treacherous uncle was completely in command of the Scotland of which he himself was the rightful ruler.

Although he started his incarceration in the Tower of London, he was moved around elsewhere at Henry's whim, to various prisons in castles and fortresses, although the Tower remained his base. Probably his favourite place of custody was Nottingham Castle, on the edge of Sherwood Forest, where Lord Grey de Codnor was his keeper, a man who was notably fond of the chase. So sometimes young James was permitted to go hunting, strictly watched of course. He had as his constant companion another youthful hostage, Griffith Glendower, son and heir of the Welsh patriot and true Prince of Wales, Owen Glendower, and these two became great friends. There was a third hostage who, however, was treated very differently – Murdoch Stewart,

Earl of Fife, eldest son of none other than Albany himself, captured at the disastrous Battle of Homildon Hill four years earlier, a handsome, arrogant but basically weak young man, whom Henry kept near his own person and treated as one of his courtiers. His cousin James came to loathe him and to resent his much greater freedom, more especially when, in 1416, with Henry IV dead and succeeded by his son Henry V, the new monarch, of warlike nature, needed money for further French adventures and accepted a £10,000 ransom from the Scots – not for their King but for Murdoch of Fife. This was a sore blow to James's hopes and pride. He had another eight years to wait for his freedom.

During the weary years of waiting he at least was comforted and sustained by one of the most famed and sung royal romances in our history – famed and sung because the captive James himself turned it into poetry, in the renowned *The King's Quhair*, the lady having 'beauty enough to make a world to dote'. She was the Lady Joanne Beaufort, daughter of the Earl of Somerset and grand-daughter of John of Gaunt, Duke of Lancaster, a son of Edward III. Also her uncle was the Chancellor of England, Bishop, later Cardinal, Beaufort. So she was sufficiently lofty as to background for a royal bride, and at the same time a talented and highly attractive young woman.

James tells in his own writings how his personal joy came to him, how one May morning, the court at Windsor and he with it, but still captive, the cuckoos were calling *their* freedom from all around and he was confined in a small tower-room. He was writing:

> 'Where spring-time sets the seal of youth on brow and
> heart,
> And I stand here, in very sooth, a man apart . . .'

When the lovely liquid notes of a nightingale came to him, and moving to the window he peered out, seeking the bird. He could not see it, but there below, on the dewy grass of the garden, a little white lap-dog came running, silver bell tinkling at its throat, to be followed by a young woman walking, quietly lovely, serene, and alone. He could not watch her for long, for his window was narrow, twist and contort himself as he would. But presently she came pacing back – and he was a man transformed. Entranced by her beauty and grace, suddenly the prisoner's horizons were vastly, joyfully enlarged. He hurried back to his paper, and his pen raced now.

James, of course, was starved of feminine company, like so much else, and his poetic talents, allied to an undoubtedly romantic temperament, rendered him particularly vulnerable to the effects of some such experience. It was not at first any idea of love that filled his deprived and susceptible heart but sheer wonder that so much beauty and delight should walk the same restricted earth as he. He wrote:

> Beauty, fair enough to make the world to dote,
> Are ye a worldly creature?
> Or heavenly thing in likeness of nature?
> Or are ye Cupid's own priestess, come here,
> To loose me out of bonds . . . ?

But when the young woman came each morning to walk her dog below his window, James fell headlong in love. He discovered who she was, a cousin of King Henry, and even contrived to see her, in company, from afar necessarily, in the great hall where she sat at a banquet, up at Henry's dais-table. He could not speak with her, of course, but saw her eyes on him more than once, and next morning when she passed below his window, he managed to drop a plucked rose to her beneath. When, the following evening in the hall, he saw that she was wearing his wilting rose on her bosom, his emotional fate, and hers, was sealed.

During dancing he contrived to speak with her, and discovered that it was in fact no accident that she had chosen to walk below his tower-window of a morning, that she had long felt for him, grieved over his state and even pleaded for him. Clandestine meetings were arranged.

Their romance was interrupted, however, not by discovery but because King Henry insisted on taking James with him on a renewal of his French campaigning. This was not out of any concern for the young King of Scots' freedom of movement or military education, but in the hope that his presence with the English army would inhibit the activities of the Scots forces fighting on the French side. For the crafty Albany could play his games with more than the English, and had sent an army to France, as part of the Auld Alliance arrangement, his younger son, the new Earl of Buchan, with it, to provide a balancing factor for Henry.

James's French excursion in 1420 was a great experience for him, even if no great success as regards his effect on the opposing Scots. France was riven between the factions of Orleans and Burgundy, and fell fairly easily to the victor of Agincourt. Henry married the daughter of the imbecile French King Charles and proclaimed himself Regent of France, inviting James to the wedding. After his fashion, the martial King Hal seems to have developed something of a fondness for his hostage.

When they returned in triumph to England, Henry found that glory could be costly. He needed more money than ever to pay for his new-found stature. Albany had at last died and the regency had been taken over by his elder son Murdoch of Fife, the ransomed one, who was now second Duke of Albany. A poor character, he lacked his father's wiles and ruthless wits, and Scotland was suffering again. Henry perceived that it might be better to have James back there, someone he could at least trust. And a new ransom would be useful. So the two kings came to an agreement. But Henry died suddenly, and it fell to his brother, the Duke of Bedford, as regent for the infant Henry VI, to effect the exchange. Somehow, James would find the enormous sum of 100,000 marks of ransom, and promised that the Scots would not assail the English rear during the difficult times caused by the King's death and the fluid French situation in return for his freedom – and the hand of Henry's cousin, the Lady Joanna Beaufort, in marriage.

So, after eighteen years of captivity, James was free – save of debt. He and Joanna were wed in Southwark Cathedral, and the happy couple set off for Scotland, James aged thirty.

And now we see a different side of James Stewart's character, a capacity for vengeance. He was still the romantic, the poet, visionary and musician, and was to prove a just an able ruler, and peace-loving. Indeed he swore: 'With God's help, if He grant me life, if He grant me but the life of a dog, I will make the key keep the castle and the bracken-bush the cow!' meaning that peace would reign in his realm. But his justice was stern where those who for so long had wrought him ill were concerned. He had little or no mercy on Albany's brood, a not very worthy lot, save for John, Earl of Buchan killed fighting in France. James was barely over the Border when he arrested Duke Murdoch's eldest son, the Lord Walter Stewart and, remembering his grim wait on the Bass Rock all those years before, confined him there to await trial for high treason. Walter had been in open revolt, even against his father, declaring that he would make a better ruler, even king, and indeed seeking to conclude a personal treaty with the French. James did not arrest Murdoch himself yet, however, for he had a coronation to go through, and Murdoch, as Earl of Fife, was the hereditary crowner – so the Duke had to suffer the humiliation of placing the crown, after such long delay, on his cousin's head at Scone amidst great acclaim.

But soon thereafter the Lord James Stewart, the Duke's youngest son, in a surprise attack captured the royal castle of Dumbarton, slaying thirty-two people in the process – because his brother Walter had been keeper there and he decided that now *he* ought to be. King James could not oust this interloper easily from the strong fortress on the Clyde; but it gave him an excellent excuse. He arrested Duke Murdoch and his second son, Alexander; also the Duke's father-in-law and accomplice the Stewart Earl of Lennox, with some others of their kin. He brought the Lord Walter from the Bass, and had them all tried for treason and condemned. Walter he had beheaded, at Stirling, one day, and his father, brother and grandfather the next. Not only that, but he winkled the proud and ambitious Duchess Isabella, Murdoch's wife, out of Doune Castle, and sent her to the Douglas hold of Tantallon, in East Lothian, opposite the Bass, there to be a perpetual prisoner.

The last of the family, the Lord James in Dumbarton Castle, saw the writing on the wall, written by a strong hand, and quietly slipped out of his fortress one night, boarded a ship in the Clyde and disappeared from history, it is thought to exile in Ireland.

So the poet-king made a fairly clean sweep – although, as time was to prove, not quite clean enough. He settled down to ruling, and ruling well. He had used the Douglases to help bring down the house of Albany, and now he had to keep *their* power from growing too great. With the unruly nobility Scotland had, divide-and-rule had always to be the policy of her kings. And he had one great disadvantage, the necessity to raise that vast ransom of 100,000 marks; for although it had been promised to Henry V, not his infant son, James was a man of honour and did not default. Also he had had to send sundry Scots lords to England as security. These facts did not add to his popularity with his nobility. He had found the Treasury empty when he returned and appeal for subscriptions produced little. The royal lands had been frittered away by the Albanys, so he introduced a once-for-all tax of 12 pence in the £ from all rentals of land – a dire imposition for the nobility, hit where it hurt.

It was not an easy reign, but James and Joanna had thirteen years given them to make the key keep the castle and the bracken-bush the cow, and succeeded on the whole pretty well. The position of a minor on the English throne helped, so that there were no real invasions of Scotland. Then, sadly, James paid the price, oddly not so much for the sternness of his vengeance as for one of his generous gestures. He released from captivity Sir Robert Graham, uncle of the late Earl of Strathearn, whom he had imprisoned early on as one of the Albany faction; and this hot-heat showed his gratitude grimly – that he was a hot-head indeed is demonstrated by the fact that, after his release, he actually tried to arrest the King during a parliamentary sitting, declaring that he had such power in the name of the Three Estates. But in his rashness he found a more wily accomplice in the person of none other than Walter Stewart, Earl of Atholl, the King's uncle. This was the youngest of Robert II's deplorable sons, the drunken one, who had outlived the rest, and now, after James's infant son by Joanna, was in fact next in line for the throne. These two got together, and plotted.

They were aided by the fact that James, having had over-much of castles and fortresses during his captivity, avoided such places now when he could, preferring to occupy abbeys and monasteries. The house of the Blackfriars at Perth was a favourite dwelling, and it was there, on a dark night of February 1437 that Atholl and Graham came for the King. Had he been in one of his royal castles, they could not have gained access; but a monastery was different. They broke in, with the aid of Atholl's grandson and heir, Sir Robert Stewart, who was in fact chamberlain to the royal household and in charge of the accommodation. As the armed intruders came clanking in, James, alone with the Queen and her ladies, was briefly warned and sought to lock the door of his chamber. But his treacherous chamberlain had tampered with the lock and removed the draw-bar of the door. It was then that the famous incident was enacted when Kate Douglas, one of the Queen's waiting-women, ran to the door as it was being forced, and thrust her own arm into the empty bar-sockets. This held up the attackers for long enough to allow Joanna to push her husband into a hiding-place. But the young woman's arm broke, and the plotters burst in. And the chamberlain, of course, knew the hiding-place; and though the Queen tried to protect him, James was dragged out and stabbed to death, Joanna herself being wounded in the savage affair. Her lady-in-waiting was known as Kate Bar-lass ever after, and there are still people today in Scotland proud to bear that name, now usually spelt Barlas.

So Scotland again suffered the miseries and uncertainties of a child-king – for the new James II was only six years old – with the warring and unruly nobles scheming against each other for power through the control of the young monarch. The most influential man in the kingdom of course was Archibald, fifth Earl of Douglas, but it so happened that this individual was highly unusual in that he was of a retiring nature and little concerned with the exercise of power. He was almost automatically made Lieutenant of the Kingdom – not Regent, since Joanna sought to hold that position, for her son's sake. But when Douglas showed no signs of taking the rule, there was the inevitable rush to fill the vacuum. Atholl and Graham and their faction had paid terribly for the late King's murder, so that what was left of the house of Stewart was at a low ebb. Into the power-struggle came two new names, Crichton and Livingstone.

These were both comparatively minor barons, Sir William Crichton of that Ilk and Sanquhar and Sir Alexander Livingstone of Callendar, keepers of Edinburgh and Stirling Castles respectively. Crichton had the initial advantage, for it was decided that the coronation of the new monarch at Scone would be too risky, so near to the Atholl and Graham country, and that for the first time it should be held elsewhere – at Holyrood Abbey, in Edinburgh. So young James was brought to that city, with his mother, and lodged in the castle there, with Crichton as keeper; and after the coronation, he just held on to them. Thus simply and at once he grasped the power – and began to use it harshly, in the King's name.

This did not suit his rival, Livingstone, at Stirling, and he contrived to get word to the Queen that she would be much better with him. So, under pretext of taking her son on a pilgrimage to the shrine of the Virgin, at Whitekirk in East Lothian, she was permitted to go, under guard, to a ship at Leith, to sail down to Dunbar. But instead of turning eastwards down Forth, the shipmaster confounded the guards by sailing westwards *up* Forth to Stirling – and Livingstone got his hands on the royal pair.

He proved to be no kinder a gaoler – for that was all he was, in fact, actually locking Joanna in a cell. These two beauties, Crichton and Livingstone, now began a tug-of-war which was to last for years, pulling their youthful liege-lord between them, heedless of his needs and feelings. Since they were so evenly matched in cunning, determination and unscrupulousness, they eventually came to some sort of power-sharing compact. Crichton should be Chancellor, that is chief minister; and Livingstone should be Guardian of the King.

In this struggle, of course the other nobles took sides, and Scotland sank into complete anarchy such as it had scarcely ever before suffered, the mailed fist unchallenged, all mailed fists, the lot of the poor and helpless almost beyond belief. And the lawlessness was not confined to the nobility. The chroniclers tell us of ordinary folk frequently being attacked in the streets and highways and their clothes even stripped off them, and by their own kind.

It looked as though there might have been a change, if not

for the better at least towards firmer control, when the Earl of Douglas died and his seventeen-year-old son succeeded to the vast potential of that great house. William the sixth Earl was a very different character, with the seeds of strength in him, and the men and resources to bring Crichton and Livingstone to heel. That pair of rival brigands saw their danger and united temporarily to overcome it. They invited Earl William and his brother David to dine with the young King at Edinburgh Castle, a royal command; and rashly the Douglases accepted. At some state in the meal a great dish was brought in and set before the Earl, bearing only a bull's head – a recognised symbol of doom. The Douglases were seized, despite the entreaties of young James, and after a mock trial on a charge of treason, beheaded there and then. This was the notorious Black Dinner which has resounded ominously down Scotland's annals:

> 'Edinburgh Castle, towne and toure, God grant thou sink for sinne!
> And that even for the black dinoir Earl Douglas gat therein.'

It might have been expected that the entire mighty clan of Douglas would have risen in wrath and swept away the perpetrators of this deed. But no – for the new Earl of Douglas was the youths' great-uncle, James the Gross, and he was almost certainly art-and-part in the murder, seeing it as the way to his own advancement. He did nothing against the killers and did in fact co-operate with them thereafter. So the unholy partnership of Crichton and Livingstone continued to dominate the country and the sad boy-king, and chaos and savagery prevailed.

Perhaps it was unfortunate for Scotland, in a way, that during this grim period England was preoccupied elsewhere and left the northern kingdom alone – for at least invasion has usually tended to unite the Scots and bring out the best in a basically individualist and disunited people. Henry VI was still only young, and the French situation was growing ever worse, until only Calais remained in English hands. So there was no threat to Scotland from the south to rally the land.

Again it was the death of an Earl of Douglas which sparked off change. James the Gross was huge, obese, and his heart gave out under the strain. His funeral at St Bride's Kirk in Douglasdale was a fitting end to him; for so heavy was the coffin that its bearers lost control of it going down the steps into the crypt below the church, and it hurtled off on its own down into the depths, to crash in amongst the other Douglas dead. Many were the foreboding heads shaken over this leave-taking.

But James the Gross left six sons and four daughters – so he had been active enough once. And the heir, William, eighth Earl, was at last the worthy descendant of the Good Sir James, lively, vigorous, strong. He quickly began to make his presence felt in Scotland – and outwith it, for he renewed the ancient and traditional Douglas feud with the Percies of Northumberland, to the extent of burning Alnwick and Warkworth. He married a kinswoman, Margaret Douglas, the Maid of Galloway, and with her gained that great province to add to all his other lands and strength. One of his brothers was Earl of Moray and another he got made Earl of Ormond; and his sisters married the High Constable and the heads of the houses of Fleming and Wallace. So power began to centre upon young Will Douglas. He was popular, able and dashing. Scotland had a figure to look to, at last.

Crichton and Livingstone saw their danger, of course, and took a number of steps to try to counter it. They could not make head-on attack against the man-power the Douglases were able to field, so their efforts had to be more subtle – and they were expert in such matters. And of course they ever sought to poison the King's mind against his most influential subject. But Douglas was aided by the fact that, as the monarch grew towards manhood, his two manipulators saw their time coming to an end and each decided that it should be the other who went down thereafter, not himself. A more obvious split developed, and the Earl of Douglas saw it and took his own advantage of it. So, judiciously, he aided Crichton to bring down the Livingstones. And after battle, Crichton, in the King's name, had Sir Alexander the Guardian, and his son the Chamberlain, executed. So now the survivor, made Lord Crichton, was supreme – for the moment. He negotiated the marriage of the King with Mary of Gueldres, and seemed almost to be turning elder statesman instead of mere brigand. But when Earl William went on a pilgrimage to Rome in 1450 – not entirely in the interests of religion – Crichton, again in the King's name, struck. He made surprise attack on, and destroyed, the Douglas castles of Lochmaben in Annandale and Craig Douglas in Ettrick, and took over the earldom of Wigtown, in Galloway, all part of an effort to divide the Douglases, particularly to the advantage of the *Red* Douglas house, of Angus and Tantallon, against the Black main line of the south-west. More effective still, he managed to convince the King that the Earl of Douglas was a threat to the crown.

So, soon after his return from Rome, the Earl found himself besieged in his main Galloway seat of Threave Castle, on its island in the Dee, by King James himself – on the pretext of having hanged there the Sheriff of Galloway, Sir Patrick Maclellan, one of Crichton's minions, for misde-meanours during Douglas's absence abroad. It was on this occasion that a famous piece of artillery first came into Scotland's story – Mons Meg. It is usually assumed that this great cannon was founded at Mons, in Flanders, because of its name. But in fact this name is only a corruption of Moll-ance, a place near Castle Douglas, where it was manufactured by a noted blacksmith called Brawny Kim of Mollance, who named the piece after his wife Meg. I imagine that it was really being built for the Earl of Douglas himself, since the smith was one of his people. But at any rate the King purloined it and turned it against the unsuspecting Earl. According to the chronicler, it took a charge of seventy pounds of powder and threw a ball 'the weight of a Galloway cow' – though both these assessments would appear to be excessive. This monster, now of course the pride of Edin-burgh Castle, allegedly sent a ball smashing through the eight-feet-thick masonry of Threave, to pass between the Earl and his Countess, the famed Maid of Galloway, as they sat at table – a nice touch this, indicating the power of the cannon, the accuracy of the aim and the *sang froid* of the Douglas pair, who sat pleasantly at their meal while the King's bombardment went on.

Be all that as it may, the assault failed in its object and James had to retire. Some sort of peace was patched up, and the King and his most powerful subject co-existed. He was no saint, but it is probably fair to say that the Douglas had no design other than to bring down Crichton and free Scotland – and himself – from that crafty rogue. But, to be sure, there was no lack of folk to tell the young King that the Earl aimed to get rid of *him* also, and to take over the kingdom; after all, the Douglases had been inter-marrying with the Stewarts for generations and had almost as much royal blood as had James himself.

The almost inevitable climax came in the January of 1453. The King invited the Earl to discuss matters with him at Stirling Castle, and, lest Douglas was suspicious, issued him with a royal safe-conduct. The Earl duly attended, and there, after a cordial supper, James in effect charged his guest with treason. When this was hotly denied, the King personally drew a dagger and stabbed the Earl, there before all the court. The body was then thrown out of a window. So far as I know, this is the only occasion when a reigning monarch with his own hand actually murdered one of his principal subjects.

After that, of course, it was war between Stewart and Douglas, war to the end. The Douglases could not capture the mighty fortress of Stirling, but before burning much of Stirling town, they nailed the King's safe-conduct to the market-cross, and then dragged it through the streets tied to the tail of the most wretched horse they could find. Then they went home to prepare their armies.

But the Douglas brothers did not have the late Will's ability and dash, and the Red side of the house took the King's side. It should perhaps be explained that the Red Douglases, Earls of Angus, descended from an illegitimate son of the second Earl of Douglas, he who died at Otterburn, by a Countess of Angus in her own right. At any rate, after more than one defeat in the field, the main Black line went down in disaster and forfeiture, their lands taken over by the crown. There were to be no more Earls of Douglas.

So Crichton triumphed in the end, but only for a short time, for he died the next year, of natural causes, like so many other villains. Nor did the unhappy James II long survive the Douglas débâcle. In view of his cannoneering at Threave with Mons Meg, it is interesting that another cannon should have been the end of him. In 1460 he decided to try to eject the English garrison from the strategic royal castle of Roxburgh which, like Berwick, they had occupied for a long time. And whilst personally helping to aim one of the pieces of artillery against the castle, the explosion drove out a wedge of the gun which killed the King. He was aged only twenty-nine. Oddly, another wedge wounded the Red Douglas, Earl of Angus, at his side.

Surely this must have been one of the most unhappy reigns in Scots history, for people as well as monarch. James left an eight-year-old son, another child-king, and another James.

Chapter 10

DESTINY AND ITS CHAIN

If James II's reign was scarcely felicitous, James III's was little better. At least the father was no weakling, however impetuous and resentful; whereas the third James Stewart was a throwback to his great-grandfather, Robert III, feeble, ineffective and directionless – at least for the times in which he lived. Perhaps, in a later age, he might have been hailed as a man to be admired, for he was much interested in the arts, matters cultural and the like. But that was not what Scotland needed of a monarch in the fifteenth century.

As a child, of course, this did not signify – and there was a sufficiency of spirit and vigour about the throne, with two strong characters striving for dominance. There was the Queen Mother, Mary of Gueldres, and the Primate, James Kennedy, Bishop of St Andrews. Unfortunately, as was so usual in Scotland, they strove *against* each other.

Insufficient has been made, I think, in our story, of Mary of Gueldres, for she was an extraordinary woman by any standards, lively, vehement and bold. On her husband's death she was not given the regency, but she retained control of her son, and all the great fortresses of the kingdom, and so was able to wield much power. A Council of Regency was established by Parliament, and Bishop Kennedy dominated this. He was a nephew of James I, and therefore a second cousin of the young King, and the ablest ecclesiastic Scotland had seen for many years. It was a pity that not only did he not get on with the Queen but he disapproved of women wielding direct power – and said so. He ' . . . found a great division in the country caused by the Queen, whom God pardon, from which there resulted a great dissention between the said queen and me, and great likelihood of slaughter between the kinsmen and friends of either party.' That has an ominously familiar sound to it.

The said Queen was admittedly not backward in asserting herself, whether in her son's cause or otherwise. She continued with the siege of Roxburgh, although her husband had been killed, and succeeded in capturing the castle. Almost immediately thereafter she personally led a force over the Border to attack the English castles of Wark and Norham. Out of her personal funds she presently built Ravenscraig Castle in Fife, the first in Scotland to be designed specifically for the use of artillery, with especially strengthened flat roofing to carry heavy cannon. She supported the Yorkist side in England – where the Wars of the Roses were now raging – and when that faction suffered temporary eclipse, she welcomed to Scotland the deposed Henry VI, Queen Margaret of Anjou, Edward Prince of Wales and the Dukes of Somerset and Exeter – and as price for sheltering and lending them troops, obtained a promise of the return of Berwick-on-Tweed to Scotland, and even the cession of Carlisle. She also indulged in an affair with the Duke of Somerset, at the same time as she was living with the already-married Adam Hepburn, Master of Hailes – and when Somerset ended the arrangement tactlessly, she sought to have Lord Hailes, Adam's father, slay the Duke. Altogether she seems to have been quite a lady.

Bishop Kennedy found it all unsuitable, for he supported the Lancastrians. On the Council of Regency his principal supporter was George Douglas, the Red Earl of Angus. So there was a constant tug-of-war again, as the fortunes of the Yorkists and Lancastrians fluctuated. Scotland's share in the Wars of the Roses is often forgotten. Incidentally during the reign of James III, no fewer than five kings followed each other on the English throne.

Queen Mary was nothing if not assiduous in her activities, for she kept up her amorous ambitions to the end, and was actually proposing marriage to Edward IV himself, the *Yorkist*, when she died in December 1463. This left Bishop Kennedy in control of the King and Scotland, and for the two years that remained to him he proved an able ruler. History has been kinder to him than to some, and probably rightly so. But there were more sides than one to his character, for although he did much good, founded the renowned St Salvator's College at St Andrews and effected a fifteen-year truce with England, he also accepted a pension of £366 per year from King Edward, and built a magnificent tomb as his own memorial monument.

But in 1465 he also died, and then the old familiar power-struggle recommenced, to hold and control the thirteen-year-old monarch. Now a new name crops up in Scotland's story – that of Boyd – to rise like a meteor, and fall just about as quickly. Robert, Lord Boyd of Kilmarnock, and his brother, Sir Alexander, and Gilbert, Lord Kennedy, brother of the late Bishop, siezed young James when he was out hunting from Linlithgow Palace, conveyed him to Edinburgh Castle, where Sir Alexander was then Keeper, and there held him in the accustomed fashion.

The Red Douglas had just died also, and there was nobody else sufficiently strong to oust the Boyds. With their kinsmen and friends they took over all the principal offices of state, especially successful being Sir Alexander's son Thomas, who managed to marry James's sister, the Princess Mary, and get created Earl of Arran. Soon he was more or less ruling Scotland. He was handsome, talented and dashing, if unscrupulous. Oddly enough it was thanks to Thomas Boyd that the Orkney and Shetland Isles became part of Scotland – for up till then they had belonged to the Norse or Danish crown. But Arran arranged a marriage for his brother-in-law James with Margaret, the twelve-year-old daughter of King Christian of Denmark, with a dowry of 60,000 Danish florins. Unfortunately or otherwise, Christian was not good at sums, and could not lay his hands on even the 10,000 deposit, much less the remaining 50,000. So he pledged the Orkneys and Shetlands as surety – and never got round to redeeming them. Nowadays, in an age dominated by money, it is hard for us to realise how little cash was used by our forefathers, and so to understand that a great and powerful monarch just could not raise 60,000 florins, and esteemed all the Orcades as of less value than that.

But in these negotiations the handsome new Earl of Arran himself journeyed to Denmark, twice, and was away for quite lengthy periods – which was unwise for a man seeking to rule Scotland. It gave opportunity to others to rise. Two in particular now did so, the Earls of Atholl and Buchan, both uncles of the King. Sir Alexander Boyd was arrested on a charge of treason – that abducting of the King at Linlithgow – and beheaded. His brother Lord Boyd managed to flee to England. And the Earl of Arran, arriving back at Leith, heard the news and promptly turned the ship round and back to Denmark.

But now James was nineteen and old enough to take over the reins of government, under his uncles' guidance, however inadequately. And his inadequacy was soon apparent. He shunned his nobility, even his uncles, and surrounded himself with a very odd lot of favourites, all low-born, which it is strange that he even had come to know. For instance, Thomas Cochrane, a mason turned architect; William Roger, a musician; James Hommyle, the royal tailor; Torphichen, a fencing-master; Dr Andreas, an astrologer; even Leonard, a shoemaker. It would not have been so bad if James had merely associated with these 'unworthy vile persouns and cubeculares'; but he made them his advisers and councillors, in place of his lords. His attitude towards the nobles, and theirs' to him, is illustrated by the account of him personally tearing up the Earl of Morton's charter, and then being forced to sew it up again by the lords.

All this made a nonsense of ruling, for of course these 'familiars' had no armed followings, like the nobility – and Scotland having no standing army or other permanent force, the King was dependent on the lords for not only national support but for internal order. This not being forthcoming in the circumstances, the state of the nation went from bad to worse, with lawlessness everywhere.

Rebellion inevitably broke out – and this time it was led by the King's two brothers, Alexander, Duke of Albany and John, Earl of Mar. For once James took swift action – or more probably it was Cochrane the mason who did, in the King's name, for he was a forceful character. Albany and Mar were apprehended and confined in Edinburgh and

Craigmillar Castles. And in the latter, John of Mar died – and Cochrane was alleged to have murdered him. Such allegation was not helped when James promptly made the ex-mason Earl of Mar in his brother's stead, a major folly to say the least. Albany managed to escape and fled to France.

Now the scene darkened further. Edward IV had come to an agreement with France and could turn upon Scotland, and decided to use the fugitive Albany as his tool. He even declared him to be Alexander the King of Scots, announcing that as Lord Paramount he had demoted James. And he sent up a fleet, with orders to do as much damage as it could on the shores of the Firth of Forth, preparatory to full invasion.

The Scots, in however rebellious mood, could not stomach this, of course, and James was forced by the popular will to act. Unfortunately, he took his entourage of familiars with him as he headed for the Border in strength. He got as far as Lauder when the main Scots army caught up with him, the armed forces of the nobility. And now occurred the famous incident which gave Archibald Douglas, sixth Earl of Angus, the by-name of Bell-the-Cat. The phrase arose out of a conference of the lords in Lauder kirk when they heard that Cochrane, the most hated of the low-born courtiers, had been given command of the artillery. This the warlike nobles just would not have. They declared that they would not proceed further if the King did not dismiss the favourites from positions of ·command. When James refused, it was crisis. The lords agreed that it was now or never. With the English marching north from York, Scotland was in dire danger. They must get rid of the familiars, especially Cochrane, the cat who manipulated the royal mouse. They must hang a bell on the said cat, the Lord Gray declared – but how to do so? Angus answered strongly that he would bell the cat.

They called for Cochrane to come to the kirk, and when he appeared, he was decked about in gold-painted armour with a gold helmet carried before him and a heavy gold chain round his neck 'worth five hundred crowns'. Angus at once snatched this off, announcing roughly that a common rope would suit him better! They held him there, whilst the lords went to the King's tent and arrested the other favourites.

And there and then, before the King's horrified eyes, they hanged them all, Cochrane first, over the parapet of Lauder Bridge. Only one was spared, a seventeen-year-old youth named Ramsay, on whom the King doted.

Strangely enough, after all this, the march on England was not proceeded with. Angus and the other lords took the King back to Edinburgh Castle and there left him a virtual prisoner in the keeping of his uncle Atholl.

The English army under the Duke of Gloucester – later to be Richard III, Crookback – and Albany, had a clear march therefore, right to Edinburgh. There they were faced with something of a quandary. They had come, after all, not so much to savage the Scots as to place Albany on his brother's throne; and they found the situation other than anticipated, James a prisoner in his own fortress and inaccessible without a major siege, and the uncles ruling the land with Douglas Bell-the-Cat. After some indeterminate negotiating, Gloucester left Albany to it and returned to England.

So there followed a peculiar interlude, with no very clear authority in the land, the royal house of Stewart at odds, with James kept more or less impotent, Albany as it were marking time, the uncles controlling the King if not the country, and Angus the most positive force. Probably it was to ensure that the Douglas did not get too strong that the Stewarts united sufficiently, presently, to make Albany Lieutenant-General of the Realm, which at least gave him some official status. But it was still an unsatisfactory situation and obviously could not last.

Albany increased in power, and presently obtained the King's release from captivity. For a little while it looked as though the brothers would manage the kingdom between them. They were even reported to share the same bed. But James feared and resented Albany, probably with cause, and the sudden death of Edward of England, Albany's supporter, gave James his opportunity. He passed sentence of attainder on his brother – after first having attempted to have him poisoned, it was said – and Albany once again fled the country, back to France – where next year he was killed accidentally by being struck by a splinter of broken lance whilst watching a tournament. His life had been a difficult and frustrating one. A much stronger character than his brother, he probably would have made quite a good king had he been the first-born. As so often with the Stewarts, the second sons were more apt for the throne than the first.

Despite all the lack of success, James III had a lengthy reign, twenty-eight years, its last years no happier for the country than were the earlier ones. His nobles grew ever more rebellious, demanding reforms. They managed to get a promise of betterment out of James, at Blackness Castle, formal enough to be called the Pacification thereof – which the King promptly went back on. In fury the lords got hold of the heir to the throne, James, Duke of Rothesay, aged fifteen, and rose in arms. The monarch gathered what support he could and marched to meet them. The two armies met at Sauchieburn, south of Stirling, in June 1488.

It was a fierce battle, with the King on one side and his elder son on the other. But James was no hero and when he saw the tide turning against him he quietly left the field, alone, and rode off, a failure to the end. He got as far as the mill of Bannockburn, ironical location for his tragedy, when, reluctant to ford the burn, his horse threw him, and crashing to the ground in his heavy armour, he was stunned. The miller and his wife found him and dragged him into a nearby stable. There, when he came to, in pain and misery, he declared that he was the King, and dying, and commanded the miller to find him a priest to shrive him ere he died.

The miller, naturally, could not produce a priest at short notice. But then up rode a party of armoured knights to whom he appealed for help. These were some of the rebel lords, led by Lord Gray, the same who had first suggested belling the cat. They had observed the King riding off and come after him. When Gray heard that the monarch was there, needing a priest to shrive him, he declared that *he* would shrive James Stewart, and going to the stable he drew his dirk and stabbed the King to death there and then.

It was shortly after this ghastly deed that the fifteen-year-old Duke was brought to the scene, and seeing his father's gashed body lying there he knew a great sorrow and regret. He had never got on with his father, but recognised how he had allowed himself to be used by the lords against him.

Turning away, stricken with guilt, he saw a length of harness-chain hanging from a hook on the stable-wall and impulsively taking this down he tied it round his waist and loins, beneath his armour and doublet, vowing to wear it there to his dying day to remind him of the part he had unwittingly played in his father's death. Some historians have scoffed at this story, as a mere picturesque legend. But if they were to consult the Lord High Treasurer's Accounts for the next reign they would discover more than one entry written: 'To ane link to the King's chain – so much': this as James IV's girth increased with middle age.

So now a new James Stewart was on the throne – and a notably different one; for despite the terrible disaster at the end, he was to prove one of the best monarchs Scotland ever had. Young as he was, right away he began to take order with the lords who had hitherto used and bullied him and even at his coronation was leaving no doubts as to who was now in charge. It is significant that from the first there was no question of a regency.

The young king faced enormous challenges. For generations the realm had been mismanaged, the nobles out-of-hand, the people persecuted and given over to lawlessness, the Highlands at war with the Lowlands, the English threat ever present. How James dealt with all this, and with a notable degree of success, makes a fascinating study – but not for recounting here. He was able, courageous, determined, and with a strong sense of humour, a keen athlete and sportsman also, and quickly became immensely popular with his subjects, who found that at last they had a king whom they could trust, admire, even love. And this greatly helped, especially in his control of the nobles. He had his faults, of course. He was headstrong, romantic and perhaps too fond of women; and in the end it was for these that Scotland had to pay the price.

He had advantages other than his character. Henry VII, the first Tudor, now sat somewhat uneasily on the English throne, and was fully occupied in putting down risings, of both Yorkist and Lancastrian origins, with the pretensions of would-be rivals such as Lambert Simnel and Perkin Warbeck. Also the French were on the upturn again. Then

James had the advice of the wise Bishop Elphinstone of
Aberdeen and the very useful support of Andrew Wood of
Largo, the admiral.

Presumably it was Wood who instilled in James the useful-
ness of having a fleet of warships, something which the Scots
had never attempted hitherto; and this became a priority with
the young King. So often English invasions had been aided,
indeed spear-headed, from the sea. Wood was a Fife laird,
but also a merchant-venturer and shipmaster – and probably
something of a pirate. At any rate, he seems to have been a
born sea-commander and was speedily to give evidence of his
prowess, for only the year after James's accession, although it
was during truce, a squadron of five English ships came up
to wreak piratical havoc in the Firth of Forth, attacking the
Scots merchant vessels. Wood put to sea with two cannon-
carrying ships, his famous *Yellow Carvel* and *The Flower*, and
in a running fight off Dunbar, at the mouth of the Forth,
not only beat the English flotilla but captured all five ships
and brought them in triumph into Leith.

This was a notable boost to Scots morale – and an equal
blow to the English. So much so that Henry could not ignore
it, truce or none, and next year sent up one of his best
captains, Stephen Bull, with three larger and more heavily-
armed vessels, to regain English command of the sea. Again
Andrew Wood went out to meet them with his two ships,
and this time had a still tougher fight on his hands, against
more powerful and more numerous guns and better ship-
handling. Starting off St Abb's Head in Berwickshire, the
battle went on all day and into the night, the vessels drifting
northwards, crowds watching from the Scottish shore. At
daylight the struggle was resumed until, off the mouth of the
Tay, Wood eventually got the upper hand. He was thereafter
able to escort all three battered enemy ships into Dundee
harbour, to great rejoicings. In a typical dashing and romantic
gesture James, who admired bravery in all men, not only
knighted Wood but pressed gifts on Stephen Bull and his
men, and even sent them back to England in their own ships
– which probably rubbed salt into King Henry's wounds.
Not all the English seamen were returned, however, for we
read that thereafter Sir Andrew Wood was allowed to use

his English naval prisoners to help build his fine new castle at Largo.

James now turned his attention to the situation which had been looking like repeating the danger to the crown which the Battle of Harlow had lifted a century before – the expansionist activities of the Lords of the Isles. In this instance the young King himself led his forces up to the north-western seaboard, and in a brilliant campaign of manoeuvre, threat and diplomacy, succeeded not only in defeating the Lord of the Isles but of effectively forfeiting the lordship itself to the crown and merging it into the kingship – where it has remained, so that today Lord of the Isles is one of the heir to the throne's Scottish titles.

It would be an exaggeration to say that women were the downfall of James IV, but women certainly played a very large part in his life and much affected his fate. He started early, with Mariot Boyd, daughter of the Laird of Bonshaw, and by her he had a son, born in 1493, when he was still under twenty. This was Alexander, destined to become Archbishop of St Andrews only seventeen years later and to die with his father on Flodden Field. James then fell headlong in love with the Lady Margaret Drummond, daughter of Lord Drummond, and her he wanted to marry – after all, there had already been two Drummond queens. But Margaret and her sister died together mysteriously one morning in 1502, poison being suspected. Henry of England was offering his nine-year-old daughter Margaret Tudor to James as wife, and it was thought that those in favour of the English match, to put it no higher, decided that they had to get rid of the Drummond girl.

James was desolate, for this was the really great love of his life. But of course there were other women, in especial the Lady Janet Kennedy, daughter of the second Lord Kennedy and grand-niece of the late Bishop (who would not have approved). She was known as Flaming Janet, on account both of her red hair and of her wild spirit. She was, in fact, betrothed to none other than Bell-the-Cat, old enough to be her grandfather, and he had made over to her the lordship and castle of Bothwell, when she was swept off her lightsome feet by King James. He did not seek to wed her, remaining loyal to Margaret Drummond; but she rejected the Earl of Angus – but not the Bothwell lordship – and this remained a sore point between Red Douglas and his liege-lord for the rest of their days.

James's character was indeed a curious mixture. Despite his need for the love and affection of women, he made the sacrifice, for the nation's sake, of entering into a loveless marriage, persuaded that Henry's renewed offer of his daughter would be advantageous, for with it came a treaty of perpetual peace with England. So in 1503 they were wed, he aged twenty-eight and she only thirteen.

Margaret Tudor proved to be no catch for the mettlesome James. Even at that age she was plain and as unattractive as to disposition as to appearance. Of all the queens Scotland had had, she was probably the least agreeable – and bride for Scotland's most romantic king.

So James continued to find distraction elsewhere, particularly with Janet Kennedy. Not to make it too blatant, he developed a habit of making frequent pilgrimages, allegedly at the behest of his conscience over his father's death – he was still wearing his chain. Probably there was truth in that, too, but it is noteworthy that the pilgrimages were to St Ninian's shrine at Whithorn in Galloway whilst Janet was living at her father's castles of Casillis or Maybole, which houses made a convenient halfway stopover, going and coming; and when, with a son born and requiring some paternal acknowledgment, James bestowed on him the earldom of Moray, with its seat Darnaway Castle, and mother and child removed thither, the King promptly transferred his allegiance from St Ninian to St Duthac of Tain, to which northern shrine Darnaway likewise was a convenient halfway-house.

Alas, James's matrimonial sacrifice proved abortive, for in 1509 Henry VII died and was succeeded by Henry VIII, and he quickly showed himself to be more of Margaret's brother than his father's son, an arrogant, petulant and treacherous young man of eighteen, vain as he was aggressive. The treaty of perpetual peace had little relevance for the new King of England.

There followed a number of pin-pricks, largely at sea,

where James's new navy was apt to clash with English ships, both frequently acting in piratical fashion. When, in 1511, Andrew Barton, one of the most prominent Scots captains, lost his ships and was slain in an engagement with the Lords Edward and Thomas Howard, the breach between the two monarchs opened wide. It was added to by the fact that Henry's Queen, Catherine of Aragon, continued to be childless, whereas Margaret next year produced a son for James, another James – and, what with the Tudors being so unprolific and the Wars of the Roses having killed off all the collateral contenders, it so happened that this infant, Henry's nephew, was male heir to the *English* throne, an unheard-of development. We all know how Henry sought to cope with *that* situation.

What brought matters to the inevitable flash-point, in view of the temperaments of these two kings, was typical of them both. Henry had made a compact with the Pope that if James invaded England he would be excommunicated. And James, religiously-minded in a conventional way, was upset by this and sought to improve his position with the Vatican, and also to demonstrate his muscular Christianity. He took up the Papal idea of a belated Crusade to liberate the Holy Land and stop the Turkish advance into Christian Europe. Pope Julius II was strong on this – but sadly, James, despite being the most remote from the scene of action, was the only prince in Christendom prepared to take this Crusade seriously, and it all fell through.

However Henry, with Europe in turmoil, saw it as an excellent opportunity to attack France, and Louis XII appealed to the Auld Alliance with Scotland to create the traditional distraction. Not only so, but the French Queen actually sent James her glove and a ring, in the romantic chivalric fashion, pleading with him to advance even three feet into England for her sake.

That was the sort of challenge which James Stewart could by no means resist, so the die was cast. He assembled a great army, possibly the greatest Scotland had ever fielded, some accounts putting the numbers at 60,000, some at 100,000. There were 17 large cannon, drawn by over 400 oxen. They headed for the Border.

There was no hurry – there could not be, with those oxen
and the numbers involved; and besides, in typical fashion,
James had sent the English commander left behind by Henry
when he went to France, the veteran Earl of Surrey, notice
that he was coming and a challenge to meet him in a fortnight's time.

So the Scots took their time. Across Tweed, they besieged
Norham Castle and took it, then went on to Wark and Etal
Castles, which they also captured, pressing on up the valley
of the Till. Still there was no word of Surrey.

The tradition goes that, to fill in the time of waiting,
James 'dallied' at Ford Castle, where lived the attractive Lady
Heron, whose husband, it so happened, was at that time a
prisoner in Lord Home's Fast Castle, hostage for his brother,
accused of the murder of some Scots. James had met Elizabeth Heron before and found her to his taste. He dallied,
therefore – and the lady, it is reputed, found his chain
uncomfortable and besought him to put it off meantime. This
is the only reported female objection to the chain round the
King's loins.

But at last the English army was reported to be coming,
and James took up a strong position on the long hog's-back
ridge of Brankston Edge, above Flodden, in the vale of Till,
to offer Surrey open challenge. But the English commander,
that 'auld crooked carle', was no chivalric demonstrator but
a cunning and stern realist. Instead of a head-on clash, he
divided his force, and sending the smaller section under his
son, the Lord Admiral, in full view of the Scots on the ridge,
round to the north of the position, he kept the greater portion
hidden, and moved in secrecy to a situation under the hill,
where they could not be got at without the Scots coming
down to them. Shrewdly Surrey gauged his opponent. There
the main English army waited.

James being James and, of course, the challenger in this
encounter, when his scouts brought him word of the situation, did what Surrey had guessed and planned for. He
could not sit up on his ridge like some besieged castle
garrison waiting to be starved out. He had come to fight. He
ordered the strong Scots position to be abandoned and his
forces to rush down the steep hill to the attack. Unfortunately

this meant leaving tens of thousands of horses up there on the high ground, for the escarpment was too steep for mounted men to descend and also too steep for the cannon to depress their muzzles. So the Scots went into battle without cavalry or artillery, save for a mounted force under the Lord Home which had been sent off on the left to outflank the Lord Admiral's corps.

James's leaders were largely of his own mind in the matter and co-operated heartily. But not old Archibald Bell-the-Cat. He protested that this was folly, in no very polite terms; and when the King insisted, he declared that he and his would have no part in it. Charged with unfaithfulness, even cowardice, the Earl in fury turned his back on his liege lord and called on his sons to follow him, with the Douglas strength, back to Scotland. None did, and the old Red Douglas walked off alone along Branxton Edge as the army flung itself forward, down the hill.

It was disaster, of course, the greatest military defeat Scotland ever suffered, led in utter folly, as Angus had said, by her beloved monarch, who did not act the general but merely the dashing spearhead of the assault. Perhaps he recollected how his father had failed to lead at Sauchieburn? Louis of France had sent a vast consignment of thousands of eighteen-foot-long pikes, as an inducement to fight, and James felt that these had to be used. They would have been invaluable in defensive hedgehog positions against cavalry; but for men hurtling down a steep rocky hillside they were worse than useless, utter menace. They tripped men up, overbalanced them, got in the way, broke, splintered and pierced – but not the enemy. And at the foot of the escarpment, the utterly disorganised rush was met by a continuing hail of English arrows, the age-old English menace. The Scots dead piled up in mile-long swatches, still far out of reach of the enemy.

Even so, it takes a long time for scores of thousands to die, in the sort of hand-to-hand fighting which eventually developed. But die they did, and James and his seventeen-year-old Archbishop son by Mariot Boyd, with them, the King on top of the youth and both on top of a mountain of the slain.

It is said that the King's body, when discovered next day,

was found not to be wearing his chain – and Scotland, in its mourning, blamed a broken vow and the Lady Heron.

There are two particularly interesting footnotes to this appalling tragedy. One is that the Lord Home and his cavalry, having won their own lesser battle with Surrey's son, might conceivably have still saved the day had they swung round from the north into the main English rear and over-run it. But instead Home chased off after the fleeing Admiral's cavalry, westwards, and was seen no more that day. The other postscript refers to the fact that, as night fell, and the fighting still went on, Surrey himself did not know that he had triumphed. Indeed as darkness made it impossible to continue, he drew back, summoned his principal lieutenants and soundly berated them for failure, inefficiency and disobedience of orders. It was only in the morning, when they discovered that only the Scots dead remained on the field, mountains of them, that he realised that in fact victory was his – and he promptly knighted forty of the captains whom the night before he had so roundly chastised in the fog of war.

Chapter 11

SCOTLAND'S GUDEMAN

The legacy left by James to his one-year-old son, James V, in 1513, was an appalling one. The nation was shattered by its losses. It was said that there was scarcely a home in all the land which did not mourn its dead, largely of course the bread-winners. Most of the nobility had died at Flodden with their King, the lords and lairds and their heirs too. Also the provosts, magistrates and councillors of many of the burghs, who had taken the field for their beloved monarch. Numbed shock and chaos reigned, the country was wide open to invasion.

If attack did not follow on a national scale, because Henry needed all his armed strength for his French adventures, there was no lack of enterprise on a more local basis. Lord Dacre, the English Warden of the Marches, led the way – and sent Henry this report: 'There was never so mekill myschefe, robbery, spoiling and vengeance in Scotland than there is nowe, without hope of remedye; which I pray our Lord God to continewe.' Everywhere raiding parties from England crossed the Border, to harry and ravish and steal, deep into Lowland Scotland. Defenceless, the people cowered.

Or not quite defenceless and not all cowering. It is significant that many of the famed annual Common Riding festivities, still such a feature of Border life, take their themes from this grim period. Selkirk, for instance, remembers the return from Flodden of only one of its contingent, the Town Clerk – trust a Selkirk lawyer to survive, as the Hawick folk would say; and Hawick itself celebrates a more positive event, the bloody triumph of Hornshole.

The year after Flodden, one of the English raiding parties, that of the Prior of Hexham no less, came burning, raping and looting up Teviotdale. It got as far as Denholm-on-the-Green, under Minto Hill, and there, glutted with the spoils, the raiders camped for the night in the riverside haugh of Hornshole, preparatory to proceeding on to attack Hawick town the next day. Hawick, like the other Border burghs, had lost its man-power, but the youth and boys of the town banded together and, with such makeshift weaponry as they could find, set out to do what their fathers would have done. They reached the bend of Teviot three miles to the east and there they found the Northumbrian camp all but unguarded, the raiders careless in their confidence, drunken, roystering or asleep. In unholy glee the youngsters recognised their opportunity, and fell upon the invaders out of the darkness, daggers, knives, hatchets, bludgeons flailing. Whatever resistence was offered was unavailing. Almost to a man the English were massacred. The youths returned to Hawick in triumph, bearing their trophies, in especial the blue flag with the golden saltire, the banner of the Priory of Hexham – which – or once it wore out, its replica – has been carried at the Common Ridings ever since, in celebration of the deliverance of 1514.

'Teribus ye Teri Odin, sons of heroes slain at Flodden,
Emulating Border bowmen, aye defend your rights
    and common!'

The Scots are always best in times of national danger, and the Borderers were not alone in their efforts at defence and defiance. Edinburgh itself was typical. Its provost and magistrates had fallen with their King, but the remaining citizenry rallied, every male who could bear arms, from mere boys to dotards, training in their use; and a great new wall was hastily erected round the city, still known as the Flodden Wall. As well that the people themselves thus took their fate in their own hands, for leadership was at the lowest ebb. Queen Margaret Tudor assumed the regency, but not unnaturally was distrusted by most, not only as Henry's sister but because of her nature. She bore a posthumous child six months after Flodden – but in another five months had remarried, this time to none other than Bell-the-Cat's grandson, aged only nineteen, now Earl of Angus, for the old man had not long survived the monarch on whom he had turned his back.

Needless to say, what was left of leadership could scarcely accept this Englishwoman and the grandson of the disgraced Red Douglas as rulers, and so sent for the next nearest heir to the throne to be Regent – John Stewart, Duke of Albany, son of the late Duke and cousin of the infant King. He took his time to come – after all, he had been brought up as a Frenchman, was indeed Admiral of France, and could speak neither Scots nor English; and Scotland was no enticing land to come to rule for a child-monarch. Meanwhile, there was all but civil war again, with the Queen's and Douglas faction against the rest, and no real government. When Albany did arrive, in 1515, Margaret and Angus fled to her brother in England.

But Albany's task was hopeless from the start, and he was no born viceroy anyway. Henry wrote and told the Scots that if they wished to retain his friendship – less than obvious as this had been hitherto – they must send Albany packing back to France. This was scarcely the way to gain his ends – but after only two years of it, Albany returned home of his own accord, in disgust. Margaret Tudor came back.

Now there was administrative chaos indeed, for Albany was still officially Regent and the Queen Mother's actions had no force in law. Moreover she had tired of young Angus and was seeking a divorce. She turned to the Hamilton Earl of Arran, who had near links with the crown – his mother was that Princess Mary who had been wed as a child to Thomas Boyd, Earl of Arran, and when he had died abroad, had married the Lord Hamilton and brought him the earldom of Arran. Needless to say, this new liaison did not please the Douglases, and open warfare erupted. That this took place largely in the capital city of Edinburgh made it the more unacceptable. It so happened that Arran was Provost of Edinburgh at the time, but on one of his trips elsewhere the Douglases managed to shut the city gates against him and he had to retire to Glasgow, bringing the two cities into a state of hostility. However there was a meeting of the Estates of Parliament in 1520, which enabled the Hamiltons to get back into Edinburgh, and in force. A major clash seemed inevitable, and the citizens went to ground. Gavin Douglas, the poet-Bishop of Dunkeld, tried to get Archbishop Beaton, a Hamilton supporter and Chancellor of the Realm, to use his authority to avert an encounter. This was the celebrated occasion when Beaton called his conscience to witness that on his oath no mischief was intended. Unfortunately to emphasise his sincerity the Archbishop beat on his breast – and there was the hollow clang of metal from hidden armour beneath the archepiscopal vestments. 'Methinks your conscience, my lord, is not a good one, for I heard it clatter!' the Douglas said.

The dreaded battle duly took place thereafter, in Edinburgh's High Street, a fierce and bloody affray in which the Douglases won hands down. Arran escaped with his life but had to flee to France. This extraordinary behaviour of the King's stepfather and the King's cousin gained the appelation of Cleanse the Causeway – a Douglas description, needless to say.

Albany came back in 1521, sent for more out of desperation than anything else. But he could achieve little in such circumstances – with the Queen Mother, for instance, who also still called herself Regent, sending to Surrey, Lieutenant of the North for Henry, to come over the Border and kidnap the young King and take him to England, a plot that fell through. After only a year, Albany went back to France in disgust, this time for good.

It is scarcely to be wondered at that James V grew up hardly the most responsible and reliable of monarchs. At fourteen he suddenly found himself being declared of full age and 'erected' to the rule of his kingdom – this partly so that his unpopular mother could pursue her latest passion, the young Henry Stewart, son of Lord Methven. More by default than choice the Chancellor, Archbishop Beaton, had to do any governing the distracted land received.

Even now James was largely a prisoner, at Stirling Castle, for Angus moved in to fill the vacuum and Beaton was not

strong enough to contain him. Gradually he filled up the
offices of state with Douglases. It is alleged that he deliberately encouraged his step-son in debauchery; and certainly
James developed a way with women which far outshone that
of his father, indeed any of the earlier Stewarts – which is
saying something – and at a remarkably early age. It is probably often forgotten how young the King was when he was
making his reputation as the Gudeman o' Ballengeich. After
all, he was only thirty when he died, after a reign of twenty-
nine years. Oddly enough, partly because later generations
have not realised just what the term gudeman meant, and
partly because James won a sort of popularity with the
common people – for he possessed the Stewart charm, was
good-looking and witty – he has garnered a better reputation
as monarch than he probably deserved. The fact is that, no
doubt more sinned against than sinning, he nevertheless
made a fairly feeble king. Gudeman has nothing to do with
goodness. A gudeman was a small farmer. And Ballengeich,
which he got tacked on to his by-name, was a tiny, rocky
croft tucked into the north face of the castle-hill of Stirling.
So, in fact, for a monarch, the title was one of derision. He
indeed behaved frequently more like a small farmer than a
king, showing no great interest in the affairs of his realm –
although of course, for long Angus did not allow him to, in
any major respect. His main preoccupation, young as he
might be, was with women; and his favourite alternative
diversion seems to have been hurly-hacket – that is, sliding
down the steep hillside of Stirling Castle to Ballengeich on
a cow's skull as sledge, using the horns as handles. At this
he became acknowledged champion.

The story has been assiduously propagated that when
Angus relaxed his grip James used to slip out almost every
evening, in disguise, to visit the homes of his ordinary
subjects, nobly to acquaint himself with their problems and
how they lived. In fact, it seems to have been his subjects
daughters that he sought, in determined and supremely catholic fashion, rich and poor alike. No monarch, of Scotland
at least, ever fathered so many bastards, and at such an early
age. One assessment is that he produced seven sons called
James Stewart, all by different noble ladies – presumably he

did not allow ignoble ones to call their sons James – and we know that other acknowledged sons were called other than James. How many daughters he sired is anybody's guess. In later years, when the Reformation was boiling up, he seems to have staffed many of the country's abbeys and priories with commendators named Abbot or Prior the Lord James Stewart.

James appears to have had a harsher side to his character too, as is displayed for us in the famous ballad of *Johnnie Armstrong*. The King had at last escaped from Angus, and helped to engineer his step-father's eventual downfall in 1528. Two years later, at the age of eighteen, he led an expedition down into the Borderland which, because of unending English invasions was in a state of more than usual lawlessness – or not quite lawlessness, for Johnnie Armstrong imposed his own laws over a large part of it. This did not suit many of the Border lords, who convinced James that a display of the royal authority must be staged.

So Johnnie was invited, in 'a luving letter', as the ballad puts it, to meet the King on a hunting-trip at the chapel of Caerlanrig, west of Hawick. Johnnie was laird of Gilnockie Tower near Langholm, a castle which still exists – indeed it has recently been restored. He was younger brother of Armstrong of Mangerton, chief of that warlike Border clan, but a much more dashing figure. It was claimed that he never rode abroad without a 'tail' of no less than thirty-six gentlemen of his own name; and could on occasion field as many as 2,000 mosstroopers. These figures may well be exaggerated, but they indicate a formidable character and explain why James used guile to meet him.

Johnnie turned up at Caerlanrig with his thirty-six esquires, more handsomely dressed and mounted than the monarch and his attendants. 'What lacks this knave that a king should have?' James demanded hotly at the sight, and dispensing with all further pretence, commanded that Johnnie and his Armstrongs should be strung up there and then from convenient trees.

Johnnie was too proud to plead for his life, but he did bargain, as one prince to another. He allegedly offered to provide the King with forty horsed and armed gentlemen to attend him at all times; he offered twenty-four milk-white horses and as much good English gold as they could carry; he offered the produce of twenty-four meal-mills annually; he offered to bring the King of Scots any Englishman he liked to name, be he duke, earl or baron, alive or dead, by any given day; and finally he offered a rent on every property between where they stood and his burgh of Newcastleton.

When all this, to be sure, only made James Stewart the more determined to get rid of so dangerous a subject, Johnnie made his celebrated valedictory speech:

> 'It was folly to seek grace at your Grace's graceless face; but had I known it, I should have lived long upon the Borders in despite of King Harry and you, both; for I know that King Harry would downweigh my best horse with gold to hear that I were condemned to die this day.'

And so the Armstrongs were hanged.

So says the ballad. But although there may be some romantic gloss on all this, the event did take place. The renowned Sir David Lindsay of the Mount, James's Lord Lyon King of Arms and author of *The Thrie Estaits*, puts these words into the mouth of a pardoner:

> 'The cordis baith grit and lang,
>   Quihilk hangit Johnie Armstrang,
> Of gude hemp, soft and sound,
>   Gude, haly people I stand ford,
> Wha'ever beis hangit in this cord
>   Neidis never to be drowned!'

Despite all his successes with the opposite sex, James's marital ventures were less felicitous. Henry wanted him married to his own daughter Mary – the same who later became the Bloody Mary, married to Philip of Spain – as an aid to grasping Scotland; but this was rejected. In 1536 it was arranged that he should wed Marie de Vendôme of France, and James set out from Galloway in great style with a train of one hundred knights. However, July storms all but wrecked the royal flotilla and they had to turn back. He tried again in September, but when he got to France he discovered the lady to be quite impossible, unthinkable as a wife, and had to beat an embarrassing retreat. However, whilst in France he met the Princess Madeleine, daughter of the King of France, and although she was very delicate, decided that she would serve. So they were wed. Sadly she died within a couple of months of reaching Scotland, and the quest had to recommence. It was scarcely married bliss that James sought, of course, but a legitimate heir for the succession. This time the choice fell on another Frenchwoman, again in the interests of the Auld Alliance, Marie de Guise of Lorraine, found for the King by David Beaton, the Archbishop's nephew of whom we shall hear much more – then acting ambassador at the French court. She proved to be a better bargain, for Marie de Guise was an able and practical women and was to be a major asset to Scotland. In due course she presented James with the lawful son he required, given the odd name, for Scotland, of Arthur. Unfortunately he was to die at an early age.

All this while the Reformation had been causing dire upheavals all over northern Europe, with the Romish Church in a grievous state of decadence. Strangely, in Scotland, where the Church's state was almost more corrupt than elsewhere, there was as yet little stirring. Henry VIII, of course, had his own reasons, scarcely religious, for falling out with Rome; and the Reformation in England was almost twenty years ahead of that of Scotland. This was by no means Henry's fault, for he quickly saw the opportunity of using incipient Protestant feeling in his own service, against the establishment of Crown and Church, with the Archbishop as Chancellor and James firmly tied to Catholic France in alliance and marriage. Henry instigated a cunning campaign, implanting secret reformers and agitators, succouring protesting priests – John Knox was one of these – bribing lords with promises of Church lands and doing all in his power to foment internal strife in the northern kingdom.

That he did not succeed in all those years was thanks largely to the efforts of one man – the aforementioned David Beaton, one of the most interesting characters in Scotland's story. Seventh son of a Fife laird, the Archbishop's brother, he had to make his own way in the world, and began it by becoming his uncle's secretary. As Chancellor was well as Primate, of course, this put young Davie in the way of learning much about statecraft and power-politics – and he was an able pupil, shrewd as he was ambitious. Quickly he made himself indispensable to the Archbishop and as the latter grew older took more and more of the decisions – and these were decisions of the State as well as of the Church. He went to France as ambassador and it is important to note that it was whilst there, and not before, that he took holy orders, and indeed through the influence of King Louis was promptly given the nominal bishopric of Mirepoix. This matter of becoming a priest has a vital bearing on what was to follow.

After James's marriage Davie came back to Scotland and renewed his more-than-secretaryship to his uncle. Now, as Bishop of Mirepoix, he had to have greater standing in this country and was given the rich abbacy of Arbroath. Much has been made of Davie's immorality, although in those days it was almost a normal state, from the King down. But Beaton's case was rather special, not only with what he was able to do, with his power-base, and the wealth of Arbroath Abbey, but because almost certainly he was already married and with a family. This is no place to recount the evidence I could quote for that assertion. It was forbidden, of course for one in holy orders to have a wife; but Davie Beaton had reached man's estate before he went to France; and there he entered the priesthood. Why did he do it, then? For one very good reason – so that he could succeed his uncle as Primate of Scotland and Chancellor of the Realm. Old James Beaton was fast becoming senile and unable to cope; and Scotland had a particularly feeble crop of prelates just then, symptomatic of the decay of Holy Church. It was said that some of them could not even recite the Lord's Prayer. And some were in the pay of King Henry. It required a strong hand at the helm of Church and State, especially with the Reformation looming. So Davie saw both opportunity and duty – and took the plunge. It meant, of course, reducing his wife, Margaret Ogilvy, daughter of the Lord Ogilvy of Airlie, to the status of mistress and having to legitimise his already legitimate offspring by her, in order that they could inherit the property he was able to give them, an expensive business. But presumably he considered it worth while whatever his wife thought, although she remained with him to the end – an apparently loving couple. It is amusing that a large number of the castles of Angus and The Mearns have the story that they were built by Cardinal (as he became in 1538) Beaton for his many mistresses and bastards. But when further detail is sought, it always turns out that the mistress was Margaret Ogilvy and the bastards her sons and daughters. John Knox, Beaton's great enemy, described her as the Cardinal's 'chief lewd', a marvellous phrase. I have come across no evidence that he had any other.

At any rate, when old Archbishop James became quite incapable, David, Abbot of Arbroath, found himself able to move quietly into the archepiscopal shoes. And since he had been doing the work effectively anyway for some time, King James was quite agreeable that he became Chancellor or chief minister also. So there was Davie Beaton, to all intents ruling Scotland – and much more efficiently that she was accustomed to.

Until 1546, then, Cardinal Beaton was busy indeed. Fortunately he had an ally in the new Queen – not in the old, for Margaret Tudor was a handicap to the last, tiring of her then husband, Henry, Lord Methven, seeking another divorce and proposing of all things to bring back the exiled Angus from England and remarry him. Fortunately, probably, she died before this could be effected. There were plenty of more urgent problems than this for Beaton to deal with, of course, especially the Henry VIII efforts at promoting Protestantism in Scotland. Coping with this was a constant battle, not so much from the religious as the political aspect. How much true religion the Cardinal had in him is a matter for debate; but he was a patriot, and his efforts, almost single-handed, at checking the English machinations were on the whole effective. He got little help from the Scots lords, whose power was at an especially low ebb. Beaton has been much blamed for burning heretics. In Scotland eleven were so burned, tragic enough; and he, as both Primate and Chancellor could not avoid responsibility. But during the same period Henry in England burned over 10,000, and yet has not been greatly criticised for *that* one of his many crimes.

Henry, of course, tried many times to get rid of Beaton, by kidnapping and by poison. He plotted his murder and offered £1,000 sterling as expenses for the job. He sent as agent a Scot named Wishart; whether this was the same George Wishart whom Beaton caught, and was soon to be martyred at St Andrews, has been endlessly debated. But the preacher *was* a pensioner of Henry's, like Knox. Some indication of Henry's virulence may be gleaned from his instructions to the Earl of Hertford, in charge of the first of his invasions:

> 'Burne Edinborough towne – when you have sacked and gotten what you can of it . . . sack Holyrood house . . . sack Lythe (Leith) and burne and subvert it and all the rest, putting man, woman and child to fyre and sword without exception.'

The Gudeman of Ballengeich was no warrior-prince, and with the awful example of his father's Flodden ever before him, he was always loth to take up the sword. But Henry's savagery and menace eventually, in 1542, drove James to retaliatory action. After an abortive attempt, at Fala Muir, when his nobles refused to proceed across the Border, he put on a smaller expedition, under the command of his current favourite courtier, one Sir Oliver Sinclair, of the 'lordly line of high St Clair'. Sinclair was in fact a no more effective general than was James; indeed the Scots were at this time all inexperienced in warfare, not having indulged in any since 1513; whereas the English were veterans of continuous continental campaigning. James chose to make his venture in the west, and the Battle of Solway Moss was the result, when the lords refused to obey the upjumped Sinclair and were shamefully routed by an English force only a quarter of their strength. It was an appalling disaster, allegedly only 20 Scots being actually slain, although many were drowned in panic flight, and 1,200 were taken prisoner, including 2 earls, 5 lords and over 500 knights and lairds, the most humiliating defeat in Scots history.

James's morale was shattered. Presumably his health was

impaired otherwise, for youngish men of thirty do not die of broken hearts, whatever the poets may say. But desperately depressed, partly over the loss of his beloved Sinclair who had been taken prisoner, he retired to his Fife palace of Falkland, pausing only briefly at Linlithgow, it is to be noted, where his Queen was awaiting childbirth again. A few days later the news arrived that he was the father of a daughter, not the son he had hoped for. Despairingly he made the only renowned statement of his life. 'It cam with a lass and it will gang with a lass!' he groaned from the bed he had taken to and refused to leave, this referring to the crown coming to the Stewarts through Marjory, the Bruce's daughter – ironical indeed for a man who had sired so many bastard sons. Then, according to the chroniclers, he turned his face to the wall and yielded up the ghost. What James died of is not clear – but he was dead within a week of his daughter's birth. And Scotland had a queen-regnant, as never before – since the Maid of Norway scarcely counted – Mary Queen of Scots, one week old. The so-familiar tragedy for the nation, of a monarch's long minority, started once more.

Fortunately this time the land had two strong figures to hold the reins of government, the Queen Mother, Marie of Guise, and David Beaton. As well that it had, for this dynastic situation provided Henry with a new theme of conquest to add to those of invasion, bribery, murder and Reformation – marriage of the baby-queen to his sickly infant son Edward, whom Jane Seymour, his third wife, had given him. This marriage the surely half-mad Tudor was determined on, and he pursued the project for the rest of his life, with his usual ruthless intensity. It became known as the Rough Wooing.

And rough it was, by a past master in roughness. By every means in his considerable power, Henry sought to get the child Mary into his clutches, and Scotland with her. He was aided by one event in especial – and whether or no he actually engineered it is still argued over. He got rid of Davie Beaton, in 1546.

The Cardinal's end was sufficiently dramatic. An account describes graphically how he was 'in his naked bed' in an upper chamber of the Sea-Tower of St Andrews Castle early one morning, when a knock came to his door – and being a prudent man, he kept his door locked. He called 'Who is there?' The answer came, 'A friend.' Still cautious, he asked, 'Which friend?' Came the reply, 'Friend Norman.' This was Norman Leslie, Master of Rothes, and hitherto indeed a friend. So Davie rose and opened the door. And in they streamed, about a dozen men, dressed as workmen, their disguise for getting into the castle, friend Norman amongst them. Only, he and the others had drawn daggers in their hands. They started to stab. But presently one of them, the Reverend James Melville, one of the Protestant divines, held up his hand, crying, 'Halt! Halt! This is not being done godly. Let us pray!' So they all knelt – but not the Cardinal, who was already on the floor – and Melville led them in prayer. Then he resumed his dagger-work and they finished off Beaton and hung his naked body by an ankle from the tower-window, facing, as they said, the spot where George Wishart had been burned not long before.

This account is testified to in John Knox's *History of the Reformation*, and he adds the significant rider. 'These things we write merrily.'

So now Mary of Guise stood more or less alone, to counter Henry. Wisely she managed to import quite large numbers of French mercenary troops to help in the process. As well that she did, for Henry promptly sent Hertford to invade again on a massive scale. The English got as far as Edinburgh, but failing to take the great fortress, turned back and were themselves besieged by a Scots-French force in the East Lothian county town of Haddington. Henry had to send up a fleet to try to relieve them. The fleet sought to land troops and munitions in Aberlady Bay, five miles from Haddington, but this was opposed by the castle of Luffness, at the head of the bay, garrisoned for the occasion by the French general de Thermes, well supplied with cannon. The ramparts which de Thermes threw up to base his artillery are still very much in evidence at Luffness. So accurate and sustained was the cannonade that the English Fleet had to draw off. Hertford had eventually to be relieved by land, at much cost in casualties – and Scotland breathed again.

But not for long. Henry, of course, was beside himself with fury and ordered a greater punitive expedition, fetching in large numbers of Spanish and Portuguese mercenaries to assist. To Scotland's relief, the Tudor died before this huge army could set out, to be succeeded by the nine-year-old Edward VI as King, with Hertford, his uncle, now promoted Duke of Somerset, as Lord Protector. Somerset went ahead with the Scots invasion nevertheless. The Scots were overwhelmed at the Battle of Pinkie, and all the southern half of the country fell to the invader. Somerset demanded the surrender of the child-Queen, but Mary of Guise's answer had been to despatch her daughter secretly to France, and safety.

Thereafter Scotland had to suffer one of the most ghastly reigns of terror she had ever undergone, particularly at the hands of the Spanish and Levantine mercenaries – with the French mercenaries, in fugitive bands, also terrorising the countryside. It is reported that it was quite a frequent occurrence for the Frenchmen to take prisoners of the local people purely to sell them to the Spanish and Portuguese for these to have the pleasure of putting them to death horribly. The years 1549 and 1550 were appalling.

In the treaty terms imposed on Scotland, one of the clauses stipulated the 'spoiling' of Luffness Castle, which two years before had prevented the relief of Hertford in Haddington. The Lord Protector had a good memory, at least.

Chapter 12

REFORMED CHARACTERS

It must have seemed scarcely possible that Scotland could ever win out of the desperate state she was in during the early years of Mary's reign. The resilience of her people, however, is never to be underestimated. The Queen Mother's influence, too, and her French backing, was a major factor, and circumstances elsewhere contributed notably. For one thing, the sickly young Edward VI died after only a brief reign, and his older sister Mary came to the throne – so there were two Marys reigning in these islands. And Mary Tudor quickly earned the grim title of Bloody Mary in her five-year reign. She had had a troubled childhood, with her appalling father, and in revulsion to Henry she became a perfervid Catholic. And, of course, for political reasons, she had been wed to His Most Catholic Majesty, Philip of Spain. So now a savage anti-Protestant regime took over in England – and the first to go to the scaffold was Lord Protector Somerset. Persecution and civil war there came to Scotland's rescue, and the enemy occupation was withdrawn. It all had another effect; it meant that the Protestant Scots, whom Henry had encouraged and sheltered, were no longer acceptable at court, and they tended to come home, for Scotland, although still Catholic, was not rabidly so. John Knox, after a brief sojourn in Geneva, was amongst the returned exiles, toughened still further by a spell as a galley-slave.

There are many assessments of Knox, his character and his impact on Scotland, some adulatory, some the reverse. Without taking sides, which is difficult, it can confidently be said that he was a great man and of tremendous driving-force. Comparatively humbly born, near Haddington, he was reared for the priesthood but early was smitten with reforming zeal. Making things too hot to hold him in Beaton's Scotland, he fled to Henry's England, where he sufficiently impressed the new Reformed Church and its royal head to be given the Rectorship of Newcastle and indeed offered a bishopric. Had he accepted it, as seemed possible, history might have been very different. But he did not. And when Bloody Mary's repressions began he fled to the Continent, and then came back to Scotland. His enemy Beaton was dead and had been succeeded by lesser men; and Marie of Guise had her Catholic hands full, and was seeking to unite rather than divide her daughter's realm.

Knox, of course, a brilliant orator as well as a forceful personality, was no peacemaker, and laboured, to great effect. Even the fairly reasonable Queen Mother could not ignore his activities, and he had to flee to Geneva again. While there, he was tried by an ecclesiastical court in Scotland, and in his absense his body assigned to the flames and his soul to damnation.

However, encouraged by the rise of Protestant feeling in Scotland, greatly daring he came back in April 1559. He was immediately summoned to appear for trial again, and before the Queen Mother herself, at Stirling. Instead he made his way to Perth, with large numbers of Protestant supporters; and there followed an extraordinary scene. He entered the great Church of St John, which gave Perth its name of St John's Town of Perth, and, although it was celebrating a Romish Mass, went to the pulpit and delivered a vehement and rousing sermon on the evils of Popery; presumably the clerics in charge were afraid of the mob, who had come in with Knox. However, when he had finished his sermon, one bolder priest went on to continue with the Mass, opening a tabernacle on the high altar. This, oddly, provoked the protest of a mere boy – whom the shocked priest turned and cuffed on the ear. The boy, according to Knox's own account, picked up a stone – although what loose stones were doing in the church is not explained – and threw it at the priest. It missed him and hit the tabernacle, smashing what Knox calls the images, presumably painted pictures thereon. At this 'sign' as it were, all hell broke loose, and the congregation surged forward and began to smash up the entire church. When they could find nothing more to wreck there, they rushed out and attacked the Greyfriars, Blackfriars and Charterhouse monastries. Knox more or less washes his hands of this riot, declaring that 'the whole multitude convened, not of the gentlemen, neither of them that were earnest professors, but of the rascal multitude.' Nevertheless, thereafter, he led the said rascal multitude on a great spree of image-smashing and pulling down of 'idolatrous shrines and buildings', even to the metropolitan religious capital of St Andrews itself. And almost everywhere in southern Scotland similar scenes were enacted, and abbeys, priories, monasteries and churches were wrecked and burned. Thus reform came to Scotland.

Knox, however, recognised that this sort of thing, however dramatic, would not change the Catholic government of the kingdom; and with shrewd understanding of the way to convert the nobility, helped to weld together a coalition of the lords by indicating that half the best land in Scotland was in the hands of Holy Church, thanks largely to death-bed repentancies over the centuries and last-minute salvings of uneasy lordly consciences by donations for priestly absolutions. If Catholicism could be brought down, what had happened in England years before could happen here, and all this land become available for the winners. This appealed mightily to the nobles, by no means all fervid Protestants, and the so-called Lords of the Congregation was the result. John Knox was most skilful in using them. Also he imported literally cart-loads of Bibles printed in English – the English were probably glad to get rid of them, in Bloody Mary's regime – and these greatly encouraged the spread of Protestantism – for of course the Catholic Scriptures were in Latin and for the use of the priesthood only. The marriage of young Queen Mary in France to the Dauphin, who presently became King, making her Queen of so-Catholic France as well as Queen of Scots, gave the reformers cause to redouble their efforts, in fear that time might be working against them.

But suddenly the situation was largely reversed. Bloody Mary's brief and harsh reign ended with her death after only five years; and her staunchly Protestant half-sister Elizabeth came to the English throne. And shortly afterwards, Marie of Guise died. At a parliament held in 1560, even though it had no royal sanction and was therefore legally only a convention, Scotland was declared to be a reformed realm; and Knox hastily made up a Confession of Faith, which was accepted more or less as Gospel.

Whilst it would be inaccurate to say that Knox now ruled Scotland, he certainly was the most significant figure therein. The Earl of Arran was made Regent, but *he* was no strong figure. It was ruled that the saying or hearing of Mass was forbidden, with confiscation of property and imprisonment for a first offence, exile for a second and death for a third, Knox declaring that it would be better for the country to be invaded by ten thousand enemies than for one Mass to be celebrated. Reform Scotland might have gained, but tolerance, no.

It was to this situation that Mary Queen of Scots came home in 1561 – although it is to be doubted whether she ever really looked on Scotland as her home, after her fourteen formative years in France. From her mother's death the year before, there were moves to have her back; but being Queen of France now complicated the situation. However, when her delicate husband died, after only a seventeen-months reign, there was nothing to keep her – save for various marriage suggestions – and commissioners were sent to arrange her return. It is noteworthy that amongst these were two who were to play a large part in her life – her half-brother, the eldest of her father's bastards, the Lord James Stewart, later Earl of Moray; and James Hepburn, Earl of Bothwell. It is also noteworthy that the new Queen Elizabeth of England refused a safe-conduct for Mary's vessel.

At any rate, on 19 August 1561 she arrived safely at Leith, to the welcome of great crowds. If Mary accepted this as an encouraging sign, there were two views on the matter, for that evening at Holyrood, when large numbers came to serenade her, Knox himself describes it thus: 'Fyres of joy were set furth all nyght and a cumpany of the most honest, with instruments of musick and with musicians gave thair salutations at hir chalmer wyndo. The melody, as sche alledged, lyked her weil.' On the other hand, Brantôme complained, in French, that when the Queen wished to go to bed in the evening five or six hundred knaves of the town came under her window with wretched fiddles and small rebecs and sang psalms so badly out-of-tune that nothing could be worse.

But Mary could demonstrate too, and on her first Sunday at Holyrood insisted upon a celebration of Mass in the chapel there – which 'grittumlie annoyit' the Lords of the Congregation, and brought from Knox the thunder: 'Shall the idoll be suffered agane to tack place within this realm? It shall not!' The French officiating priest had to be escorted to his chamber afterwards through the angry Protestants by two more of the Queen's half-brothers, both Protestants, Robert and John, Commendators of Holyrood and Coldingham.

So the stage was set for confrontation. Mary was beautiful, high-spirited, courageous, but pleasure-seeking and injudicious. So much has been written about her short reign – for she ruled in Scotland only from 1561 to 1568 – that little in the way of elaboration is called for, or possible, here. She has been given more attention than any other Scots monarch – and, as a ruler, certainly does not deserve it, however intriguing and dramatic her story as a woman. She issued a proclamation the very next day declaring that none should seek to alter the state of religion prevailing, on pain of death; but equally that none should interfere in the religious observances of herself and others, also on pain or death. On the face of it this sounds fair and reasonable – but it must be recollected that Parliament had specifically prohibited the saying of Mass in Scotland, again under pain of death. So here was the sovereign of the said realm, in her first public pronouncement, declaring that she, and those who thought like her, would do just that. It other words, she challenged the authority of both Parliament and Kirk.

There was uproar straight away, of course, Knox thundering and Arran, the late Regent, declaring that to participate in or defend the Mass was more abominable in the sight of God than was murder.

Nineteen-year-old Mary sent for forty-seven-year-old Knox to appear before her at Holyrood, and there followed the first of those public encounters which have fired the imagination of so many generations, the young, beautiful and captivating woman and the stern, eloquent zealot, the one as determined as the other. Neither of them pulled any punches. Mary led off by accusing Knox of raising her subjects against first her mother and now herself, and also for his attitude to women in his notorious writings in *The First Blast of the Trumpet against the Monstrous Regiment of Women*, in which he had declared women to be weak, frail, impatient, feeble and foolish creatures, and that any rule by them was contrary to God and repugnant to nature. To this admittedly shrewd thrusting, the man replied that if she, the Queen, behaved well and did not bring the realm to disaster, he would not disallow her rule. But she must not interfere in matters of religion. He in fact compared the position of her Scots subjects to that of children whose father had gone insane. For himself, he would be as content to live under Her Grace as Paul was to live under Nero.

All the court listened enthralled and appalled to this astonishing battle between sovereign and subject. There could be no agreement or compromise, obviously, although Mary kept her hot temper surprisingly well; and though she shed tears at one stage, it was thought to be of anger rather than of grief. The confrontation, which in any other monarch would probably have seen Knox led off to imprisonment or worse, ended in a draw and indication to fight again another day, but with a sort of wary mutual respect, the Queen saying that she perceived that he would have her subjects obey him and not her, and he that it was not himself but God and His Kirk they must obey. When she asked was it not the Kirk of *Rome* which nine-tenths of Christendom obeyed, he sadly ended with, 'I fear of right knowledge ye have none!'

That interview, in fact, set the tone for much of Mary's reign. Her position was all but hopeless from the start. Mary had failings, but it was sad that it was her real virtue as a faithful, honest and determined adherent of her own faith which ensured her ultimate failure, the Catholic monarch of a Protestant land. The contradiction of her situation was exemplified by almost the first major action of her rule when she was forced by her Council to make an expedition into the North to put down the power of the Catholic Earl of Huntly, the chief of the Gordons. Huntly was something of a fool, admittedly, overbearing, arrogant and unrealistic, even suggesting that his third son, the handsome and dashing Sir John Gordon, would be a suitable husband for the Queen, and acting more or less as an independent prince in the north. But he was her principal Catholic noble and had offered 'to set up the Mass in three shires'; and it must have been galling indeed for her to have to take arms against him. But his son, the said Sir John, had got himself involved in an unsavoury scandal against the Ogilvies, and something like civil war loomed. So, at the same time as making a progress into the Highlands to show herself to her people in those parts, she was manoeuvred into the position of challenging Huntly in fight. The Battle of Corrichie was the result, in which Huntly himself expired, not of wounds but from apoplexy, falling from the saddle in a rage, and Sir John was captured. Thereafter the son was executed at Aberdeen in Mary's presence, the Gordon calling out that he was solaced by her being there since he was to suffer for love of her. To make matters worse, the executioner made a botched job of beheading the prisoner, and Mary collapsed in tears, one of the few occasions when she gave way to physical weakness, and had to be carried to her chamber. Huntly's dead body was later set up in court on a charge of treason, so that he could be declared guilty and his lands forfeited. Mary's eldest half-brother, the Lord James Stewart, Commendator of St Andrews, who was largely behind the entire business, got most of the Moray lands and was created Earl of Moray.

Poor Mary was not finished with reproachful executions, for returning south she put up one night in Burntisland Castle – now called Rossend and recently restored – and there the romantic French poet and courtier Chastelard hid himself under the bed in the room allocated to the Queen just before she retired. There, fortunately or otherwise, he was discovered, dragged out, and would have been despatched by the guards, there and then with their daggers, had not the new Earl of Moray come to intervene and declare that this would not do, that all should proceed lawfully and properly – he was a notable proponent of law and order was this James Stewart – and that Chastelard should be taken to St Andrews and there tried and punished for the crime of *lèse-majesté*. So there, next day, the unfortunate lovelorn poet was duly condemned to death – apparently he had done the same thing on a previous occasion and got away with it – and once again Mary was forced to witness an execution, with Chastelard crying out, 'Adieu, thou most beautiful and most cruel princess in the world!'

The fate of these two does not seem to have discouraged other admirers of the Queen's beauty and vivacity from seeking her favours. Nor does she appear to have discouraged them. Her personal entourage was notably gay, colourful and indiscreet, however frowned upon by the godly – and preached against by Knox consistently. It is noteworthy, nevertheless that the people, by and large, were less condemnatory, gaining much interest and amusement from the goings-on at court, an aspect of the Scots character and behaviour which has always tended to raise the ire of the puritanical.

A husband, of course, *was* sought for the Queen, for reasons of the succession, for there was no near heir to the throne, despite all the illegitimate half-brothers. Various suggestions were put forward, including the Archduke Charles of Austria and Don Carlos, son of the King of Spain – both of which Queen Elizabeth let it be known would offend *her;* and her own candidate was her personal favourite Robert Dudley, Earl of Leicester. But Mary's choice fell on her distant cousin Henry Stewart, Lord Darnley, son and heir of the Earl of Lennox. This was a sample of Mary's lack of judgment, both in matters of the heart and of statecraft; for although Darnley was as good-looking as he was well-born, he was weak, vain, effeminate and petulant; moreover, his mother, the Countess of Lennox, had been Margaret, daughter of the Earl of Angus and Margaret Tudor, and therefore even closer to the *English* throne, so that Elizabeth was almost bound to look with grave suspicion on the marriage of two possible claimants to her virgin crown. From the point of view of Scottish-English relations almost any match would have been better than this. But Mary had fallen headlong in love, and would hear of no other.

They were wed, and Darnley quickly showed his true character. He wanted the crown-matrimonial, that is the rank of king, not prince-consort, and sulked until he got it, in face of Mary's and the Council's reluctance. Then he started to interfere in affairs of state, offending almost everyone. Mary very soon tired of him, on discovering that there was little to him but his looks, and they drifted apart, all in less than a year of marriage.

The Queen, to be sure, did not lack for other male company, many of her courtiers and nobles being frankly in love with her, for whatever else she might be she was a most attractive, indeed magnetic young woman – a magnetism which has survived down the ages; it was said that even Knox himself was not proof against her charms and that this might be partly at the back of his abiding harshness towards her, in a sort of love-hate relationship. He was already a married man, of course. Amongst the most assiduous of her admirers was the dashing, brigand-like James Hepburn, Earl of Bothwell, whose headstrong masculinity appealed to Mary, especially in contrast to Darnley. Also she spent a lot of time in the company of David Rizzio, her personable Italian secretary, necessarily perhaps. If as secretary that was not to be wondered at, there was no lack of those who would suggest that there was more than that to it. So much so that a group of prominent nobles actually stabbed Rizzio to death in front of the now-pregnant Queen, at Holyrood, with Darnley indeed holding her there to watch it being done – the ghastly deed which was thereafter blamed for King James VI's life-long and inordinate fear of cold steel and dread of assassination. It was even suggested that the child Mary was bearing was not Darnley's at all – that he was indeed incapable of fathering a son – but Rizzio's. This was possibly baseless scandal, but it is typical of the atmosphere prevalent at Mary's court. And it is significant that when the child was being christened with great ceremony at Stirling Castle, Darnley absented himself. Also that thirty-seven years later, when King James was trapped in Gowrie House, Perth, at the time of the Gowrie Conspiracy, the Perth mob surrounding the house shouted continually, 'Come down thou son of Signor Davie, come down!' It was, presumably, purely coincidental that the child James grew up short in body and notably sallow in complexion, quite unlike Darnley, Mary herself, or any of the previous Stewarts. And later Henry IV of France declared that James could well claim to be the modern Solomon, since he was the son of David.

The child James was born in June 1566, after a long, difficult and painful labour, amidst great national rejoicings at having an heir to the throne. But it took Mary a long time to recover full health. Indeed she was still suffering after-effects a year later, which makes all the more extraordinary and significant her behaviour in the October, four months after the birth. She was at Jedburgh holding a justice-eyre or circuit court when she heard that Bothwell had been wounded in an affray in Liddesdale – he was Warden of the Marches – and had been taken to his remote castle of Hermitage. In doubtful health or not, she set out to ride the twenty-six or so miles over hills and rough moorland, in bad weather, to Bothwell's bedside, spent a couple of hours with him and then rode back to Jedburgh, over fifty miles hard riding in very difficult conditions. She was an expert horse-woman, of course; but even so it was an astonishing feat for a woman, but surely again indicates lack of judgment. Soaked and weary she fell direly ill thereafter, and those with her feared that she would die. She herself later was to say 'would that I had died at Jedworth!' Yet, despite having over sixty fits of violent vomiting and many lapses into unconsciousness, the Queen recovered – and Moray, who had been laying hands on her silver and valuables, had to relinquish them. Darnley was absent in the west.

Tragedy was never far away from Mary Stewart. Darnley's own death at Kirk o' Field, in Edinburgh, is of course one of the great mysteries of history. Was Mary involved therein, guiltily? We know that the murder was plotted at Whittinghame Tower, in East Lothian, a Douglas stronghold by the Douglas Earl of Morton, Bothwell, Maitland of Lethington, the Queen's Secretary of State, and the local Douglas laird, under the famous yew-tree, which still exists. According to Morton, later, it was Bothwell's suggestion, and they sent Douglas of Whittinghame to the Queen at Edinburgh asking if she would give them some written authority for the despatch of her now thoroughly unpopular husband; but he returned with the equivocal answer 'Show to the Earl of Morton that the Queen will have no speech of the matter.' Whether or not this was true we cannot tell, for Morton was certainly no trustworthy authority. But others, highly-placed, were undoubtedly concerned. The house Darnley was sleeping in – he was not with the Queen at Holyrood – was blown up one night, but his all-but-naked body was found lying nearby, apparently undamaged by fire and explosion, but strangled, and his clothes beside it, an inexplicable circumstance. The page with whom he had been sharing the house lay beside him, also strangled.

Whether or not Mary was aware of the plot, and there is confusing evidence for and against, at least she did not make much show of mourning, for she attended a wedding just two days later, and within a week was entering into archery contests at Seton Palace. Bothwell was summoned for trial for the crime, but arrived at the hearing backed by a company of his Border mosstroopers and was promptly acquitted.

No one can pretend that all this was other than disreputable on the part of all concerned. But more was to follow. After his acquittal, Bothwell lost no time in waylaying the Queen as she rode in Lothian, and carried her off to his castle of Dunbar. Again Mary's co-operation is suspected; certainly there were no attempts at resistance or rescue. While at Dunbar hasty arrangements were rushed through for Bothwell's divorce from Lady Jean Gordon.

What happened in Dunbar Castle can only be guessed at, although Sir James Melville, who was there at the time, wrote, 'The Queen could not but marry him, seeing he had ravished her and laid with her against her will.' It was on 24 April 1567 that Mary was abducted, and on 6 May they returned to Edinburgh together, apparently on the best of terms, his divorce being published the next day. They were married a week later. Mary did not give Bothwell the crown-matrimonial but she did create him Duke of Orkney. This was all only a few months after Darnley's murder. Life was lived fast in Mary's brief reign.

There was no let-up, even then. Moray, who had been away in England during this interlude, returned, and stirred up the nobles against the new duke and his wife. The pair had gone to Borthwick Castle in Midlothian, and there the lords surrounded them with armed force. Bothwell, scarcely gallantly, contrived to make his escape in the darkness, alone, leaving Mary. However, whatever else, the Queen seldom lacked for spirit, and next day she had herself lowered on a rope from a castle window, dressed in the clothes of Lord Borthwick's son, and managed to make her way through the besiegers' lines and across the moorland some miles to Cakemuir Castle, where Bothwell had taken refuge. Together they rode off to Dunbar again.

But now things had gone too far to be patched up, and the people as well as the Protestant nobles had lost all confidence in Mary. It had become a trial of strength, brute force. Bothwell raised his Borderers and such as remained loyal to the rash Queen; and the Lords of the Congregation, led by Moray and urged on by Knox, mustered their greater power. They met at the Battle of Carberry Hill, near Mussel-burgh, on 15 June of that same eventful year, and the royal army was defeated. Bothwell galloped off to Dunbar, but Mary gave herself up to the lords. It was the last the pair were to see of each other. Mary was carried captive to be immured in the Douglas castle on an island in Loch Leven, a prisoner in her own kingdom. Moray now ruled the land and Knox the Kirk. Bothwell fled to Denmark.

Even at Loch Leven there was drama. Morton, who took charge, brutally forced Mary to sign documents of abdication in favour of her infant son, James VI, protest as she would, Moray looking on. She was still only twenty-six. Moray was named Regent. He must have cudgelled his sour but cunning wits as to what to do with his hapless half-sister now.

She solved the problem for him by effecting her excape. Mary retained all her powers of attraction for the other sex, whatever else she may have lost. George Douglas, the laird's brother, and young Willie Douglas their cousin, were both in love with her. They contrived her flight by boat from the island stronghold by night to where her faithful Catholic friend Lord Seton, father of Mary Seton, one of the Queen's

Four Marys, awaited her, and conveyed her to his castle of Niddrie Seton near Winchburgh. She had been eleven months a prisoner, during which time the infant James had been crowned.

So now there were two monarchs in the land, the realm hopelessly split. But Bothwell, outlawed and harried, had departed overseas, and Mary had few powerful supporters left. She called all who would hear her to her side, renouncing her abdication as made under duress, and prepared for the inevitable battle.

This took place at Langside, near Glasgow, and proved disastrous for Mary's forces. Largely Hamiltons and Borderers, they had no adequate military leadership, whereas the Regent's army had Morton and Kirkcaldy of Grange, both proven soldiers. But although many of her prominent supporters, including the Lord Seton, were captured, this time the Queen was not. She fled southwards for the Border, crossed it and threw herself upon the mercy of Queen Elizabeth. Mary might have known the quality of Tudor mercy – but then, she was ever an optimist, against all reason. So commenced her eighteen grievous years of captivity in England, leading to her final execution at Elizabeth's hands.

That, then, crammed into seven short years, was the rule of one who has been called the most romantic figure in Scots history – not the *reign*, for Mary had been reigning since the week after her birth. Romance is a matter of interpretation, I suppose – but it is not the description I would use. No one could claim that she made a good or effective queen, and to be sure her follies were legion. But she was as much sinned against as sinning, undoubtedly; and certainly she lived in dire times, and landed in Scotland into the clutches of as unsavoury a collection of scoundrels in high places as this country has ever assembled at one time – a parcel of rogues they have been called, and that is perhaps being over-kind. It is, of course, fair to remember that elsewhere in Christendom, in the second half of the sixteenth century, conditions were little better and morality at a low ebb.

Poor, brave, foolish, beautiful Mary.

CHAPTER 13

THE WISEST FOOL

So it was regent's rule for Scotland once again. The governance of Scotland, indeed, seems to have been oftener in the hands of regents than of monarchs of full age. And what regencies these were. Young James VI who was to become renowned as the Wisest Fool in Christendom, was particularly unfortunate in this respect – although he learned the hard way how to cope with them. He had four of them before he was twelve years old.

His uncle Moray was the first. Of course, he had in effect been ruling Scotland for years, and once in undisputed power he did so reasonably efficiently. He was a strong character, reminding one of his ancestor the first Duke of Albany. He was the eldest known son of James V, and had he been legitimate he probably would have made quite a good king. But he was not, and resented his situation all his life. He was able, cunning, ruthless but sour, and could be treacherous. His behaviour towards his half-sister Mary was, on the whole, shameful. He was a man who, so far as can be gathered, displayed little affection in his life and aroused no more. But he knew how to govern. It was probably unfortunate for the infant King when Moray was shot dead by a disgruntled Hamilton in the High Street of Linlithgow less than two years after Mary's flight into England.

He was succeeded as Regent by young James's grandfather, the old Earl of Lennox, Darnley's father, whose palsied hands held the reins of power for only a year when he too was slain, this time in Stirling. Next followed the Earl of Mar, the child-King's guardian, Keeper of Stirling Castle,

153

where James passed his childhood. Mar was probably the best in character of the regents, but he was no ruler, and the ship of state yawed and veered. However, he lasted the least time of all, less than a year, dying, it was suspected, of poison administered by Morton.

Whether he was the poisoner or not, James Douglas, fourth Earl of Morton, succeeded to the dangerous regency – towards which he had been aiming for a considerable time. And now Scotland had for ruler one of the most fearsome characters even her story can produce. His background is interesting. He was a brother of the Red Douglas Earl of Angus, and married a daughter of the third Earl of Morton, chief of the Dalkeith branch of the Black Douglases, her mother being an illegitimate daughter of James IV. So he was born into intrigue and violence. He was as unscrupulous as he was coarse, harsh as he was unlovely, a boor of a man but shrewd and effective – and notably ambitious. He now ruled Scotland, with an iron fist and belly-laughter, for six years. His portrait, which hangs in the National Portrait Gallery in Edinburgh, in the same building which houses his Maiden – of which more hereafter – shows a blunt-featured, high-coloured, hot-eyed, red-bearded individual, with one hand covering his dirk and the other on his sword-hilt – all in all probably a pretty fair picture of the man he was.

Yet those six years were not all grim. Scotland has always needed strong rulers, and Morton was strong enough. Whilst he held the power, lesser rogues lay low. It is reported that he suffered none to be as rapacious as himself. This had the effect of making depredations on the common folk less normal, so that the people in general more or less approved of Morton, although none could ever love him. And he knew how to deal with Elizabeth Tudor – after all, he had been dealing with her, one way or another, for most of his life.

Morton made two grievous errors of judgment, however. He incurred the enmity of the Kirk by continued and blatant confiscation of properties belonging to the old Catholic Church, constituting himself collector, and much of the collection sticking to his own fingers – this to the hurt of the new reformed parishes. And he made no attempt to show a kinder disposition towards his young monarch, like so many others underestimating that extraordinary character, who even then was displaying precocious abilities. And these two errors coalesced, in that one of the most noted reformed divines was James's tutor and guide at Stirling Castle, George Buchanan, and he loathed Morton and all his works, 'spoke evilly of him in all places', and schooled the boy-King to be his Regent's enemy.

We get few glimpses of James at this stage of his life and reign. We know that Buchanan made a very severe tutor, having no compunction about beating his royal charge for the most trifling misdemeanours. There was the famous occasion when the Countess of Mar, almost James's nurse, protested to the schoolroom tyrant, to be answered, 'Madam, I have whipped his arse. You can kiss it if you like.' Buchanan worked the boy hard indeed – with results which were to impress all who came in touch with the King all his days – for the divine was a most notable scholar, historian, theologian and even poet. James, despite the sternness of the regime, acquired a great thirst for knowledge and a remarkable linguistic ability. Never had a Scots monarch – and few other monarchs, for that matter – had such an education. It is recorded that by the age of eight James knew Latin, Greek and Hebrew as well as he did his broad Scots mother-tongue, which prevailed with both Buchanan and the Mars, and could extempore read a chapter of the Bible out of Latin into French and out of French into English. He was also proficient in theology, astronomy, demonology, geography and other disciplines. Sadly, Buchanan also taught him to hate and despise his mother as an adultress and murdress, something which James never outgrew.

Morton took notice of the boy only when it served his purposes to do so. There was the occasion when, at the age of five, the Regent required his royal presence at a parliament in order to give certain plans of his own added authority. He seated the lad in a rickety throne under a tattered canopy, and as proceedings were about to begin, the child-sovereign startled everyone by glancing up at the canopy and observing sapiently that this parliament had a hole in it – as indeed any parliament master-minded by Morton would be apt to have.

At any rate, by the age of twelve, the young-old King

revealed something of his mettle, outwitting Morton at his own game. The Regent decided that it would much increase his power and ability to control all if he had James in his own keeping and not in that of the Mars at Stirling Castle. So he devised a scheme, suggesting that the King was now old enough to rule on his own and no longer be kept all but a prisoner in this fortress. To achieve this, and outmanoeuvre the Mars and other nobles, he himself would resign the regency, James would announce his personal assumption of rule, and they would both go the *Edinburgh* Castle, which Morton held, and there he, Morton, would aid and advise His Highness on the business of government. It was a subtle plot for a man who did not usually deal in subtleties; but he had reckoned without the present occupant of the throne. James seemed to go along with it, made public acceptance of the Regent's resignation, announced his personal rule – and then told Mar and the others what Morton had proposed, and why, and refused to move out of Stirling Castle. Morton found himself no longer Regent or in power, and at twelve James was ruling his kingdom – and using the threat of Morton's return to keep Mar and the rest of the nobles co-operating. This was the first major demonstration of the kind of character Scotland now had for monarch.

Morton was not so easily disposed of, to be sure, and began to use his more normal methods to regain power, threatening, ravaging and raising an army. But at this critical stage a wholly new figure appeared upon the national scene, not entirely fortuitously – Esmé Stewart of Aubigny arrived in Scotland from France. This was the nephew of the late Regent Lennox, and therefore a cousin of Darnley, wholly brought up in France, a handsome, cultured and talented individual, who was sent by the King of France to try to restore the French influence in Scotland, to aid the captive Mary's cause, and if possible to help revive the Catholic religion – a heavy programme indeed. But Esmé Stewart did not take all that too seriously, and he had his own ideas and methods. He put such projects into cold-storage meantime and set about captivating his young second-cousin. And well indeed did he succeed in that aim. James as good as fell in love with him – James's emotional needs were all his life somewhat odd. Esmé was all that the gawky, pedantic boy admired, brilliant, witty, polished and affectionate, even a poet and musician, all in the greatest contrast to most of the nobles around the King. It quickly became a case of hero-worship. But James did not entirely lose his over-large head to his cousin, if he lost his affection-starved heart, for he promptly sought to use him against Morton, and to excellent effect.

So now the ageing Morton had a foeman worthy of his steel – or rather, the steel was on the other side, a rapier against a bludgeon. The Douglas was outwitted time and again. Esmé did not seek regency or official position, but James created him first Earl and then Duke of Lennox, and together they sought to rule the land, the King learning statecraft and how to outwit men as quickly as he had previously acquired book-learning. It was probably the happiest period of this James Stewart's life.

With Esmé at his side, the King rode in triumph from Stirling to Edinburgh for his first true Parliament, amidst great rejoicings. Lennox arranged for James to have fine clothes, for the first time, and all the trappings of royalty.

Morton, of course, was not inactive. He was in constant touch with Queen Elizabeth, who was much concerned over the rise of French influence in Scotland, and who urged Morton, her pensioner, to lay violent hands on Esmé Stewart. However, Esmé got to hear of this, and struck first. He contrived Morton's arrest at a meeting of the Privy Council, on the old charge of being art and part in the murder of Darnley, thirteen years before, rushed through a trial and had the ex-Regent executed. It was ironical that he should lose his head on the Maiden, as it was termed, a sort of guillotine which Morton himself had invented many years earlier for the efficient despatch of people he did not like.

James's joy was now at its height, with his new Duke arranging that he should have everything that he wanted. But it could not last, it was all too foreign to the Scots temper and traditions – and of course, to the Reformed religion, for Esmé was a Catholic although he pretended to be converted to Protestantism. The nobles resented this Frenchman and the Kirk saw him as a menace, with the possibility of turning the young monarch to Catholicism. Knox had died in 1570 but he had left numerous stern successors, and these clashed with Lennox.

Matters came to a head in 1582, with the Kirk accusing the King of having neglected Christ's true Church and his own realm for shameful traffic with France and the Catholics. And in the climate of opinion thus engendered, with the charges being thundered from hundreds of pulpits, certain of the Protestant lords struck. Esmé, for once, was careless, and allowed James to go hunting insufficiently guarded, near Perth; and Mar, the Earl of Gowrie, chief of the Ruthvens, and the Master of Glamis and others, took the opportunity to kidnap the King and carried him off to the Ruthven seat of Huntingtower nearby, and held him there captive. It was the old, old story, once more – those who held the monarch could rule Scotland.

Esmé, Duke of Lennox was lost. Without the King, he had nothing, no power, no focus, no party. He went back to France – and, strangely, died there shortly afterwards although only in his mid-thirties.

James was held in Huntingtower, or Ruthven Castle, for a year, in what became known as the Raid of Ruthven – and in no gentle hands. Typical of his treatment was the occasion when, going to pass through a doorway, the Master of Glamis thrust out his leg to bar the way and the King tripped. In his humiliation he burst into tears of shame and anger – at which Glamis exclaimed, 'Better bairns weep than bearded men!'

But the sixteen-year-old monarch did more than weep. He perceived the uneasy alliance of his captors, their weaknesses and rivalries, and worked on them to cause dissention. Apparently accepting his state, he schemed to end his detention. He had messages smuggled out to other lords and factions, especially the Catholics, amongst them the Lord Seton who had once rescued his mother. And, at length, using his very fondness for the chase which had led to his capture as a means of ending it, he contrived a hunting expedition eastwards in which he got away from most of his guards and into the arms of those with whom he had been corresponding. They then all rode post-haste for St Andrews and freedom.

One of those who helped to mastermind this dramatic escape was Patrick, Master of Gray, eldest son of the fifth Lord Gray, great-grandson of the Gray who had finished off James III after Sauchieburn. So now appears one of the most fascinating figures ever to perform on the Scottish stage, a man who makes even Esmé Stewart's brilliance look dim by comparison, and who for many years was to play a significant if by no means always reputable part in the nation's affairs. Patrick Gray was known both as the handsomest man in Europe and the Machiavelli of Scottish politics. Unlike most of the other nobles of the period he was polished, elegant, highly-intelligent and educated – yet quite unscrupulous. And he largely stepped into the vacuum left by Esmé, and for the rest of James's reign in Scotland played a greater or lesser part, as often behind the scenes as on them. He was an extraordinary mixture, the greatest dandy, with rouged cheeks, ear-rings and scented gloves, yet courageous and capable of the most dramatic actions, a schemer of the most involved plots, a believer that the end justified any means whatsoever, a silver-tongued rogue possessed of the utmost charm, yet by his own odd lights consistent. He held, whatever else, to one great aim throughout his career, the eventual placing of James on the throne of a united kingdom of Scotland and England and the end of centuries of warfare, and was prepared to use every means in his considerable armoury to achieve that end. It has been said that the Master of Gray would betray everything and anyone save this ultimate goal. The irony of it all was that when in 1603, with Elizabeth dead at last and all the other possible candidates for her throne eliminated, at Berwick-on-Tweed on his way south, James turned to the Master, in his great train of nobles and courtiers heading for London, and told him to go back home, that he would not need him in England. In Scotland all these years he had needed a great rogue to berogue lesser rogues; but in England he would find him one of their own rogues to serve a like duty!

Patrick Gray never forgave that, and is thought to have

blackmailed the King over his mother's injudicious Casket Letters for years thereafter.

But that was twenty years on. Meantime James made use of Gray and Gray made use of James – but subtly. He refused all high office, contenting himself with being Master of the Wardrobe, which of course enabled him to be ever close to the King, but prevented greater nobles from becoming over-jealous. He frequently was as good as Chancellor, or chief minister, but never was called that, although on occasion he presided over meetings of the Privy Council, which was a duty of the Chancellor; and many times he acted as personal ambassador. Gray was content, whilst being very strategically there, at court, to help steer the ship of state as it were not from the bridge but from the stern, while the prominent lords strutted, postured and plotted so much less effectively. In especial, two new bearers of titles already all too familiar, the Earls of Bothwell and Huntly.

The new Bothwell was a nephew both of Mary's third husband and of Mary herself, a flamboyant and extraordinary character who dabbled in witchcraft, and twice attempted to kidnap the King. Much of his behaviour, indeed, was scarcely credible, yet he was close enough to James to be a very real nuisance. Huntly was the grandson of the earl who died at Corrichie and nephew of the executed Sir John Gordon. These two constituted an especially sore trial to the much more clever and directionful schemer, the Master of Gray.

The new Bothwell's fall came about oddly, to say the least, considering how much more blatant and dangerous had been his activities hitherto. In 1589, having married Anne of Denmark by proxy, and his bride having twice been driven back by storms from crossing over to Scotalnd, James decided to go to Denmark himself to collect her – a most singular proceeding for so physically timorous a character. He was away for all that winter, having a fine time in Denmark with the young King Christian, Ann's brother, 'drinking and dryving in the auld manner', as he himself put it; or, as another observed, 'Our King made good cheer and drank stoutly till the spring time.'

At any rate, at the end of April 1590 James and his new fifteen-year-old Queen sailed for home. This time they had rather better weather, until they got to the mouth of the Firth of Forth when, according to the King's own story, a sudden storm blew up in the vicinity of the Bass Rock, off North Berwick, and the ships were in dire danger of capsising. So close to his own kingdom – of which no doubt James had been boasting to Anne – he was much offended as they were driven off northwards. Moreover, apparently, he personally perceived a crew of witches in the guise of hares, sailing in a sieve around his labouring ship. Whether anyone else was vouchsafed this remarkable sight is not reported – perhaps the winter's drinking and dryving may have enhanced the King's perceptions. But he was naturally upset, especially as witches had been tried and burned in Denmark earlier for causing the storms which had delayed Anne's coming.

When at last they won into Leith and the official reception, James was much preoccupied with Satan's obvious campaign against him, the Lord's Anointed. Sundry known witches were arrested and put to the question, and more than one of them implicated Francis Hepburn Stewart, Earl of Bothwell. Significantly, North Berwick appeared to be the epicentre of the witchcraft proceedings, and of course, this was Bothwell country, near to the Hepburn seat of Hailes Castle in Haddingtonshire. Clearly to James that storm was the making of that thorn in his flesh and cousin, hares in sieves and all. Something would have to be done about it.

The King took personal charge. The evil-doers must be caught in the act. He organised an expedition down to North Berwick from Edinburgh one suitable night – presumably his spies were able to inform him when these coven-assemblies were apt to take place – and the King and his party secreted themselves around the old parish church of St Andrew out near the harbour, the ruins of which are still there although the site is no longer an islet as then, joined to the mainland by arches. And in due course, by moonlight midnight, the coven gathered, a great company of ninety-four witches and six warlocks or wizards, flitting in from the shadows, to perform in the kirkyard and in the kirk itself all sorts of shameful things, the females all having their breasts exposed and dancing to the music of one Geilie Duncan's Jew's Harp, celebrating the Black Mass in the church and, worst of all, to line up, skipping and cavorting, to kiss the bare backside of the horned and hooved president of the proceedings, who could be none other than Francis, Earl of Bothwell himself who, 'startit up himself in the pulpit, like ane meikle black man and callit every man by name, and every ane answerit, "Here, Maister." They then openit up the graves, twa within and ane without the kirk, and took off the joints of their fingers, taes and knees, and partit them amang them; and the said Agnes Sampson gat for ther part ane winding-sheet and twa joints, whilk she tint negligently.' This last was evidently too much for the monarch, who gave the signal to pounce. The royal party leapt out of hiding and the unseemly revellers were rounded up and for the most part captured, although unfortunately the evil genius of it all escaped.

Thereafter James Stewart showed still another side of his character. He took charge of a large-scale investigation into the entire theory and practice of witchcraft, the findings of which were duly enshrined for posterity in his famous book on demonology, personally supervising the interrogations – he preferrred to call them justifications – of witches and warlocks. He devised an ingenious method of extracting the required information from the witnesses by tying a rope around their brows and then inserting a dirk-blade and twisting until the scalp was lifted off the skull. By this means he had little difficulty in gaining all the confessions he needed, including of course verification of the implication of Bothwell. James ordered the arrest of that individual, but he took refuge in the wild Borderland where it seems the King's writ hardly ran, and was able to remain at large there for a considerable time, even making still another attempt on James's person at Holyroodhouse on one occasion, until finally forced to flee the country. He ended up in Italy where, incidentally, amongst other pursuits, this extraordinary character studied architecture to such good effect that when eventually he could return to Scotland, with the King gone to London, he built the handsome extension to his castle of Crichton, the only Italianate fortalice in the land.

The other high-born trouble-maker was George Gordon, Earl of Huntly. Despite him being the Catholic leader and a born plotter and intriguer, James always seems to have had a soft spot for him. He needed all the royal friendship a couple of years later, with the murder of the Earl of Moray – this was the theme of the popular ballad, *The Bonnie Earl o' Moray*. All that was behind this affair has never been fully ascertained. The ballad makes it all cut-and-dried, of course, but there are wild discrepancies of fact. The song says that Moray was the Queen's true love, and that he might have been the King – presumably if James could have been disposed of. This is nonsense. This James Stewart was the son of one more of James V's bastards, the Lord Doune; and he had married the daughter-heiress of the late Regent Moray, his uncle, and gained the earldom with her. He could never have been the King, both because of illegitimacy and because Anne was not a queen-regnant but only a consort and had no ability to pass on the crown to anyone. Anne seems to have been a bit of a flirt – with the odd husband she had, perhaps this was almost inevitable – but there is no real indication that she was inordinately fond of the good-looking and sport-loving Moray. King James may have been jealous, nevertheless.

Anyway, Huntly set out to trap Moray, his hereditary enemy – it will be remembered that the Regent had won all his Moray lands from the Gordons. How much of this enterprise was at James's instigation is not clear but Huntly went with a royal writ empowering him to 'execute justice on the accomplices in Francis, Earl of Bothwell's raid on Holyroodhouse' aforementioned. Was Moray involved in that? Moray had a castle at Donibristle in Fife. Huntly and a company of Gordons set out from Edinburgh and crossed Forth at Queensferry – and it is significant that the ferry thereafter was closed by royal command, so nobody could follow. He proceeded to Donibristle, surrounded the castle, and challenged Moray to come out. When that man prudently refused, the Gordons laid brushwood all round the tower's base and set it alight. This was a cunning move, for although these sturdy stone fortalices of Scotland were practically impregnable to all but heavy artillery, there was a new-fangled weakness at Donibristle, as in some others, namely a garderobe-flue in the thickness of the walling, with an exit at ground-level – this an elementary form of sanitation whereby the contents of garderobes or mural loos at upper levels could drop down these shutes instead of having to be carried in buckets through the house. But, sadly, sanitary improvement had its handicaps, for the shutes could act like chimney-flues, and fires lit at their base sent the smoke billowing up, to make the upper storeys untenable. This happened at Donibristle and Moray had to try escape by letting himself down by rope from an upper window. He was seen, through all the smoke, and pursued. He ran to the nearby shore, but was chased, caught and cut down. His dying words were, 'Huntly . . . you Hieland stot . . . you ha' spoiled a better face . . . than your own!'

There was a great furore of course, the entire influential house of Stewart up in arms, the Protestant lords furious. But the King undoubtedly protected Huntly, for whatever reason – he had married the beloved Esmé Stewart of Aubigny's daughter. The ballad makes him say 'Wae be to thee, Huntly, for wherefore did you say, I bade you bring wi' you and forbade you him to slay!' Whether or no there is any truth in this, James did advise the Gordon to ward himself voluntarily in the royal castle of Blackness, on the West Lothian coast – which was of course an excellent bolt-hole where no reprisal-seekers could get at Huntly – and there he remained in comfort for a few weeks until the fuss died down, the King reputedly sending him delicacies from his own table.

Meanwhile the slashed and naked body of Moray lay in a sort of state at the parish church of Leith, for all to see and note; and the Earl's mother, the Lady Doune – she who looked down from Castle Doune no more to see her son come pounding through the toun – paraded Edinburgh's streets with the bloodstained shirt as banner, demanding vengeance. It is notable, however, that the Earl's wife, the Countess of Moray, seems to have taken no part at all in all this; perhaps she believed that there might have been more between her late husband and the Queen than mere idle flirtation?

There was no vengeance for poor Moray, in the event. Huntly in due course quietly left Blackness for his northern Strathbogie fastnesses, and was never punished for the murder. In fact he was soon back at court, and was created Marquis a year or two after, living on to involve himself in other plots.

The Master of Gray has been much blamed for his Machiavellian policies and manoeuvres in seeking to steer the ship of state to some extent at this period; but considering the conditions prevailing, it would surely require a certain dexterity as to methods and a nimbleness as to conscience, to keep Scotland on any sort of even course. He obtained an ally at this time, Ludovick Stewart of Aubigny, come from France, the son of Esmé and now second Duke of Lennox, who was to become and long remain the King's closest associate.

Another new influence on the scene was occasioned by the birth to the Queen of a son, and heir to the throne, something which ought to have been as great satisfaction to the King as it was to the nation at large, the succession at last looking more assured. Unfortunately, however joyful the event, all too soon the infant became a bone of contention between James and Anne. Even at the christening, at Stirling Castle, there was trouble. James wanted the boy to be called Henry, after Henry VIII of England – this was to please Queen Elizabeth and to help ensure her goodwill now and also towards James's eventual accession to *her* throne; but Anne desired her son to have the name Frederick, after her father, King Frederick of Denmark. Neither would give way, and the only compromise reached was that the prince should have both names. But which first? James insisted on Henry Frederick, Anne on Frederick Henry, and at the actual baptism both gave the unfortunate celebrant, the Bishop of Aberdeen, strictest royal commands as to the order of his naming. The poor man, at his wits' end, finished by making mumble of it, twice – but whether the first mumble was Henry Frederick or Frederick Henry no one quite heard – although each proud parent was satisfied that it was *their* version. This was only the beginning, for James, with memories haunting him of his own unhappy childhood, grabbed for by this ambitious lord or that, ordained that Henry Frederick must remain continuously safe in that great fortress, irrespective of his mother's wishes or her whereabouts. As the Queen could by no means live permanently at Stirling, which she hated anyway, this was to force separation between mother and child – something which Anne never forgave. She actually concocted a plot to steal her son from the care of the Earl of Mar at Stirling, the Lord Home and Sir Robert Ker of Cessford aiding her. Unfortunately or otherwise she also confided in Maitland of Thirlstane, acting Chancellor at the time, whom she believed her friend, nephew of Mary's Secretary of State, Maitland of Lethington; and he, whilst seeming to support her, secretly informed James, who was hunting at Falkland. The King furiously put a stop to it all. He made an official decree that the prince was not to be delivered by Mar to anyone, neither the Queen nor the Estates of Parliament, until he reached the age of eighteen, even if he himself, the King, was 'called to God'. So the heir to the throne became as much a prisoner as ever his father had been, and the rift between the King and Queen widened.

James was, undoubtedly, the strangest monarch Scotland had ever had, an extraordinary mixture of shrewdness and credulity, of cunning and simplicity, of moral and intellectual courage and physical cowardice, of religiosity and demonological dabblings, and with distinctly homosexual leanings, although pruriently interested in women's anatomies but scarcely their intelligence. He got himself involved in some very strange activities, many of them scarcely regal. One of the most odd was what became known as the Gowrie Conspiracy, of 1600, just three years before Elizabeth Tudor at last died and James made his long-awaited translation to London.

The Gowrie affair, at Perth, had its origins long before 1600, when the Lord Ruthven – involved in the murder of Rizzio and mastermind of the Ruthven Raid when James, as a boy, was kidnapped and imprisoned in Ruthven Castle or Huntingtower – became Lord Treasurer and was created Earl of Gowrie. James, who was not of a forgiving nature, never forgave Gowrie, and in due course brought him to his death by execution – but not before he had managed to borrow £85,000 from the Treasurer. Gowrie had two sons, John and Sandy Ruthven. John, who succeeded as earl, probably wisely distanced himself from his peculiar monarch and went overseas to Padua where, a studious and able young man, he distinguished himself by becoming Rector of that famous university by the age of twenty-one. But less wisely, for some reason, he came home in 1599 to claim his inherit-ance – which was very great. He was also indiscreet enough to remind the King that he owed him £85,000 plus interest.

James devised his own involved way of dealing with this situation. On a hunting-trip at his beloved Falkland, he announced that Sandy Ruthven, the brother, had informed him that they had apprehended a strange dark mannie with a pot of gold, and stories of more, and confined him in a room of Gowrie House, Perth; and that he, the King, was going to ride there right away to interview this intriguing character. Despite the astonishment of Ludovick of Lennox, Mar and the rest, James promptly set off on this lengthy ride of fully twenty miles. He was always a keen horseman, of course, however poor a walker. The bewildered courtiers followed on.

Just what was at the bottom of this unlikely story has never been explained. The King and his party duly arrived at Gowrie House, the Ruthven town-lodging – they were hereditary provosts of Perth. There, notably, hospitality had not been prepared for the visitors, and while something was being produced at short notice, James and his current young man, or page, John Ramsay, went to an upper room of the house with the Earl and his brother. And from a window thereof, presently, the King's agitated voice came down to his courtiers in the garden with pathetic cries of treason, treason and that he was being murdered. Needless to say there was a concerted rush up the winding turnpike stairs to the chamber, where they found the door locked and shouting coming from within. Sir Thomas Erskine, Mar his cousin, Lennox and the rest at last broke in. And there they found the monarch blood-spattered indeed – but not with his own blood. Both Ruthvens lay on the floor, both unarmed but stabbed to death by young Ramsay, dagger in hand. All rushed to comfort the endangered King, who babbled of another man, a right savage and terrible man, presumably he of the pot of gold – but of him there was no sign. At any rate, the unharmed sovereign now got down on his knees, as must all others, to lead in prayers of thankfulness for his deliverance, amidst great excitement.

The excitement soon spread outside and before long a mob of Perth citizens were surrounding Gowrie House, in threatening fashion – for young Gowrie was popular – shouting, 'Come down thou son of Signor Davie – come down!' The King, in fact, had to make an undignified escape through the garden and a private door on to the bank of Tay.

Whatever was behind this scarcely believable happening, it all fell out very conveniently for most, if not for the Ruthvens. The £85,000 debt could be written off; the great Ruthven estates were forfeited, partly to the crown and partly to Sir Thomas Erskine, who was suspected of having contrived the whole affair, and who was created Lord Erskine of Dirleton, Viscount Fentoun and then Earl of Kellie; and the page Ramsay was knighted. The mannie with the pot of gold was never heard of more.

So much for the divine right of kings, one of James's most cherished theories. Three years later he went to practice it on the unprepared English.

Chapter 14

RULE AT LONG RANGE

The removal of the monarch to London, as it turned out for good – or not so good – inevitably had a profound effect on Scotland, the oldest kingdom of Europe suddenly deprived of its resident King and subjected to a totally new kind of government, at long range. This realm now became of only secondary importance to its ruler. The King of Scots had always been just that, however inadequate so often – much closer to his people than were the Kings of England, France or otherwise, the title 'of Scots' not 'of Scotland' significant. In Parliament and government, in the administration of justice, in even living conditions and sport and entertainment, the monarchy was an integral part of the national scene, not a rarified institution nor lofty figurehead. Now all that was abruptly gone. Personal rule had ended. James still reigned but others had to rule, usually favourites, sent up in the King's name from London. It was almost like a permanent regency now, and Scotland had had all too much of that; but then at least the Regent was able to be got at, reached and affected by the expressed will of the people. And in the past the Regents had usually been strong men, however self-seeking, who grasped the dominant position by their own power and driving force. Now it was otherwise; court favourites were seldom of that sort, and Scotland ever needed strong government.

There was one great advantage, of course – the threat of armed invasion seemed to have gone for good in the new United Kingdom of Great Britain – that is, until Cromwell, Monk, the Duke of Cumberland and others came along.

169

So Scotland was governed by a succession of James's chosen minions, and as time went on these tended to act more and more on their own, as the King lost touch with his ancient realm and inevitably became more absorbed in the problems of England. In fact, James returned to Scotland only once thereafter, in 1617. Nevertheless his shrewdness did not desert him and he allowed no too powerful figures to monopolise the rule in the north. He ensured this through the system of having three different hands always at the helm. The Chancellor, or chief minister, remained, to deal with the day-to-day running of the country and preside over the Privy Council; the Secretary of State was the more direct mouthpiece of the monarch, in constant touch; and the Lord High Commissioner, senior to them both, acted as a viceroy and opened and presided over Parliaments in the King's stead, but was only sent up from London for such and other specific occasions. These three had their underlings, of course, and there could be rivalry between them; but they did serve to keep each other from becoming dangerously powerful.

This system evolved probably as a more effective form of government than prevailed in England, where the Parliament of Lords and Commons held much more power, particularly in control of the purse-strings, and which could and did greatly counter James's style of personal rule. But it did permit of minor tyrannies and corruptions on a scale never before experienced in Scotland, with ultimate authority so far off and divided.

Another aspect of the new situation was the need for Scots ambitious for preferment and honours to go to London for them, to the fount of honour himself, and this effected a great change in the Scots nobility and aristrocracy, tending to turn their eyes southwards. A steady trail came to be beaten to the court at Whitehall. And this was expensive, requiring long journeys with coaches and escorts; quarters to hire in London; costly clothing, especially for the women-folk, to vie with the fine English fashions; and James, ever kept short of money by his English Parliament, apt to charge sweetly for his goodwill. The Scots ruling class had never been rich in money nor even concerned with it. Land and man-power were their real wealth. Now, suddenly, they needed cash; and the only way to get it was to sell or mortgage land. But to whom? Only a very few were in a position to seize the opportunity – to advance money on the security of lands and estates, in the nature of things much of which would never be redeemed, and it happened that two such entrepreneurs were cousins, although very different types of men – George Heriot and Sir Thomas Hamilton of Priestfield.

George Heriot, Jinglin' Geordie as his monarch called him, of course was famous as a crony of the King's long before he went to London. He was in fact, although of lairdly stock, the royal goldsmith, a tradesman – although goldsmiths in those days were frequently also bankers, money-lenders. Queen Anne was passionately fond of jewellery and apt to buy more than she could pay for, so that she, and perforce her husband, were almost permanently in debt to Geordie Heriot – who was wise enough not to be too fussy over payment after the fashion of the unfortunate Earl of Gowrie. James indeed made a personal friend of Heriot, especially after the celebrated occasion when in Geordie's office one cold day, the monarch complained that he would have thought of his means would have afforded a richer fire, whereupon Heriot took the King's newly-written note-of-hand for £2,000 and tossed it on to the fire, suggesting that this might better warm His Grace somewhat.

Heriot saw the opportunity of supplying cash to the Scots *en route* for London in exchange for land, and in the process amassed an enormous fortune and became one of the greatest landowners in Scotland – part of which fortune he left to found the famous school in Edinburgh which bears his name, in emulation of Christ's Hospital in London which he much admired; and much more than the school itself, which the present writer had the privilege of attending. Heriot was no mere court favourite but an enlightened, able and far-seeing man, modest and refusing all titles. Would that James Stewart had had more like him as advisers.

He had, however, Tam o' the Cowgate, as Sir Thomas Hamilton was commonly known, a red-faced, burly bull of a man, but with wits as sharp as those of his cousin and, moreover, a bounding ambition. He was to play one of the most consistently important roles in Scotland over a long period. If the term Tam o' the Cowgate sounds lacking in dignity, let it be undersoood that his house in the capital's Cowgate was in fact all but a palace, indeed large enough to entertain the King and his court on occasion.

Hamilton, who was the son of another Sir Thomas, Lord Priestfield, of Session, despite his less than genteel ways, early showed both his mettle and his ambition, getting himself appointed Lord Advocate at the extraordinarily early age of twenty-four – and it is recorded that the man he was succeeding, MacGill of Cranstoun-Riddell, died of grief when he heard of Tam's appointment. Five years later he was himself a Lord of Session, in 1592, although he seems to have continued to exercise the functions of Lord Advocate, prosecuting for James in Parliament House, on the famous occasion when, some time after the Gowrie Conspiracy, the accused were the two exhumed bodies of the Ruthven brothers, stinking as they were, and he had them not only duly forfeited for treason, their heirs and family and all their wealth, but managed to implicate too that curious adventurer Logan of Restalrig and all *his* oddly-gotten wealth, who allegedly had also been blackmailing the King over the notorious Casket Letters of his mother. James never forgot his debt of gratitude to Thomas Hamilton. By 1612 he was Secretary of State and Lord Clerk Register and four years later Lord President of the Court of Session, passing on the Lord Clerk Registership to one of his brothers. His three other brothers did not do badly either; one became a Lord of Session also; another Under-Secretary of State; and the youngest a general of artillery. Tam himself was created Lord Binning and Byres in 1616 and Earl of Melrose in 1619, getting this changed to Earl of Haddington a few years later. This was the sort of situation which could develop under an absentee monarch – although Sir Tam's abilities were never in doubt.

Another character who gained great power in the land at this period was Archibald Campbell, 7th Earl of Argyll, who was given almost complete hegemony over the Highlands and Islands, and who was responsible for the proscription of the clan of MacGregor. The Campbells had been systematically ejecting the MacGregors from their Argyll lands around Glen Orchy and Loch Awe for centuries, to the fury of the smaller clan – who of course, were fiercely proud, claiming descent from the early Celtic kings, as their style of Clan Alpine indicated, Alpin being the father of Kenneth I (MacAlpin) and Gregor his brother. To be harried and dispossessed by what they looked upon as jumped-up newcomers like the Campbells was intolerable, and they did not fail to strike back as far as they were able. They in fact became a very warlike lot, with something of a persecution mania; and did not confine their resentment wholly to the Campbells, others under the general protection of that great clan tending to suffer also in areas bordering on the ever-reduced MacGregor lands. Matters rather culminated in 1603, when after a raid called the Slaughter of Lennox, wherein many Buchanans were killed and Luss burned, the MacGregors slew 200 hundred Colquhouns at the clan-battle of Glen Fruin. This coincided with James's departure for London; and the Campbell chief, the Earl of Argyll, who was hereditary Lord Justice-General, had his own methods of carrying out the royal commands for justice – aided by a parade of Colquhoun women through Edinburgh's streets bearing the bloody shirts of their late menfolk. The Campbell ordered the chief of the MacGregors, Glenstrae, to come to the capital with an explanation, granting him a safe-conduct – without which undoubtedly he would never have ventured out of his own mountain fastnesses – but once there, he and his escort of thirty-five clansmen were hanged out of hand. Thereafter a declaration of fire-and-sword was issued against the clan, whereby anyone and everyone had not only the right but the duty to slay, harry, burn and dispossess any MacGregors they might find weak enough to let them do so, without recourse to the authorities. This was followed by a unique dictate, the proscription of the very name of MacGregor. Thereafter none might legally call themselves by that name. If this sounds more of a nominal penalty than an actual one, consider that it meant that no property could be held in that name, nor bought or sold, no document so signed was lawfully valid, no one thus named could marry or be buried, and so on. This extraordinary proscription made it legally necessary for every MacGregor to adopt another surname; and this remained the position in law until 1774. The MacGregors, of course, continued to so call themselves privately and in their own wild territories around Loch Lomond and the Trossachs, Glen Gyle and Glen Dochart; but in their dealings with others they had to use a great variety of names to sign themselves – Greig, Gregory, Grier, Grierson, Carse, Cass, Fletcher and many another, including of course other clan names from round about. The famous Rob Roy, for instance, used Robert MacGregor Campbell, his mother being of that clan.

This Earl of Argyll distinguished himself elsewhere, as Justice-General, twice making savage punitive raids on Islay in the name of the King – the territory, of course, of the Campbells' other hereditary enemies the Macdonalds. Also, by a ruse, he enticed a number of Highland chiefs to Iona, where he promptly arrested them and forced them to agree to what was known as the Covenant of Icolmkill of 1609. This provided for the establishment of non-Romish churches, the predominance of the English tongue instead of Gaelic, the banning of firearms, the suppression of beggars and vagabonds – this to get rid of travelling bards and storytellers who kept the Gaelic culture alight – even the distilling of whisky being forbidden as was the importation of wine. Needless to say, all these alleged reforms were less easily enforced than promulgated.

But as far as Lowland Scotland was concerned, undoubtedly the principal preoccupation of James's rule from London was his decision to impose episcopacy on his northern kingdom. James was scarcely a religious man by normal standards, but he was intensely interested in theology and of course autocracy. In England he found the rule of bishops in the Church as admirable, and conducive to the exercise of his own authority; so he determined that the Scots Kirk should have them also. The Kirk did not want them. So started a long drawn-out struggle which neither side really won and which continued well into the reigns of his successors, Charles I and II. James appointed bishops and archbishops and ordered that they have seats in the Scots Parliament as they did in the English House of Lords. This was anathema in Scotland where, since the Reformation, no churchmen sat in Parliament, they having their own authoritative General Assembly. Most leading Scots divines refused to accept the role, just as most parish ministers refused to accept their authority. Some very odd characters were appointed, in consequence, and these became known as Tulchan Bishops, a tulchan being a calf's skin stuffed with straw, used to induce a cow to give milk. To try to bring the Kirk to heel, James refused to call General Assemblies, which required the royal recognition. The bishops became the most unpopular men in Scotland, shouted at and mobbed in the streets. The King summoned Andrew Melville, who had more or less succeeded Knox as Scotland's foremost religous leader, to London, with his nephew James Melville, to instruct them in the royal will.

It must have been a dramatic encounter, in the palace of Whitehall, between these fiery Calvinists and the slobbering but shrewd and scholarly monarch, all equally determined and voluble. The King, whose King James's version of the Bible is still the standard translation, was of course well-versed in the Scriptures, however individualistic his personal interpretation; and the Melvilles were unable to stump him with texts and quotations, in a duel of wits and rhetoric before much of the court and the English Church hierarchy. The wordy battle went on for hours, James claiming Biblical authority for his doctrine of the divine right of kings, his position as Christ's Vice-Regent and Coadjutor in this part of the earth, and his royal right to appoint overseers over the Church of which he was God-anointed head; the Melvilles accepting none of it, asserting the independence of the Kirk from all earthly rulers, the authority of presbyters under a General Assembly, and Andrew reiterating his celebrated statement that: 'there is Christ Jesus the king of the Church, whose subject James the Sixth is, and of whose kingdom he is not a king nor a lord nor a head but a member, God's silly vassal!' Whoever won in this battle-royal of dialectics, the King saw to it that he won on a procedural level, for thereafter the divines were not permitted to return to lead further trouble in Scotland. Andrew was confined in the Tower and not freed for five years, when he was allowed to go to France; and his nephew was exiled, oddly to Newcastle-on-Tyne, and forbidden to travel beyond ten miles of it. So much for theology.

James made only the one return to his ancient northern kingdom, in 1617 when, with a vast train of courtiers, he spent three extraordinary months in Scotland, largely to the consternation of its people. He had Communion celebrated at Holyrood according to the English rite, by an English bishop causing much of the congregation to walk out; he expended considerable time and ammunition firing off cannon from the castle – for a man who hated war and cold steel, he had an inordinate fondness for artillery; he spent more time hunting deer at Falkland than in any other activity, even neglecting a scheduled visit to Aberdeen to continue with his sport, although allowing a considerable and bewildered body of English courtiers to travel north in his stead – something which Aberdeen never forgave; and in visiting the coal-mines and salt-pans of Sir George Bruce at Culross, in Fife – in the interests of money-making, over which he was always preoccupied – he allowed himself to be conducted down a pit which went on under the Forth, and came up a shaft contrived as a loading-place for shipping out in the estuary and immediately, on seeing himself surrounded by water yelled, 'Murder! Treason! We are dead!' and, sure that it was all a plot against his life, refused either to travel to land in a boat or to return underground the way he had come, eventually having to be carried bodily down to the vessel.

Much more could be recounted of this memorable visit. Scotland, which had waited eagerly for fourteen years for her monarch to make his return, heaved a sigh of relief at his departure.

James died in 1625, having been a king for fifty-eight of his fifty-nine years.

The accession of Charles I made little difference to Scotland. Although he behaved with so much more dignity than had his father, he lacked James's shrewdness and the common touch. He left the secular government of Scotland much as it had been, in the hands of favourites, but otherwise

showed little interest. But in one item, ever to grow in importance, he outdid his father. Where James had sought to
impose bishops on Scotland, Charles went much further and,
in his efforts to co-ordinate religious observance in the two
kingdoms, imposed Anglican-style *worship* which was a vastly
more serious matter. He even ordered a prayer-book, Laud's
Liturgy, composed by the Archbishop of Canterbury, to be
used in all Scottish churches, than which nothing could have
been more unpopular, resulting in widespread unrest and
refusal to obey. The reaction of one Edinburgh worshipper,
Jenny Geddes, a kail-wife of the Tron, is famous. When the
Dean in St Giles in his surplice opened the controversial
prayer-book, Jenny rose to shout, 'Deil colic the wame o'
thee! Out! Out! False thief – dost thou say Mass at my lug!'
and picking up her stool – there was no seating for worshippers in those days – she hurled it at the alarmed cleric. This,
in 1637, was, one might say, the initial stroke of the Civil
War, as far as Scotland was concerned.

A great deal worse was not long in following. Bishops
and priests were rabbled, burnt in effigy, even tarred-and-
feathered. The military were called out to defend them and
punish the attackers. It was not only the common folk and
their mobs who rebelled, the lords and lairds were almost
equally outraged.

It is typical of the Scots that while they will accept with
only grumbles and growls a great deal of misgovernment and
even tyranny, any assault on their religion or metaphysical
predilections can arouse them to fury and action. By 1638 a
great National Covenant, or declaration of religious freedom,
was drawn up – although not forgetting to condemn Popery
– in the 'Great Name of the Lord our God' but disclaiming
any attempt against the King's greatness and authority,
indeed swearing to defend 'our dread Sovereign the King's
Majesty'. The first to sign this covenant was that handsome
and influential nobleman, James Graham, Earl of Montrose.

King Charles in London, stubborn and out-of-touch, saw
it all only as a plot against himself, and sent up his tool, the
Marquis of Hamilton, as High Commissioner, to bring the
protesters to heel. At a great General Assembly at Glasgow

he was defied, and he retired, threatening drastic reprisals. The pen and the word had failed; it now had to be the sword.

So the Wars of the Covenant started. These have been much misunderstood. They were not a revolt against the King's person nor even his government – otherwise Montrose, for one, would not have signed – but against religious dictatorship from London and the imposition by royal command of an alien form of worship. The term Covenanter came in time to have a rather different connotation – and time had its importance here, for fifty years on the Covenant troubles were still in progress.

The Covenant military leadership was divided between two very different commanders. Alexander Leslie, later Earl of Leven, was a dour, stern veteran of the foreign wars, a general under Gustavus Adolphus of Sweden; and the aforementioned Montrose, destined to become one of the transcendant names in Scotland's story, aged twenty-seven, was no trained soldier but a born strategist and brilliant leader of men. These two seldom saw eye-to-eye. A third leader, although scarcely a military one, was Archibald Campbell, eighth Earl of Argyll, son of James's Lord Justice General, a very different character, devious, cunning and ambitious – ambitous enough to aim to rule Scotland. He and the almost too honourable Montrose were bound to clash.

As the Covenant supporters rallied to arms, King Charles led an army up to Berwick-on-Tweed. Leslie hurriedly took a scratch force to the Border to oppose him, their banners inscribed 'For Christ's Crown and Covenant'. The two armies faced each other across Tweed, the first time this had happened since the Henry VIII Rough Wooing. Both sides were reluctant to fight, however – the Scots against their Stewart king, and Charles having trouble behind him in England where he was little more popular. A treaty called the Pacification of Berwick was patched up. But all knew that this could be only a temporary lull, for it resolved nothing. Charles would not give way over his episcopacy.

Meanwhile Montrose had marched north. Aberdeen had become the episcopal capital of Scotland, its university's 'Aberdeen Doctors' strong in that cause. Moreover, this was the Gordon country. Their chief, the Marquis of Huntly, was the principal Catholic in the land, and Charles had unwisely made him Lieutenant of the North. He had taken over the city in the King's name. So Montrose went to teach them the error of their ways, and at the Battle of the Brig o' Dee won the first encounter of the Civil War, and thereafter occupied Aberdeen. Huntly was sent a prisoner to Edinburgh.

This was just the first, and most minor, of Montrose's victories. But, strangely, the others were all to be rather different, in that they were fought *against* the Covenanters, not for them. He has, of course, been accused of changing sides, of treachery, in this war; and on the face of it, that might seem to be the case. But in his own judgment, and that of most historians and biographers thereafter, it was not so. Montrose was essentially an upright man, noble to a degree, and a loyal subject of the King, to whom as earl he had made vows. He had taken up arms reluctantly in favour of a limited object, religious freedom. But when the Covenanters presently gained what they had wanted from Charles – now beset with his English problems, which were to culminate in his downfall and execution – Argyll stepped in and prevailed on the Covenant leadership to continue the fight. King Campbell, as he was now being called, was determined to win control of Scotland for himself. Montrose objected. They had gained what they had banded together for and had no further quarrel with their anointed monarch, to whom they owed allegiance. He gained others to this point of view and they issued a declaration known as the Cumbernauld Bond – and out of this Argyll trumped up a plot allegedly to kill him. He arrested and imprisoned Montrose. King Campbell was well on his way – for Leslie was only a professional soldier and did what his paymasters ordered, and Argyll was now paymaster.

The King came hurriedly back to Scotland, this time without an army. Worried now about a Scots coalition with his English rebels, he talked no more of episcopacy but came offering gifts, not war. He gave in all along the line, created Argyll Marquis and Leslie Earl of Leven, and gave sundry others similar honours – and, happily, he got Montrose out of prison. Then he departed again, thinking Scotland pacified.

Argyll had no desire for pacification. He decided to take the part of the English parliamentarians, now in open opposition to Charles, and persuaded the Scots parliament and the Kirk to this cause. The Solemn League and Covenant was the result, 'a platform of public worship and government wherein England and we might agree.' Part of the agreement was for a Scots army of 20,000 men under the new Earl of Leven to cross into England, at the costs of the English Parliamentarians, as threat to the King. What Charles had dreaded was come to pass, despite his liberal shower of honours.

Montrose hurried south to the King at Oxford, to offer him his services as a loyal subject. Charles, after some delay, on grim news from the north, made him Viceroy of Scotland, created him Marquis, and sent him back home to save his Scots kingdom for him – but without an army or the funds to create one, and even disguised as a groom.

And so the Year of Miracles, 1644, began. Not since the days of Wallace and Bruce had one man set out alone to win a kingdom. Montrose had his friends and well-wishers, of course, and others felt as he did, although not so vehemently and purposefully. He sent out the Fiery Cross, and somehow scraped together a force, scarcely an army, from his own lands and those of his friends, but mainly from the Highlands. For two reasons the first test of strength took place near Perth. One of his oldest friends and fellow-clansmen, Patrick Graham of Inchbraikie, lived quietly at Tullybelton in that area; and here the King's new Lieutenant for Scotland made his headquarters. More important, into these parts came Colkitto, a name which was to feature large in the coming struggle. Alastair MacDonald, son of MacDonald of Colonsay, commonly known as Coll Keitach, Coll who can fight with either hand, had invaded Argyll, the territory of his clan's hereditary enemies the Campbells, from Ireland, with a force of seasoned Irish fighters, gallowglasses as they were called. He was a kinsman of the Marquis of Antrim, another MacDonald, whom Charles had appointed Lieutenant of Ireland, and although a fiery and unpredictable character, was a brilliant guerilla fighter. He had been pursuing clan warfare rather than the King's service in the Campbell country, and having made things rather too hot for himself and his men, moved eastwards across the land into Badenoch and north Atholl, the Campbells in pursuit. Montrose heard of this and sent urgent messengers northwards. The result was a link-up, at Blair Atholl, and agreement to work and fight together. Montrose suddenly had a cadre of over 1,000 veteran fighters to stiffen his untrained levies, although under a distinctly difficult and independent-minded leader.

But the Campbells were not far behind and, more important, Covenant forces of over 8,000 men under Lord Elcho were approaching from the south. A clash could not be long delayed.

It came on 1 September 1644, at Tippermuir near Methven in Strathearn, Montrose choosing the ground – with his strategic flair – to win a major victory although outnumbered three to one. He used the soft ground of Methven Moss to bog down Elcho's cavalry. It was reported that scarcely a dozen men actually fell in the battle but nearly 2,000 died in the rout that followed.

This was the start, then. There followed the most astonishing series of victories and forced marches, across the length and breadth of Scotland north of Forth and Clyde – Aberdeen, Fyvie – where the ballad *The Bonnie Lass o' Fyvie* reminds us: Inverlochy, after an incredible march through the winter mountains, where he defeated and humiliated Argyll himself; back eastwards to take Elgin, where Montrose's fourteen-year-old son, with him on campaign, died and was buried at Bellie kirkyard, a dire blow, youthful victim of the pace and harsh conditions of this extraordinary warfare. Then more victories at Auldearn and Alford, where the Lord Gordon fell; and on south now to the greatest battle of all, at Kilsyth, in the waist of Scotland a mere thirteen miles from Glasgow, where the royalists defeated the main Covenant army. Argyll galloped a score of miles to Queensferry where he fled by boat south to join Leven's forces in the north of England. The other Covenant leaders also fled.

Suddenly, Montrose was master of Scotland. He entered Glasgow and, as the King's Viceroy, called a Parliament. But things had not been going well for Charles in England. The defeat of Marston Moor was followed by the disaster of Naseby, with Cromwell's Ironsides far outsoldiering the Cavaliers. Charles threw himself into the hands of the Scottish army at Newark, but Leven handed him over to the English on receipt of arrears of pay for his army. The King's long captivity had begun.

Now, of course, the Covenant army in England was free to return home, and Montrose hurried south to meet them at the Border. But much of his army had melted away, seeming to have won their war, and it being September the Highlanders as always were preoccupied with getting in their harvest for the winter-feed of their cattle. Worst of all, Colkitto had chosen to go off to harry Argyll in the Earl's absence. So Montrose faced the Covenant's best general, another Leslie, with a very depleted host, and was defeated at Philiphaugh, deserted by the Border lords on whom he relied. From supreme power he was a fugitive again, fleeing northwards.

So Scotland was back under Argyll's rule, and savage were the reprisals meted out to all who had supported the King's Lieutenant.

Montrose sailed from Stonehaven to Norway, and from there travelled through Europe to France before joining the other royalist exiles at the Hague. He was surprised to find himself a hero everywhere that he went. In Paris he was offered the position of Marshal of France, and in Prague made Marshal of the Empire and acclaimed as foremost soldier of the age. At The Hague he found young Charles, Prince of Wales, who welcomed him him enthusiastically. Then, on 30 January 1649, King Charles was executed by Cromwell and his Parliamentarians.

Montrose was shattered – as indeed was all Scotland. Such an outcome had never been envisaged by the Scots, who, however much they might object to a King of Scots' policies, could never contemplate the execution of their monarch – and Charles had been King of Scots as well as of England. The climate of opinion which developed was such as to encourage Montrose to return to Scotland to renew the struggle, urged on by the new Charles II and with promises of support from many sources. He sailed for Orkney in March 1650.

That last campaign was brief and a disaster. The promised support did not materialise, save for a very few loyal volunteers. Charles himself failed the man whom he had just reappointed Viceroy. There was only the one battle, at Carbisdale, in north-east Ross, a dire defeat for the small royalist force. Suddenly Montrose was once again a hunted fugitive.

Making his solitary way back towards Orkney he took refuge at Ardvreck Castle, in Sutherland, where he was betrayed and handed over to his enemies by its laird, Macleod of Assynt. Shamefully maltreated, he was tied, in peasant's clothing, to the back of a saddleless broken-down nag, feet roped under its belly, and with a herald and trumpeter going before and shouting, 'Here comes James Graham, a traitor to his country,' he was led southwards, a spectacle for all the land to see, by Tain and Inverness and Stonehaven to Edinburgh. It was not all humiliation, however, for at Skibo Castle, for instance, where they spent one night, the lady of the house beat General Holbourn, in charge of the escort, about the head with a steaming leg of mutton for not inviting Montrose to occupy the seat of honour. And at two other houses, Pitcaple Castle in Aberdeenshire and House of Grange near Dundee, the ladies thereof sought to have him escape, but at each the captive courteously refused.

At Edinburgh there was no trial; Montrose had already been condemned to death in his absence. On 25 May he was hanged at the Mercat Cross, meeting his death with great dignity and making a parting speech of notable eloquence in the King's cause. His body was then cut up, to be exhibited all over the kingdom. Argyll, who master-minded all, watched his enemy being led to his end from a window of Moray House, in Edinburgh's Canongate.

The Covenant had won. Indeed it had another somewhat doubtful triumph the following month when the new King arrived at Speymouth, too late to save the Viceroy he had failed to support. From the start he was shown who was master in Scotland, bullied and slighted, forced to subscribe both Covenants and preached at interminably. It all may have confirmed Argyll in power but it sent Charles south, to defeat at Worcester, with a hatred of Scotland which he was never to forget.

But the Covenant triumph was short-lived. Cromwell now marched up, to bring the northern kingdom into his Commonwealth. He defeated David Leslie, victor of Philiphaugh, at Dunbar in September that same eventful year – the same extreme Covenant divines who had demanded the slaughter of the royalist prisoners after Philiphaugh now commanding Leslie to leave his strong position and go down and smite the Amalekites, against his better judgment.

The iron fist of the English Parliamentarians now ruled the land, and Archibald Campbell assisted at the ceremony of proclaiming Cromwell Lord Protector and signed an engagement to support the usurper's government.

Chapter 15

THE KILLING TIMES

When Cromwell died in 1658 and was succeeded by lesser men, even England had had enough of the harsh and joyless regime of the Puritan Parliamentarians, and called for Charles to return from the Continent. The Restoration dawned. Scotland shared in this; indeed General Monck, who had governed the northern kingdom for Cromwell, saw the writing on the wall and actually led a Scots force south to aid in the Restoration – and was rewarded by being made Duke of Albemarle.

The King did not forget how he had been treated in Scotland, and sent up the Earl of Middleton, a former Covenant general turned royalist, as High Commissioner to a Parliament which was to wipe the slate clean. At last, Archibald, Marquis of Argyll, paid the price, and was executed at the same spot where Montrose had died eleven years before. Such remains of his late enemy as could be collected were assembled, given a great state funeral, amidst pious laudation and 'the honest peoples loud and joyful acclamations', and buried in St Giles Kirk in a place of honour. James Graham may well have watched from Paradise and smiled ruefully.

And now a very different chapter commenced in Scotland's story, on the face of it a great improvement but in fact more of an ominous lull before inevitable renewed trouble. The Merry Monarch, with so much lee-way to make up in comfortable living, and the dire example of his over-zealous father before him, was not only uninterested in Scotland but was not really interested in government at all, or even in religion. So, since government of some sort there had to be, others filled the power vacuum while Charles enjoyed himself. For Scotland his meant the untrammelled rule of favourites, worse than in James VI's day. John Maitland, second Earl and presently first Duke of Lauderdale, became uncrowned King of Scotland; and John Leslie, seventh Earl and later Duke of Rothes, his right-hand man. Lauderdale was the grandson of James's Chancellor Maitland and grand-nephew of Mary's Secretary Lethington; and Rothes the grand-nephew of the Norman Leslie who led the party to assassinate Cardinal Beaton.

Why Lauderdale should have gained such an ascendancy with Charles is not clear, for he was gross, coarse and debauched. But he was shrewd and learned and unscrupulous, a type which Scotland has never lacked. He had been strong for the Covenant but his hatred and fear of Cromwell changed him into a royalist. As for Rothes, he was tough and uncouth and noted for being seldom sober. These two, as Secretary of State and Lord President of the Council respectively, managed Scotland for Charles, between them for a long time. It was basically Privy Council rule, with Rothes, as President, ordering all at Lauderdale's commands from London – although ordering may scarcely be the correct word, for the Duke of Hamilton reported of the Council that 'they were all so drunk that day that they were not capable of considering anything that was laid before them and would hear of nothing but executing the law.' And the Law the Privy Council executed that day was to eject 271 parish ministers from their parishes, for refusing episcopal patronage. Of these 87 were in the Synod of Glasgow and Ayr, which left only 35 ministers there.

The first Parliament, of 1661, also known as the Drunken Parliament, was nothing if not drastic. It sat intermittently for six months and passed 400 acts, the principal of which was the oddly-named Rescissory Act, which cancelled all acts passed by the years of Covenant Parliaments. It declared the King to be the head of the Church and episcopacy the compulsary form of Scots Church government, restoring the Book of Common Prayer. And since there were no bishops left in Scotland, it sent four divines to England to be conse-

crated bishops and to come back and themselves consecrate
incumbents for the remaining ten dioceses. The leader of
this quartet was James Sharp, minister of Crail, created in a
moment Archbishop of St Andrews and Primate of the
Church – the same who in 1679 was to be waylaid and
murdered on Magus Muir in Fife.

This was when the term Covenanter began to assume a
different meaning. When Lauderdale and Sharp instituted
fines for non-attendance at parish churches under the new
episcopal incumbents, the military collecting the fines, long-
suffering Presbyterian worshippers at last were roused to
revolt, especially in the south-west – ever strongest for the
Covenant – where they were known as Whiggamores, from
the Scots word for sour whey and from which the political
term Whig derives. A large number of these, mere peasants,
in the Dumfries neighbourhood rose in wrath. They marched
north through Ayrshire to Lanark, gathering strength till
there were about 3,000 of them. Then they headed east for
the capital; but in the Colinton area they learned that they
were being followed by the dreaded veteran General Tam
Dalyell of the Binns, with his dragoons, and they lost heart
– as well they might – and decided to return to their own
territories via the Pentland Hills, their numbers dwindling.
Dalyell and his troopers caught up with them at Rullion
Green, high on the south flank of Turnhouse Hill, where
two plantations of trees still mark the site of the two sides to
what was really no battle but a massacre. The Covenanters
had no chance against trained cavalry and were mown down,
and Dalyell, who had learned his soldiering in the Russian
wars against the Poles and Turks, was not the man to show
mercy. Savage was the slaughter. Many of those taken prisoner were tortured with the Boot, a horrible device for
crushing the feet, before being executed, Archbishop Sharp
foremost in the cruel proceedings. Rothes wrote of the
victims as 'damd fules and incorrigibeable phanaticks'. This
pathetic affair was known as the Pentland Rising, and Tam
Dalyell was appointed to the Privy Council on the strength
of it.

So commenced the grim period that became known as the
Killing Times. Lauderdale reacted to the sad Pentland affair

as though it had been a major and criminal assault on government. Even harsher new measures were enacted. The only places where subjects might congregate were the parish churches under the 'King's Curates', and attendance at them was obligatory, so that even lairds, farmers and all employers of labour were fined if those whom they employed failed to attend church. It became an offence even to speak to absentees from episcopal-style worship or to let food or shelter be given to them.

The Presbyterian congregations or Covenanters – now become a term of obloquy – reacted in turn by holding secret outdoor services officiated at by their ousted ministers, which got the name of conventicles; and these became the prime targets of the government's wrath, with large military forces recruited to put them down. These troops and their officers, under the overall command of General Dalyell – who announced that he personally would spit and roast those who disobeyed – gained an unenviable reputation for savagery, and certain names besides Dalyell became especially hated throughout the land, notably Grierson of Lag and Graham of Claverhouse.

This last makes an interesting character-study, a man of great talents, generally loathed at the time, who has become something of a national hero in retrospect – Bloody Clavers on the one hand, Bonnie Dundee on the other. John Graham, a kinsman of the great Montrose, was another brilliant soldier who had learned his craft in the foreign wars, where early he distinguished himself and indeed had saved the life of William Prince of Orange at the Battle of Seneff. Brought home to help cope in Lauderdale's campaign against the Covenanters, he quickly demonstrated not only his efficiency but a ruthless streak much out-of-keeping with his debonair good looks and charm of manner. In Galloway and the south-west his name is still execrated for the atrocities he and his men allegedly perpetrated on the defenceless population, far beyond the mere putting down of conventicles. To save time the Privy Council made these officers also sheriffs, so that they could arrest, try and execute without reference to any higher authority. The occasion when he is said to have tied two women, one over sixty, the other under twenty, to stakes in the Solway sands off Wigtown and watched them slowly drown as the tide came in was said to be repeated elsewhere, as when his soldiers pushed more women back into the River Nith at Dumfries when they tried to clamber out. Men Graham preferred just to shoot. Perhaps he has been painted blacker than he deserves, for this was the man who was to lead the Jacobite cause in Scotland, as Viscount Dundee, with great gallantry, the victor of Killiecrankie, sung about by generations of Scots:

> 'Then all cavaliers who love honour and me,
> Come, up wi' the bonnets o' Bonnie Dundee.'

If Scotland had to be governed by villians, as so often it was, I suppose that it could be said that John Graham made a more personable one than did the gross Lauderdale or the drunken Rothes.

But Bloody Clavers had one humiliating set-back in his resounding military career. In 1679 he approached a conventicle being held at Loudoun Hill in Ayrshire. But the Covenanters were learning to defend themselves, and on this occasion they had a guard of about 250 armed men, 40 of them horsed. This proved more than Claverhouse's troop could tackle and he drew off to collect reinforcements. But two could play at that game, and, encouraged by his retiral, the Covenanters also called in armed help and, marching north after Graham, actually routed the soldiers at Drumclog, near Strathaven. One of the Covenant leaders here was Hackston of Rathillet, in Fife, who only the month before had been one of the slayers of Archbishop Sharp.

It was only a modest victory of course, but it had an enormous impact, encouraging the oppressed majority. Everywhere there were repercussions, not least in the government, for this comparatively minor battle actually at last signalled the fall of the great Lauderdale. The Privy Council, in a panic, appealed to Charles in London, who sent up his allegedly illegitimate son, the Duke of Monmouth and Buccleuch, to be Captain-General and Viceroy, replacing Lauderdale, with much increased military strength. Monmouth was no villain, but much that was deplorable was done in his name. With ample forces now at his command,

Claverhouse recovered his soldierly reputation by winning a victory over the Covenanters at Bothwell Brig which effectively put an end to their hopes of armed success. Four hundred were slain and 1,200 taken prisoner, to be chained two-by-two and herded like cattle the forty miles to Edinburgh where they were penned, still like cattle, into Greyfriars kirkyard, and there left under guard but without shelter or food, by order of the Privy Council.

For five months the unfortunates remained there, overcrowded and untended amongst the tombstones. Edinburgh citizens smuggled some food to them, although this was forbidden. Monmouth at least refused to give orders for wholesale execution. But many died of exposure, wounds and starvation, in the very place where the Covenant had been signed. Eventually, when Monmouth was recalled, some few survivors recanted and were released; some were executed, but hundreds were shipped off to the West Indies for slaves. They never got there, for the ship into which they were packed sank with all hands off Orkney.

Such was the state of Scotland in the later seventeenth century. Change was on the way, but scarcely for the better. Charles was ailing, worn out by his style of living, and more and more his brother, James Duke of York, was coming to the fore in matters of state. His was a very different character, better in some ways, stronger, moral, but obstinate and humourless – and a perfervid Catholic. Since Charles acknowledged no legitimate offspring, James was heir to the throne, and his Catholicism was a major headache in England as well as Scotland, especially as Charles was acquiescing in his brother manoeuvring numbers of his Catholic friends into positions of influence. In these circumstances the Duke of Monmouth, who always claimed that he was legitimate and that Charles had secretly married his mistress, Lucy Walters, the Duke's mother, at The Hague during his years of exile, began to assert *his* right to be heir instead of his uncle. He being a strong Protestant, his cause was taken up enthusiastically by many of the prominent in England – too enthusiastically perhaps, for the rumour got around that it was planned to assassinate both the King and his brother in the Ryehouse Plot. Monmouth had certainly nothing to do with this, for he was an honourable man; but it served as an excuse for strong measures by the Duke of York, in the King's name. Monmouth had to flee back to Holland, where he had been born, and his more vocal supporters were rounded up and some executed.

This might seem to have little to do with Scotland, save that James of York rather overdid it, and fears of a Catholic take-over in England grew so strong that Charles thought it best that his brother should depart the scene for a while. James was sent up to Scotland as High Commissioner and Viceroy.

And so, suddenly, there was a new dispensation in the northern kingdom. After Lauderdale's downfall, Rothes had been promoted Secretary of State as well as Chancellor, and created Duke. But he suffered a fit and died that same year as James came up, 1681 – and these two who had ruled Scotland for so long had seen to it that there were no strong men on the Privy Council to oppose their wills. So there were only comparative non-entities in power on the civil side when James arrived, although the military were all too strong. This suited the new Viceroy admirably. He took over the reins of government personally, with Claverhouse, with whom he got on well, as his lieutenant and with a seat on the Privy Council. In effect, thirty years after Cromwell had departed, Scotland had military rule once more.

James called a Parliament, and under clear armed threat passed the acts he wanted, one cancelling the requirement of only a Protestant succession to the throne, and the other, called the Test Act, requiring everybody in authority and official position to sign their support for the first act – which of course was to guarantee James's accession to the throne on the ailing Charles's death. This Test Act was highly unpopular in the nation at large, but refusal to sign was to face execution. The boys of George Heriot's School in Edinburgh demonstrated the general attitude. They took a dog, smeared a copy of the Test Act with butter, and got the animal to swallow it – and thereupon hanged the dog. Similar reaction developed all over the land. But for those in official positions it was not so easy. Even MacCailean Mor, the eighth Earl of Argyll, son of the executed Marquis, who declared that he did not understand the Act – and indeed it was contradictory in its wording – and therefore could not sign it in all honesty, was imprisoned in Edinburgh Castle under threat of execution. But he managed to escape, dressed as a page escorting his own daughter when she came to pay her farewell visit. He fled to Holland, where more and more of the Protestant leadership of two kingdoms were in exile. Claverhouse's iron fist gripped ever harder, on James's orders.

Then, in 1685, Charles II died and James the VII and II went to London to ascend the throne. Swiftly he showed England what he had already shown Scotland – what it meant to have a strong and fervently Roman Catholic ruler. Everywhere his co-religionists were placed in power, and repression of all opposition was fierce. Irish Catholic troops were brought over, since the English ones could not be relied upon.

Monmouth, now openly asserting his legitimacy and right to be King, supported by William of Orange, who was married to James's elder daughter the Princess Mary, and Protestant, started his ill-fated rising. First he sent Argyll to win over Scotland to his cause and establish a base. But the Earl was no better a soldier than had been his father, and his attempt failed miserably, the Campbells being hardly the best choice to lead a popular and dangerous revolt. When Monmouth himself invaded the south of England he was no more successful, matters were bungled and before long his uncle James captured and executed him. He left sons in Scotland by his Duchess, who had been Countess of Buccleuch in her own right. Their position was interesting.

But James's oppressive rule in England, offensive to the vast majority, could not last long without upheavals, especially with the reign of terror conducted by his minion the infamous Judge Jeffries after the Monmouth Rising, and whom he made Lord Chancellor of England. William of Orange himself was urged on all hands to come over and unseat James – for as well as being married to James's daughter his mother had been a sister of Charles and James. He descended on England in force, a very different affair from

Monmouth's, with the Dutch fleet and army at his disposal, and the so-called Glorious Revolution commenced.

After considerable manoeuvring but no real battles, James fled to France, but without abdicating. The English Parliament declared that he had deserted the country and forfeited the throne, and proclaimed William and Mary King and Queen conjointly. But the Scots Parliament could claim no such authority. For one thing, to be effective it constitutionally required the King to call it; also, the King of Scots, once crowned, could not be unseated alive by anyone save God. It was a demonstration of the essential difference of the two kingdoms, the one feudal in origin, the other patriarchal, like the clan system. And James VII was still King of Scots. He appointed Claverhouse his Captain-General and created him Viscount of Dundee.

So the strange situation developed, with Dutch William, Protestant, King of England and claiming to be King of the United Kingdom also; and Catholic James, in France, claiming to be King of Protestant Scotland. Something had to give.

The people of Scotland themselves were divided. The Lowlands, of course were preponderantly Protestant, and the Covenanters especially, hated James and all his works. Yet there was still a residual loyalty to the house of Stewart. And the Highlands were still mainly Catholic, the Reformation never having really caught on there – partly accounting for the unpopularity of the Clan Campbell who *were* Protestant. So the country dithered. But Claverhouse, Bonnie Dundee, was strong and strongly placed, and the Catholics still held the reins of government. James sent word that he would raise more Catholic troops in Ireland and bring them to Scotland, preparatory to an assault upon England.

This never eventuated. William, whatever else he was, was a good soldier. He decided that he could nip this dangerous situation in the bud. He personally sailed for Ireland with his army, met James before he was ready, and defeated him soundly at the Battle of the Boyne – which the Protestants of Ulster have been celebrating ever since, to the praise of King Billy. James fled back to France, this time for good, and his now rather forlorn cause got the name of Jacobitism.

Meanwhile, the returning Scots exiles from Holland strengthened the hands of the Protestant majority of the Lowlands, and William sent an army north to assist them, and called a parliament. There was much confusion inevitably, since only the King of Scots could call an effective Parliament and William was not yet King of Scots. Since some sort of assembly or convention was going to gather, Dundee took the initiative and announced that King James had called it and *he* was the High Commissioner. So there was the spectacle of two Lords High Commissioner confronting each other in Parliament House in 1689, each claiming to be in charge – for William had nominated the Duke of Hamilton his deputy. Amidst uproar a vote was demanded and taken, and Dundee lost decisively. He stormed out, declaring that this was no Parliament only a convention, and that its decisions therefore had no value. He called on all Catholics, all Jacobites, all supporters of the ancient royal house and all loyal men, to follow him out, and promised to return with a Highland host to overturn that traitorous decision and vote with their broadswords – surely one of the most dramatic scenes that even that ancient building had ever witnessed. William's army was still only at Durham. This was the background to the ballad:

'To the Lords of Convention 'twas Claverhouse spoke,
Ere the King's crown goes down there are crowns to
    be broke!'

The Battle of Killiecrankie was the outcome, fought at the gateway to the Highlands by the said Highland host against William's force under General Mackay, and John Graham won handsomely, this his last battle – for he was killed at the moment of victory, as his clansmen cleared all before them in a typical and terrible Highland charge. Thereafter, lacking his leadership, the victors did not follow it up, the clan chiefs, as typically again, quarrelling amongst themselves.

King William lost the battle but gained Scotland. What our history would have been had that stray musket-ball not killed John Graham, who knows?

Chapter 16

THE END OF AN AULD SANG

And now a totally new situation faced Scotland, with Jacobitism simmering in the north but with Catholicism down and
the religious controversy muted for the first time in over a
century. William III, although a Protestant, was not greatly
concerned with episcopalism, nor with Scotland – nor indeed
very much so with England either, for he was essentially a
soldier and, still being Stadtholder of the Netherlands, the
foreign wars were his main preoccupation. So Scotland was
largely left to get on with her own affairs. With the country
sickened with religious wars, other influences came to the
fore.

Commerce, oddly, largely succeeded religion as a cause of
friction. The seventeenth century, now ending, had seen
great strides in colonial development on all hands, which in
turn stimulated trade and industry. A new prosperous
merchant class had sprung up, in Scotland as well as elsewhere – but the Scots did not have colonies of their own to
exploit, although they had taken a large part, since 1603, in
founding the English ones. But now, despite it being a United
Kingdom, so-called, the English merchant interests and
colonists sought to exclude the Scots from their markets and
ventures, and were supported by their government. It was
even insisted that all goods for the colonies be carried only
in English ships. William's government, still concerned about
a possible Jacobite come-back in Scotland and the separation
of the thrones, saw an important union of the two nations as
the answer, and recognised that this issue of colonial trade
could be constituted a useful pressure to that end. If the

Scots would agree to union they could share in the new
colonial prosperity; if not, they would continue to be
excluded.

There were other pressures towards a union. It was felt
in England that the threat of James and his Jacobites could
be more effectively countered if it was not left to the Scots
– who had a different attitude towards the Stewarts, their
ruling line for over four centuries, as against less than one
century for the English; and Highland Catholicism was also
seen as a menace. And, of course, there was the ages-old urge
to dominate the stubbornly independent smaller northern
kingdom. So a campaign for union developed.

In Scotland, at first, there was little enthusiasm or even
apprehension. The new commercial class was in the main
for it, but the ordinary people were much against the idea.
The lairds and gentry, still very strong, likewise were
opposed. But the nobility were prepared, on the whole, to
consider it. Ever since James VI had gone south, they had
been having to look to London for preferment, promotion
and privilege, so this idea was less foreign to them. And
William's politicians worked on that, concentrating their
attention on the Scots aristocracy. This was an effective
strategy, for owing to the different Scottish parliamentary
set-up, they could affect the constitutional processes irrespective of public opinion. This, of course, was because the Scots
lords all had seats in the Parliament, in no way proportional
as to numbers with the rest. It was the crown's and only the
crown's, privilege to create lords, peers as they were called
in England, Lords of Parliament in Scotland. So the King
could make as many new lords as he liked – and each could
have a vote in the Scots Parliament.

It was probably as well that William's interests were mainly
elsewhere, and that he was apt to be away fighting in the
wars of the Spanish Succession, or the union campaign would
probably have been rushed through even more urgently and
unscrupulously. It gave time for an anti-union movement to
grow in Scotland, led by Andrew Fletcher of Saltoun, Lord
Belhaven and Stenton and others, with the Duke of Hamilton
playing a rather inconsistent role, blowing hot and cold.
Fletcher, the real leader, was an extraordinary man, deter-

mined, absolutely honest, gifted but hot-tempered, an East
Lothian laird of broad acres who sat in Parliament for that
county. His uncompromising honesty had got him into
trouble with Lauderdale and Claverhouse and he had had to
flee the country, eventually to Holland, where he had become
the Master of the Horse to the Duke of Monmouth. But at
the very start of the Monmouth Rising his hot temper had
in fact probably saved his life, for in a quarrel over a horse
he had shot dead the man in charge of the Duke's commis-
sariat, who had actually taken his horsewhip to Fletcher. This
affair caused Monmouth reluctantly to dismiss him, and he
sailed for Spain – and thus was not amongst the casualties
when the rising collapsed shortly afterwards. After many
adventures on the Continent – including becoming a colonel
in the Emperor's forces against the Turks and distinguishing
himself in battle – he was called upon by William of Orange
to take a leading part in *his* invasion. But he quarrelled with
William over his high-handed attitude to Scotland, and came
home to lead in his country's new-style fight for
independence.

Andrew Fletcher was not all fire and temper however, for
he had a good brain. At The Hague he had met, and been
impressed with the ideas and abilities of, one William
Paterson, a Dumfries-shire man of lowly birth who had
developed from being a colonial trader and alleged pirate to
become a money-lender and banker, and to whom many of
the exiles, including Monmouth himself, were temporarily in
debt. Paterson was in fact a financial genius and presently
became the founder of the Bank of England. It was hardly
that which interested Fletcher, however, but another scheme,
and in the colonial sphere. In his wanderings Paterson had
discovered what is now called the Isthmus of Panama and
was then known, when it was known at all, as Darien.
Immediately he perceived its possibilities. Here the American
continent was in fact only thirty-odd miles wide, level, with
no mountains – and the territory had not so far been grabbed
by any of the colonial powers. Now the riches of the New
World were nearly all to be found on the west or Pacific side
of America, in Mexico and Peru and the rest, and of course
Spain had become the wealthiest country in the world by

exploiting this treasure – with others at the same game, including England. But the treasure-ships had to be routed thousands of miles to the south round the dreaded Cape Horn to reach Europe – through the stormiest seas in the world, where a proportion were apt to be wrecked in voyages which took many months. Paterson's idea was that if a system of porterage was established at Darien, then shipping on the Pacific side could unload cargoes there, to be transported across the few miles to the Caribbean and there loaded on to Atlantic ships, saving months of sea-passage and the dangers of Cape Horn. That was his first plan; the second was to dig a canal across the isthmus, using the skills the Dutch had developed in the great canal-system of Holland. That would come later. If Scotland was to take over Darien as her own colony, and her colonists organised the porterage business on a commission basis, large profits would accrue and a thriving foothold be established on the American continent.

Fletcher saw this as a wonderful opportunity for the Scots, not only to start their own colonial empire but to increase prosperity at home, gain a bargaining point against the English merchants' prohibitions and so counter the pressures for union. With William refusing to limit the English bans on Scots trade, and Scots citizens being treated as aliens in England, Fletcher threw himself enthusiastically into the promotion of the Darien Scheme.

A comparatively vast amount of money – for a small country where money had never been in great supply – was required to organise, equip and support an expedition, purchase and fit out ships and pay for land. The chance to invest was deliberately thrown open to all, great and small, for this was to be something of a national crusade in a time when commercial fervour was ousting religious. Fletcher became one of the main sponsors, putting in £1,000 of his own money, a great sum in those days. He and his friend Lord Belhaven stumped the country raising cash and explaining the scheme. Somehow the necessary funds were raised.

There was opposition, of course, especially from the London-looking authorities, of whom the principal was now

John Dalrymple, Master of Stair, Secretary of State – although his father, the first Viscount Stair and Lord President of the Court of Session, invested. The Master was an able, ambitious and ruthless man, wholly for union. Fletcher and he were enemies from the start.

An example of Stair's power and ruthlessness occurred in 1691 when he launched a campaign to bring the Jacobite Highlands to heel by having all the chiefs and leaders of the clans compulsorily to sign an oath of allegiance to King William, before their local sheriffs, by the end of that year. Some naturally delayed, for this was not the sort of thing that clan chieftains took seriously; but threats of military reprisals had their effect and most signed. Old MacIan, chief of the MacDonalds of Glencoe, delayed to the last moment, but turned up at Fort William just in time, in a snowstorm – only to be told that the venue had been changed and that he would have to go all the way south to Inveraray to do his signing, and before a Campbell sheriff. In those wintery conditions it took a considerable time to get through the mountains to Inveraray in Argyll, the Campbell capital and there on 6 January 1692 the old chief made his submission and returned to Glen Coe. In Edinburgh, however, his signature was rejected as too late, and an arrangement was made between Stair and the Earl of Breadalbane – who was Campbell of Glenorchy, and who had received from the government £20,000 to purchase the allegiance of the Highland chiefs, most of which had stuck to his own fingers. On 1 February, 120 military arrived in Glen Coe – and they were Campbell militia, under captain Campbell of Glenlyon. At first they said that they were only there for shelter while they carried out tax-collecting duties in the area. Then, after a fortnight's hospitality with the MacDonalds, living in their houses, Glenlyon received his orders to strike. All were to be slain, without exception, men, women and children, on the King's and Secretary of State's command.

The details of the Massacre of Glencoe are too well-known to require recounting here; they represent one of the most shameful episodes in Scotland's history. In fact, quite a number escaped, although some of these died of exposure in the snow-bound mountains. But 38 were killed – including

MacIan and his elderly wife, who had played host to Glenlyon himself – all in cold blood.

It all aroused a great outcry in Scotland, even in the Lowlands where normally Highlanders were scorned and thought unworthy of consideration. The authorities realised that they had gone too far, and Stair had to retire from the scene for a while. But he was never punished; indeed it was not long before he was back in command and promoted Earl of Stair. William himself could not escape responsibility, for he had given orders to 'extirpate that sect of thieves', on Stair's advice.

Meanwhile the struggle for and against union went on, in Parliament and the country, the tide ebbing and flowing. The Darien Scheme suffered a set-back when the English Parliament ruled that it was an unlawful project, partly because it countered *Spanish* interests. All English investors in the scheme were ordered to withdraw their money under pain of impeachment – and these suddenly had to be paid back to the tune of over £300,000. Not only so, but English ambassadors were instructed to convince foreign subscribers, in Hamburg and Holland where Paterson had links, also to withdraw. So Scotland had to find another half-million to repay them, when already the barrel had been scraped. It is said that the money subscribed for Darien in the end represented more than half the total actual cash in the country. Somehow it was raised, Fletcher foremost in the task. At last, in July 1698, the great day came and the expedition's three ships sailed from Leith, with 1,200 colonists.

Alas for all the high hopes. Troubles afflicted the enterprise from the start. Too many lairds' sons were involved, who had not crossed the ocean to do manual labour. The trade goods taken were of the wrong sort for the natives – a vast quantity of wigs, for instance, were included. The English North American colonists, Virginia and the rest, were forbidden to aid the settlers or even to trade with them. The Spanish fleet attacked, and the English fleet stood by, watching. And of course the heat and the climate were unhelpful. By the time that the second instalment of settlers

The End of an Auld Sang

arrived, they found the colony abandoned and their forerunners dead or dispersed. In all nearly 2,000 died.

Scotland was shattered by this desperate failure, the country all but bankrupt, hopelessness abroad. The Edinburgh mob broke the windows of government supporters. But amongst the upper classes a feeling was growing that England held all the trump-cards and that union was inevitable. Which was, of course, what was planned all along.

Thus unhappily the eighteenth century dawned, and two years later the situation worsened dramatically when King William fell from his horse and died. The Queen had died, childless, in 1694, so that now the new monarch was Anne, her sister; and Anne too was childless – at least, she had had many infants by her marriage to Prince George of Denmark but all had died. So suddenly the succession was in question and Protestant England alarmed. James himself died in 1701, in France, but his son, Anne's half-brother, now called himself James the VIII and III – although he is better known as the Old Pretender – and he was a Catholic like his father. What urgently worried the English government was that if and when Anne died – and she was delicate – Scotland would have the right to choose its own monarch and might plump for this James Stewart, Catholic or none, whereas the English Parliament settled the succession on the German Prince, George, Elector of Hanover, far-out indeed. He was the son of Sophia, who was herself the daughter of Elizabeth of Bohemia, the Winter Queen, Montrose's friend, daughter of James the VI and I, and there was no question but that the Scots would not want German George, Protestant although he might be. Their idea of kingship was not so elastic as that.

So union, an incorporating union, became all the more important for England, in order that there would be no Scots Parliament able to call on James from France, or even on Monmouth's sons, and so separate the crowns again. The Scots Parliamentarians, led by Fletcher and his Country Party, got an Act of Security passed – against the opposition of Stair and his pro-English lords – this Act asserting Scotland's right to choose its monarch from the ancient royal line, although it safeguarded the Protestant religion. It was supported by the Presbyterian and Covenant sympathisers, many Episcopaleans, and of course the Jacobites and Catholics.

The English government was furious, declared that the act was a menace to Queen Anne, and persuaded Anne not to sign the duly-passed Scots Act, an almost unheard-of situation. Anne was a weak woman and wholly under the thumbs of her English ministers. Their counter-move was to have the Queen appoint Commissioners to Treat of a Union of Parliaments, and to emphasise their anger the English Parliament passed an act which declared that if the Scots did not accept the Hanoverian succession by Christmas 1705, all Scots would become aliens in England, with all the legal sanctions that involved. The English fleet would blockade the seas, to prevent all Scots trade with the Continent, as already was the case with the colonies and the New World. Eighteenth-century England was not so very different from the old England of the eleventh century onwards.

Nor was Scotland more united or better served by her leaders. Money poured from the London Treasury into the pockets of the Scots lords, to ensure their vote for union. Even the Duke of Hamilton, who was considered to be assuredly anti-union, appalled Fletcher and the others by proposing, and persuading others, that the new Commissioners for Union should be selected as well as appointed by Queen Anne herself – which meant by her English ministers.

So the tug-of-war developed in earnest. The Scots people as a whole were solidly against union and losing their ancient Parliament, but the forces for union were strong in position, influence and money. Of the thirty-two Scots commissioners appointed to work out a scheme for union, only one was anti-union. Threats, pressure, spying, blackmail were the order of the day, and the bribery money flowing northwards became a flood. It was extraordinary how little some of the Scots lords and provosts were prepared to accept in the form of pensions in return for their votes. Lord Elibank, for instance, sold his for £50; the Earl of Findlater, a new peerage, for £100; Lord Banff for only £11 2s. Even the Marquis of Montrose, great-grandson of the hero, accepted

£300, Lord Justice Clerk Cockburn of Ormiston £200 and the Earl of Balcarres £500. The Provost of Wigtown got £25, though the Provost of Ayr did better at £100. Some did handsomely, of course, the Lord High Commissioner himself getting £12,325 10s, plus an English dukedom, as Duke of Dover. Ironically Stair, who had largely masterminded everything, got nothing, for he died suddenly on the day all was decided. Many new lords, of course, were created for the occasion.

Fletcher and his colleagues fought long and hard. Recognising that at best it would be a near thing, they prepared a second line of defence, that if union was voted for, it would be a federal and not an incorporating union, allowing Scotland still to have a Parliament of some sort, although the English were never really prepared to consider this.

At last, on 16 January 1707, the day of decision came for the Scots Parliament. Up till the last minute the thing was uncertain, depending on how a number of prominent members unconnected with either lobby chose to vote – although Fletcher went fearing the worst, especially when the Duke of Hamilton said that he had toothache and would not be able to attend. Fletcher's fears were well founded, and most of the doubtfuls had been got at. The Act of Union was passed by 110 votes to 68, and – the shame of it – a considerable number did not vote at all. It was an incorporating and not a federal union, to be sure.

The thing was done. Scotland's age-old Parliament had voted itself out of existence. From now on, Scotland would be ruled from London. As even the Earl of Seafield, the Chancellor, announcing the decision, remarked: 'There's an end to an auld sang!'

It is only fair to say that there was a body of opinion in Scotland which sincerely believed that the union would be a good thing for the country, not only amongst the aristocracy but in the new commercial classes. It is significant, for instance, that 17 of the 66 burgess or burgh representatives did not vote at all. But the great majority of the people were wholly against it, and the country rose in uproar and outrage as the decision was announced – so much so indeed that the pro-union members were in danger of their lives in the streets of Edinburgh thereafter, and the administration leaders had to go secretly to a mere summer-house in the grounds of Moray House, in the Canongate, to affix their signatures to the hated Treaty. But it was all too late, and only gave the authorities the opportunity to move in swiftly with the military. The anti-union leaders were arrested and mostly transported down to London for trial as Jacobites – although most were not that. Andrew Fletcher found himself locked up in a cell in Stirling Castle, where some of his friends got him immured, as being a deal safer than the Tower of London or banishment to the plantations. His friend Lord Belhaven was one who died in English custody.

Scotland as a nation continued to exist, of course – and still does. But as a state, a self-governing entity, older than a united England or France, or Germany or Italy and the rest, she ceased to be.

Chapter 17

THE FIFTEEN

From the start the union proved manifestly unsatisfactory for most Scots – even for the lords who had so solidly voted for it, for only 16 of them were allotted seats in the House of Lords, out of some 200, not one in ten – although those who had been Commissioners for Union were rewarded with English peerages which allowed them to sit. The rest found themselves no longer legislators. The Scots to be elected to the House of Commons amounted to only 45, and these speedily found themselves to be very second-rate members – and, of course, able to be outvoted on any and every issue by the vast English majority.

A new burden was promptly laid upon Scotland – taxation. Hitherto the Scots had known little of real taxation, as an imposition on all classes. Their economy was just not geared to support a large central authority. Suddenly that was changed and the country became liable for a share in maintaining a standing army, a navy, a foreign and colonial service, a bureaucracy and all the panoply of state deemed suitable for a major power. This would not have been quite so bad if trade had increased as a result of union, as had been promised; instead trade actually dwindled, and many Scots merchants found it more profitable to move to London and operate from there. Also many clauses of the Treaty of Union were a dead letter from the start, and broken at will, redress all but impossible in a House of Commons hostile to the Scots. Even in Scots law, which most specifically had been protected in the Treaty, there were prompt breaches – for instance in 1710 the House of Lords casually reversed a decision of the Scots Court of Session.

All this and much more, in arousing the Scots people to wrath, greatly encouraged the Jacobite movement, and many who were not Catholic nor Highland or particularly dynastic-ally-minded turned to look towards the Pretender in France. The new James Stewart, the Chevalier St. George, however, was a very different man from his father, hesitant and unsure of himself. The urgings of his supporters eventually got him screwed up to making the attempt – and he was probably not wholly to be blamed for putting it off over an attack of measles when all was ready for a rising in Scotland; but it did not do his credit any good. And then, when in 1708 he did sail north, with a fleet of thirty French ships, the expedition got only as far as the mouth of the Firth of Forth and there, for some reason, hove-to off the Isle of May until an English fleet appeared on the horizon, whereupon the French admiral discreetly set sail for the open sea and then turned south, taking the Pretender and his soldiers safely back to France. This may not have been James's fault, but it certainly did not improve his reputation. His Scots Jaco-bites had mustered, ready for action, and things had come to such a pass that a leading government supporter reported that 'the Jacobites appeared so uppish in the streets of Edin-burgh that I durst hardly look them in the face!' Left in limbo, as it were, however, they became easy targets for their enemies, and suffered heavily, in morale as well as in arrests.

It was at this stage that a name very well known in Scotland's story came much to the fore – Rob Roy MacGregor or Campbell. He had been prominent formerly too, but in a rather different sphere. A younger son of Colonel MacGregor of Glengyle, in the Trossachs area – who had fought with Dundee at Killiecrankie – he was an extraordinary character with a great admixture of qualities, and a sense of humour. With fiery red hair and a mighty frame, at first sight he did not seem so tall as he actually was because of his enormous width of shoulder, and the fact that his arms were so long that he could tie his garters without stooping. A born leader and of an acquisitive bent, he had perfected the traditional MacGregor preoccupation with their neighbours' cattle into the forerunner of the protection racket, or if you prefer it, the insurance industry. His system was to set himself up as the guardian of the flocks and herds of a great area of central Scotland, instead of the alternative predators, but to charge a premium for his services, assuring his clients that their beasts would be safe if a given proportion of their value was paid to him annually – but he left all in no doubt that they most assuredly would not be safe if this was not done. Not content with this, he took advantage of the government's anti-Jacobite fever – although he was himself a confirmed Jacobite – to set up an armed force, with government help and money, called the Glengyle Highland Watch, in theory to patrol the said Trossachs area and put down Jacobite rebels, but in fact to operate the cattle business. Out of this Highland Watch idea grew the well-known Highland regiment, the Black Watch. It says something about the state of Scotland at the time that amongst Rob's more or less contented clients were Lord Aberuchill, the Lord Justice Clerk, and others almost as influential.

Rob was greatly aided by a geographical feature which still exists although on a much reduced scale – the Flanders Moss. This was the upper strath of the River Forth, lying just below the mountains of the Highland Line, and stretching almost from Stirling itself, where the first crossing of Forth was possible, for twenty miles westwards to the wild MacGregor stronghold country at Aberfoyle. Here the Forth had flooded the level strath all the way, for a width of some five miles, so that there was an impassable wilderness of about 100 square miles of bogs, moss, lochans and scrubwoodland, with islets of firm ground in it – impassable, that is, to all save the MacGregors, who knew the secret, twisting ways through it, and which they used to drive their stolen Lowland cattle, a great asset, their 'moat' behind which they were all but impregnable. West of Stirling there was just no way across this Flanders Moss for the uninitiated, right to Loch Lomond and beyond – even the Romans, magnificent engineers as they were, had been stumped by it. Now mainly drained, of course, largely into the great Lake of Menteith, it is today excellent farmland, the work of the so-called Moss Lairds of later years. But in the eighteenth century it was the major barrier between Highlands and Lowlands – and could have affected the entire history of Scotland, and therefore of Britain, if Rob Roy had had his way seven years later.

Queen Anne died in 1714, and the anticipated upheavals commenced. George of Hanover, distinctly reluctant to leave his Germany, was proclaimed King in London, and the Scots were outraged. He spoke little English, he knew nothing of Scotland and never visited it. A less acceptable monarch than the 'wee German lairdie' would have been hard to imagine for the most ancient throne in Christendom. This was the great opportunity for the Jacobites and all others who hated the union. Within the year, the Rising of 1715 was under way.

Having learned, from 1708, not to rely on James or the French, this rising was home-grown, and Rob Roy MacGregor had a large part to play in its preliminaries, he with his cattle-trading connections – for he bought and sold beasts from all over the Highlands as well as 'protecting' them – and so was a convenient liaison-officer between the clan chiefs and the central direction. This direction was assumed by the sixth Earl of Mar, great-great-grandson of James VI's foster-brother, Johnnie Mar. He had the unfortunate nickname of Bobbing John, this referring to his agility at changing sides. He actually was Secretary of State when the new King George snubbed him, in London, and it was this that sent him hurrying back to Scotland, a new Jacobite. However, the Earl of Mar was a suitably prominent name to head up a rising, and *Lowland*, which was important, also a Protestant. So Bobbing John took charge.

Amidst great enthusiasm the standard was raised at Braemar on 6 September, James VIII was formally proclaimed King of Scots, and contingents flocked in from all over the land, a focus for discontent and disillusion at last. There was much alarm and despondency on the government side, well aware how unpopular they were, and at this stage getting little help from a London preoccupied with George's unpopularity there. The then MacCailean Mor, John, second Duke of Argyll, grandson of Monmouth's Argyll, and a talented soldier, was appointed Commander-in-Chief in Scotland, to deal with the rising – and there were even doubts as to *his* allegiance, for he was in constant touch with Rob Roy. Known as Red John of the Battles in Scotland, in England Pope wrote of him:

> 'Argyll, the state's whole thunder born to wield,
> And shake alike the senate and the field.'

He had been a general in the French wars. But now he was not sure of his troops or cause. He had four regiments of foot and four of cavalry, the latter including the famed Scots Greys; but he did not know how these would behave if told to fight against their fellow-Scots. For the rest he had mainly German mercenaries, Hessians, whom he neither liked nor trusted. He moved this force to Stirling, and in no very confident state, more concerned with using the Forth as a defensive barrier to protect Lowland Scotland than with attacking the Jacobites.

From Braemar Mar struck out in three directions. He was no soldier himself, but he had lieutenants who were. Gordon of Auchintoul, a general in the Russian wars, he sent with Clanranald westwards to capture Fort William and hold the Highland West for King James. The Master of Sinclair he sent to take Fife; and he himself led the main army south to make Perth his base – and so, with Sinclair, to control both Forth and Tay. It was probably a sound enough strategy.

In contrast to Argyll, Mar had mustered a fine army, almost entirely Highland. The clans did King James proud. The Earl of Seaforth was there with 700 Mackenzies and Macraes; Mackintosh of Borlum had 500 of his clan; there were 400 Frasers; there was the Atholl Brigade under the Duke's two sons; Lord Drummond's Regiment; the Earl of Strathmore's Regiment; and so on. The 250 MacGregors under Rob Roy were the best equipped of the entire army, for they had the Highland Watch arms and moreover had been attacking government garrisons and units and stealing their weapons. But this great force lingered at Perth instead of marching south before Argyll was ready for them. They were waiting for King James to come, and bring with him the Duke of Berwick, his illegitimate half-brother and a renowned soldier and Marshal of France, who was to take command of the Jacobite forces in the field.

James and his half-brother delayed. Fretting with impatience typical of a Highland army, a tactical diversion was set in motion. Mackintosh of Borlum, with 1,500 men, made a surprise crossing of the Forth estuary from Fife – now firmly in Jacobite hands – to the East Lothian coast, on 13 October. They landed successfully and marched on Haddington, which they took. Next day they headed for Edinburgh itself. Argyll rushed back from Stirling and took command in the capital. Mar, of course, should have attacked then, but did not, waiting for news and for King James. Mackintosh wisely decided that he could not take Edinburgh unaided, under the guns of its citadel, and turned and took the port of Leith instead. Argyll, leaving Edinburgh strengthened, hurried back to Stirling. There was no doubt who held the initiative.

Mar was persuaded by the impatient chiefs that he must advance – without any more waiting; especially as word came of the arrival in the Clyde of an English force of warships which were reputed to be going to land troops to sail in the ships' boats up Loch Lomond, and so to try to outflank the Flanders Moss barrier. Some of the MacGregors were sent to counter this move, since it was their country – but under Gregor of Glengyle, Rob Roy's nephew. He himself was sent to prospect and hold the Fords of Frew, the only possible crossing of Forth for Argyll's cavalry, seven miles west of Stirling. On arrival there he found government dragoons holding the south bank, and sent back word to that effect. But he also assured Mar that he could guide a Jacobite force secretly through the Moss further west and so get behind Stirling and turn Argyll's front. He strongly urged this course.

But Mar had already moved as far south as Dunblane, and Argyll marched to meet him. Mar decided on a head-on clash, rejecting the idea of a flanking move through the Moss, and recalled Rob and his MacGregors.

The two armies met on Sheriffmuir, near Dunblane, with their respective right and left flanks based on the Allan Water, on 13 November, and a most confused day-long battle took place. The style of it may be judged by the address of one clan chief to his men. 'There stands MacCailean Mor for

King George, and here stands Maclean for King James –
charge!' Militarily the two sides were fairly evenly matched,
for though the Jacobites had the advantage in numbers and
spirit, Argyll had a great superiority in artillery and in trained
cavalry, most of Mar's cavalry having gone to Fife. As the
hours passed, now one flank gaining a limited success, now
another, no clear victory emerged. And all this time Rob Roy
and his MacGregors were forced-marching back to the Allan
Water valley from the south-west.

They arrived as the short October day was drawing to a
close, and found the weary fighters flagging indeed, in fact
withdrawing on both sides to lick their wounds. Some urged
Rob to attack there and then, that his reinforcements, small
as they were, might save the day. But though the MacGregors
were fresh to the fighting, they were anything but fresh
physically, having forced-marched for fifteen miles to get
there. And Rob, a born tactician, taking in the overall situation from a commanding height, made his famous decision:
'If they canna do it without me, they'll no' do it with me!' –
a remark which, unfairly, was later used to blacken his
character and courage. He nevertheless used his MacGregors
skilfully to cover the retiral of various Jacobite units for
regrouping.

Night settled on Sheriffmuir, without victory or defeat
being evident. It was like Flodden, only with the situation
reversed. The morning showed the Jacobites to be left in
command of the field, Argyll's forces having retired on Stirling in the night. But unlike Surrey at Flodden, Mar, while
thankfully claiming victory, did not press his advantage as an
experienced commander would have done. Instead, he
ordered a return to his base at Perth, there to reorganise –
and to await James and the Duke of Berwick.

This, of course, was a grievous error, tactically and psycho-
logically. Mar himself was not a Highlander, but he should
have known that any Highland army, brave and brilliant in
advance, was at its worst in retreat and idleness. Once the
excitement and challenge of battle was over, the mood of the
clansmen was always to slip away back to their glens, their
families and their herds. After all, they were all unpaid volunteers, there out of loyalty to their chiefs. This happened now.

Steadily the numbers drained away, taking their wounded with them. At Leith, Mackintosh of Borlum saw that there was going to be no link-up with the main army, and disgustedly set off for Berwick-on-Tweed and over the Border on a small-scale invasion of his own. Fife remained Jacobite-held; and Gregor MacGregor drove back the English boat-expedition on Loch Lomond. But King James and his duke never turned up, momentum was lost, and Bobbing John had shot his bolt. The year 1716 dawned and the Fifteen Rising petered out, high hopes not so much dashed as frittered away. If the Stewarts had had a Dundee or a Montrose in their service in 1715, all would have been very different. James came at last, too late, stayed six weeks, and left for good.

The Jacobite cause was not dead, of course, but the set-back was grievous; and Lowland Scotland more or less resigned itself to Hanoverian rule – although the Highlands never did. There was no major reprisal campaign, the government was not strong enough for that. Indeed only four years later, in 1719, there was another Rising, which has attracted little notice in the history-books. This took place up in Kintail in Wester Ross, and once again Rob Roy was involved. This time the initiative came from Spain more than from France, for England was now at peace with France and overt support of James by the latter would have jeopardised the fragile accord. In May, three foreign ships appeared in Loch Alsh, Mackenzie and Macrae country, two Spanish frigates and a small French vessel. On board were the Earl of Seaforth, the Mackenzie chief, who had fled to France after Sheriff-muir, the Earl Marischal, the Marquis of Tullibardine, Atholl's heir, and Mackintosh of Borlum who had had adventures in England, been captured but escaped from Newgate. There were also a few hundred Spanish soldiers. They were come to rouse the clans again. And coinciding with this, there was to be a major descent on the English west coast by a Spanish fleet under the Irish Marquis of Ormonde.

This affair had not been nearly so well prepared as the Fifteen, and the clans took a long time to assemble. Rob Roy, for instance, only heard about it after the Kintail landing, and hastened north-west with a mere 40 MacGregors. The same half-cock reaction prevailed elsewhere. After nearly a month only some 1,200 had assembled, and word came that the large Spanish attempt on England had come to naught, a great storm having dispersed and damaged much of the fleet. At this news the Spanish Kintail soldiery decided that they too wanted to go home; but the Earl Marischal, who seems to have been in command, sent the ships away secretly, to prevent any such desertion by the troops.

In these not very hopeful circumstances, General Wightman, the government commander in the Highlands, marched west from Inverness with some 1,600 men, and the two forces met in Glen Shiel on 11 June 1719. It was an odd place for a battle, a narrow steep-sided glen with lofty peaks rising all around and a rushing river at the foot, all very well for an ambush but scarcely for set fighting. If anything, it should have suited the Highlanders best, if not the Spaniards. But again artillery played a fairly important role – on this occasion mortars, not cannon, and of course they were all on the government side, the Spanish ships having brought only 2,000 muskets and 5,000 pistols. The half-hearted Spaniards did not like those mortars.

The first day's fighting was indecisive, most of it done high on the side of Sgour Ouran, one of the notable Five Sisters of Kintail. When the short June night ended, the engagement was resumed; but things now went badly for the Jacobites. There was bad blood between the Highlanders and the Spaniards – and not only the Spaniards, for the Macraes refused to fight alongside the MacGregors, owing to some clan feud. Worse, by a grievous misfortune the Earl of Seaforth was wounded, and his Mackenzie clansmen, much more concerned for their long-exiled chief than for the Stewart cause, insisted in escorting him off the field *en masse* to safety. Since this was the Mackenzie country and there were 600 of them, half the total force, the situation was transformed. Thereafter the Jacobite front collapsed, the Highlanders melted away into the mountains, and the unfortunate Spaniards were left to be taken prisoner. That was the end of the Rising of 1719.

The question remains, of course – was all this failure of the Stewart cause a bad thing or a good thing for Scotland as a whole? It is still a matter for argument and discussion. Leaving aside the Jacobite and Catholic situation, and the romantic gloss which has developed over the entire subject, it is not easy to come to a conclusion. Many would say, especially in the Lowlands, that it was all just as well, that with a Catholic Stewart monarch restored to the Scots throne, there would probably have been renewed armed conflict with England. And if the Stewarts had managed to regain the English throne as well, there might well have been religious warfare again. Putting the clock back, they would say, seldom works. On the other hand, the union was working grievously against Scottish interests, and this would have been reversed. Managing their own affairs, the Scots would almost certainly have built a better and more balanced state to enter modern times than rule from a not-very-interested London achieved. Nor would the Scots, presumably, have lost almost entire generations of young men in fighting England's wars – and this became an actual government policy. And so on. The 'if onlys' of history make fascinating if unprofitable debating-ground.

It was not all Jacobite struggles, to be sure, in the first quarter of the eighteenth century. A new development had arisen to split at least the upper ranks of the nation, this dissention imported from England and arising out of the United Kingdom Parliament – Whigs and Tories. This idea of party politics was something the Scots had not known previously, divisions being religious, dynastic or purely causal. But being perhaps the most disunited race on earth, this new opportunity for argument and division was eagerly siezed upon, and was to prove an excellent method of keeping the Scots fighting each other rather than combining for a common cause – and still does. Whig and Tory administrations, from London, succeeded each other in ding-dong monotony, the supporters of each much more concerned with getting the others out than with improving the failures and injustices of the union. Everyone was happy except the ordinary people of Scotland.

One typical act of government did arouse much indignation, even in the Lowlands. The prisoners taken in Mar's failed rising were, of course, entitled to be tried in their own country, by Scots law, since the offence had taken place in Scotland by Scots citizens. But they were ordered to be tried at Carlisle, in England. In the event, the sentences there were comparatively moderate, thanks to a change in government policy, but this major breach of the Treaty of Union was much resented.

Argyll now became the uncrowned king, although he had periods when he was out of favour in London – largely probably because he was insufficiently harsh, for on the whole he used his power well. Even in the Highlands he was less unpopular than most of his line, for instance retaining his links with Rob Roy, and seeking to disarm the clans rather than to repress them, being a clan chief himself. The Disarming Act, strengthened in 1725, could have been either an intense provocation or a dead letter, prohibiting the clansmen from owning the arms which were their very birthright. The Act was passed at Westminster, of course – but it had to be carried out in Scotland, and Argyll went about it wisely. Instead of sending fire-eaters into the glens, he sent General Wade, an Englishman but an engineer rather than a fighting soldier. And Wade, no doubt on MacCailean Mor's advice, was more interested in pacifying the trackless mountainous land by building roads than by collecting arms. He did carry out this part of his task, after a fashion; but the clansmen were adept at palming off old and comparatively useless weapons on him and hiding their real armoury, as often as not in the reed-thatch of their houses. Certainly when 1745 came and another rising, there was no lack of weapons. Wade took his other duty much more seriously, and made more permanent impact on the Highlands than any soldier before or since by his road-building programme. Hitherto there had been only drove-roads for cattle, and mere tracks, north of the Highland Line, and precious few bridges. Wade changed all this, in his most ambitious project, laying down a total of 260 miles of good roads and building between 30 and 40 bridges, many of these still in use. All this in an eleven-year stint, opening up the country in an extraordinary degree. The original scheme was to link the government garrisons of Crieff, Inverness and Forts William, Augustus and George, so that the troops could move quickly between them. This was in time much extended, in the interests of 'policing' trouble spots. Although the Highlanders were at first hostile, they inevitably came to find these roads a great convenience, for anybody could use them, everybody became more mobile – and even the Jacobite chiefs recognised that the roads could help them move their forces about equally with the government's. A notice set up near Fort William reflects all this:

'Had you seen these roads before they were made,
You would hold up your hands and bless General
    Wade!'

Whilst this was going on in the Highlands, the Lowlands were having to cope with a different sort of London edict, the Malt Tax. This, as applied to Scotland, meant a burden of 3*d* being put on every bushel of malt for brewing, which forced up the price of ale, a dire imposition on the common people and forerunner of the present-day duties on wines and spirits. It aroused great fury. Edinburgh brewers refused to brew, and in Glasgow there were riots. Few measures made London rule so unpopular. That this sort of imposition was sufficient to arouse such wrath, after all the savagery and bloodshed of previous years, was a measure of changed conditions.

George I died in 1727 and was succeeded by his son George II, also German-born and with little more to commend him to the Scots than had his father. He too never visited his northern kingdom. So nothing was changed. Jacobite plotting went on, but with James being so spineless and unexciting a Pretender, that was all it amounted to. In fact, probably, these were fairly good years for Scotland, in that there was no warfare, no actual oppression, and the Scots were largely left to get on with their own affairs by an uninterested government far away. Taxation was still the main source of friction, deeper resentments only smouldering.

But even taxation and similar impositions can give rise to violence in a proud and discontented population, as witness the Porteous Riot of 1736. This arose initially out of another highly unpopular tax, that on imported tea, wines, and brandy. This interference with free trade and the people's enjoyment led to a great deal of smuggling, a new offence. The government countered by setting up customs officers, and these became much hated. Some of them in an excess of enthusiasm, arrested two individuals named Wilson and Robertson at the little port of Pittenweem in Fife, and brought them to Edinburgh for trial. Condemned to be hanged, they were subjected to the usual sermon in the Tron Kirk before execution. Wilson, a large fat man, flung himself upon the guards as they were being led out, not unaided by the congregation, to enable his partner to make his escape – this because previously, with the mob's aid, they had made an escape attempt in the Tolbooth, the grating from a narrow window having been removed from the outside, and Wilson, having preceded Robertson in the effort, got stuck so that neither got away. The Town Guard, under a Captain Porteous, were not gentle towards the citizenry on either occasion. And when poor fair-minded Wilson was duly hanged in the Grassmarket, the crowd were incensed and stones flew. Porteous ordered his men to open fire and half-a-dozen of the mob were killed and a score or so wounded, some of them women. At the popular outcry over this, with crowds parading the streets demanding vengeance, something had to be done. Porteous was brought to judgement. He was condemned to be hanged; but London intervened. George was away in Hanover – which he much preferred to England – but his strong-minded wife Queen Caroline, acting regent, ordered a reprieve for Porteous. So, at two in the morning the Edinburgh crowd broke down the Tolbooth door, disarmed the guard and took Porteous out and hanged him. The Scots were not yet wholly subdued.

The government was furious, as was Queen Caroline. The House of Lords declared that the Lord Provost be imprisoned, the Town Guard disbanded and replaced by military; and three Scots High Court judges were brought to stand before their English counterparts. The Queen is reputed to have angrily told Argyll that she would make Scotland into a hunting-ground; whereat the Duke informed her that, 'In that case, Ma'am, I will go north to prepare my hounds!' Since his hounds consisted of some 5,000

Campbells, even the Queen saw the point. But Edinburgh had to pay Mrs Porteous £2,000 compensation, a vast sum in those days.

Chapter 18

BONNIE PRINCE CHARLIE

For better or for worse a new situation was developing on the Jacobite front. James had two sons by the Polish Princess Clementina Sobieski, and the elder of them, Charles Edward Stewart, as he grew to manhood, proved to be a very different man from James, as he himself had been from his own father – spirited, personable and handsome. It was only a question of time until dynastic matters would again be put to the test.

Things came to a head in 1745. Argyll had fallen from power in 1742 and the war with France had been resumed the next year. Charles was twenty-five, and made his famous descent upon Scots soil, to commence the most written-about and romanticised interlude in Scotland's story – so well-recorded, dissected and argued over that there is no need for any general recapitulation here. Only a very brief résumé and one or two of the less well-known details might profitably be considered, with the resultant effects on the nation.

Compared with the other attempts, this was in fact very modest in its genesis, preparations at a minimum, giving the impression of a young man's impatience. Charles, borrowing some 220,000 livres from a banker, and pawning his mother's jewels, arrived at Loch nan Uamh, in the Cameron-Clanranald country of Arisaig, in the small French frigate *La Doutelle*, on 1 July 1745, with no supporting force but only a small group of personal associates, seven in number, who became known as the Seven Men of Moidart. Some knew that he was coming, of course; indeed he had sent word in especial to two very important Highland chiefs, MacLeod of

MacLeod and MacDonald of Sleat. Sad to say these both failed the Prince, asserting the attempt ill-considered and untimely – indeed MacLeod went so far as to send information of the attempt to London, and later even brought out his clan *against* the Prince. Despite this inauspicious start, Charles was not downcast and soon was cheered by the adherence of Young Locheil, son of the Cameron chief, and Young Clanranald, the two local clans.

This entire campaign tended to be the opposite of that of 1715, vigour and haste instead of caution and delay. Landing in 12 July with only his seven men, on 19 August the Prince raised his standard at Glenfinnan in front of a force of 2,000 cheering clansmen. Without delay he marched eastwards. Learning that the government commander, Sir John Cope, at Stirling, on hearing of the attempt was marching northwards for Fort Augustus in the Great Glen to nip the rising in the bud, Charles, nothing daunted, took the bold course of heading to intercept. Near the great and grim Pass of Drumochter he waited. Cope got as far as Dalnacardoch, in north Atholl, just south of the pass, learned of the Jacobites blocking his path at Corrieyarrack and, prudent man, decided to avoid trouble at this stage and changed course, heading now for Inverness instead of Fort Augustus. So the two forces by-passed each other only a few miles apart. Charles cheerfully headed southwards for the Lowlands, to reach Perth on 4 September, where for the second time his father was proclaimed king.

Still there was no lingering, as had been the case in 1715. With the Highlanders now flocking to his standard, the Prince marched on Edinburgh, without any real opposition, reaching there on the 17th, to find chaos reigning. Locheil managed to get 900 Highlanders into the city by the Netherbow, and there was no organised resistance. The representatives of government made themselves scarce, and the city welcomed Charles with cheering crowds. Thereafter followed the extraordinary development of Charles Stewart establishing himself in the Palace of Holyroodhouse and there giving a great ball and holding court for the youth and beauty of the capital – this only a few weeks after his landing at Loch nan Uamh.

From Inverness the alarmed General Cope had hastened to Aberdeen, there to embark his troops on ships and sail for Dunbar, at the mouth of the Firth of Forth. When the Prince heard of this he interrupted his jollifications and set off eastwards to challenge the Hanoverian army. This time Cope could hardly side-step, and the two forces met on 20 September, between Tranent and Prestonpans in East Lothian.

It was, of course, a great victory for the Jacobites, the government side distinguishing itself by incompetence and poltroonery – save for the celebrated Colonel Gardiner who died heroically. Even Cope, oversleeping and surprised, after only quarter-of-an-hour's battle fled the field and headed for Berwick, leaving behind his money-chest to fall into the Prince's hands. The popular song:

'Hey Johnnie Cope are you waukin' yet?
Or are your drums a-beatin' yet?'

reflects the situation, and is still sung in celebration. This must have been perhaps the only battle where a high estate-wall played an important tactical role, for the government soldiers, retreating before the Highlanders' charge, found themselves up against this nearly mile-long wall of Preston-grange House, still there, too high to climb over, and there died in their hundreds – 1,200 were killed and wounded that day and 1,800 taken prisoner, with only a small loss on the Jacobite side, Charles behaving most magnanimously towards the defeated enemy.

Back in Edinburgh the Prince waited for a month, almost like a reigning monarch, although he himself desired immediately to press on down into England. But 6,000 French troops were promised, and also funds from the King of France, and both would be a great help. His officers persuaded him to wait.

Now the debate begins. Should Charles have been content to have won Scotland for his father, and James to have become King of Scots only, the crowns separated again? If so, how different might have been the outcome. But it was the United Kingdom throne which James claimed, James III as well as VIII – and presently, with no sign of the French reinforcements or cash, the army marched southwards. Or south-westwards, rather, into England by Carlisle, for the main English Jacobite support was reputed to be in their north-west.

Alas, although Carlisle surrendered after a brief resistance, English support was very feeble, only some 300 altogether joining the army from England and Wales, a notable disappointment, where it had been hoped that there would be a general uprising. Nevertheless, the government reaction was feeble also, astonishingly so, since the Jacobites proceeded, by way of Penrith, Kendal, Lancaster and on to Preston and Manchester, without any major clash. Still lacking real opposition they got as far as Derby, only 130 miles from London, and there they got news of conflicting significance. King George had packed his bags and was ready to flee the country, and the government was in a panic; on the other hand, three different armies were assembled against them – General Wade at Wetherby in Yorkshire, behind them; the Duke of Cumberland, a son of the King, at Lichfield, north of Birmingham; and a mixed force at Finchley, north of London.

A council-of-war was held at Derby on 7 December, and although the Prince was again for pressing on, the majority opinion, led by Lord George Murray, was for turning back. Murray, who had joined them at Perth, was an able soldier, brother of the Duke of Atholl, and with the Drummond Duke of Perth was joint Lieutenant-General of the army. The most experienced military man there, he judged that the small Highland force, so far from home, with its lines of communication so stretched, just dared not risk going on and being trapped between three armies. It was conventional military wisdom; but then, conventional military wisdom would never have let them get this far anyway. Charles's instinct was probably more accurate in fact, for, although they did not know it, the London Finchley muster was little better than a frightened rabble; and Wade, no thruster, was too far behind to have caught up before London; also young Cumberland – he was only twenty-four – cannot have been in any confident state, with his father and the administration at his back making preparations to flee. However, Charles bowed to the majority view, and the great retiral commenced.

And now, to be sure, the usual contrary influences came into play; a Highland army, if not in retreat, in retiral, with its objectives failed; and morale sinking, not least the Prince's own, for he was now resentful. All the way south he had marched at the head of his men; now he rode a horse. Scotland was a long way off. The weather was grim. And of course the opposition took heart, and Cumberland at least pressed on, with 10,000 men. There were still no battles, only skirmishes at Shap and Clifton. But the sense of pressure had replaced the euphoria of advance. All was not lost, of course, for the 6,000 Frenchmen were still expected in Scotland, and with the gold from the French king, the army would be put into a better spirit – for it had not been paid for a long time, there was no money to buy food and forage, and the men were stealing what they could and making themselves unpopular. At Carlisle Charles left a garrison of 200 to hold the castle and town, and pressed on across the Border, heading now for Glasgow. There he learned that no French reinforcements had arrived and no money either. But he held a review, to rally Scots spirits.

Then they heard that the government's General Hawley, who had replaced Cope, was advancing westwards with 8,000 men, from Edinburgh. Charles, with only half that number now, decided to try to capture Stirling ahead of him. They met at Falkirk, and the Jacobites won resoundingly.

But now the snow-covered Highland hills were in sight, and the glens called inexorably to the hungry, ragged, unpaid clansmen. Many decided to go home to their wives, families and flocks for a while, and to rejoin the Prince later.

So, with much reduced numbers, Charles headed north, by Atholl and Drumochter again, the Spey valley and Moy of the Mackintoshes – where was enacted one of the most extraordinary affairs of even Scotland's military history. The Prince had ridden ahead to Moy Hall, with only a small escort, to be well received by Lady Mackintosh, or Colonel Anne as she was known, the chief's wife. The Earl of Loudoun, the government commander at Inverness, learning of this, set out with 1,500 men to capture Charles. But Lady

Anne sent Donald Fraser of Moybeg, the local blacksmith
and four others, in the darkness to take up selected positions
at the narrow place of Creag-nan-Eoin, where the government troops must pass. When they heard them come up,
Fraser shouted loudly for the Mackintoshes, MacGillivrays
and MacBeans to form the right, the MacDonalds to take
the centre and the Frasers the left. Then all five of the
hidden party fired off their muskets, and one of the troops
was hit. Loudoun fancied that he was confronted by an entire
division of the Highland army, and ordered speedy retiral –
and a panic set in. It is reliably reported that the regiment
fled headlong not only to Inverness itself, but across the
Kessock ferry into Ross.

It is a strange feature of this period how even at such late
stage and after all the major efforts and disappointments, the
fighting initiative remained with the Jacobites. They had, in
fact, never been defeated in battle and now, weary and greatly
reduced in numbers, they still retained the military superiority and dash. From Moy, Charles directed three thrusts,
all successful. He himself went forward to capture Inverness
and its castle, Loudoun only just managing to escape, fleeing
to Skye of all places. Fort Augustus was also taken, after a
two-day siege. And Lord Lewis Gordon soundly defeated
the pro-government MacLeods at Inverurie. But these diver-
sions, although heartening, did tend to disperse and weaken
the main Jacobite force still further – and Cumberland with
his 10,000 men was not far behind. He had not taken long
to capture Carlisle, thereafter executing half the surrendered
garrison – in marked contrast to Charles who, when he had
taken that place, had allowed all the enemy garrison to go
free.

The blame for Culloden has been variously and interminably argued, the Prince and Lord George Murray
disagreeing as to tactics. Here is no place to dissect that
tragic affair and to apportion responsibility. Anyway, almost
certainly Cumberland's great superiority in artillery had a lot
to do with it. The clans stood for an hour, taking the deadly
cannon-fire, before receiving the command to charge. So
fierce, even so, was their assault that they broke right through
the government front; but the second line, and more artillery

mowed them down and in twenty-five minutes the day was lost. It was the Jacobites' first defeat – and their last. It was also the last real military battle to be fought on British soil.

Yet, if I may put it this way, Culloden was a very minor affair as battles go, the numbers involved being very small, and this only the first military reverse for a hitherto highly successful force. Charles was in the midst of his own Highlands, and support for his cause had not evaporated. *Cumberland's* lines of communication were now as stretched as the Jacobites' had been at Derby. Why then, did the rising so totally collapse?

It is a hard question to answer convincingly. Sheer weariness undoubtedly had a lot to do with it, the fatigue and exhaustion of men who had marched and counter-marched continually for nine months and covered well over 1,000 miles. Some have blamed the savagery of Cumberland's terrible reprisals and inhumanities on the prisoners and wounded, as well as on the Highland population, in a shameful reign of terror, as numbing the Jacobite support – as undoubtedly was intended; but the Scots, especially the Highlanders, are not the folk to be numbed for long by even such Germanic brutality, indeed the reverse probably applies. I think that the answer must be looked for in Charles Edward himself. We know, from his life thereafter, that although gallant, brave and dashing, his was not really a strong character – and once down he was apt to be very down. I suggest that the real moment of defeat for the Stewart cause was not at Culloden at all but at Derby, when the Prince had been so grievously disappointed, his high hopes dashed when he saw his goal in sight. All the long road back to the Highlands he was a different man. And although there were minor triumphs for his arms, the basic failure was there. He had had the United Kingdom throne for his father almost within his grasp, and had had to turn back, against his own judgment. Moreover, when he got back to Scotland there were none of the promised French troops nor the gold either. Culloden was just the last straw for Charles's military resolution. If he had retired into the glens temporarily, to rally his support again, to reorganise and reform, he could still have resumed the campaign – after all, the total losses at

Culloden were only one-fifth of the army he had led to Edinburgh and Prestonpans. The support was still there. But no; Charles reluctantly leaving the battlefield, with tears in his eyes, fled the scene, turning himself into a hunted fugitive, and kept on fleeing, ever westwards. It is significant, surely, that he made for the very place where he had landed, the Arisaig coast, via Stratherrick, Invergarry and the Cameron country, and from that coast, with only six companions, set off in an eight-oared boat for the Outer Hebrides, as though putting himself as far away as he could from any renewal of the struggle. He came back, of course, but not to fight – and then it was too late.

Charles's wanderings in the Hebrides, and later on the mainland, make a romantic and in its own way gallant tale, beloved of storytellers – how he went from island to island, helped on his way by loyal and admiring folk, how he met Flora MacDonald, stepdaughter of MacDonald of Armadale, who was actually a government officer, and how she dressed him in woman's clothes, as her maid, and so enabled him to cross to Skye from South Uist in safety, the theme of that other well-loved ballad:

> 'Speed, bonnie boat like a bird on the wing,
> Onward the sailors cry,
> Bearing the lad that was born to be King
> Over the sea to Skye.'

Generations have read and thrilled to the Prince's hair's-breadth escapes, his privations, his endurance and the self-sacrificing loyalty of so many, of how although £30,000 had been offered for his capture, not one of the hundreds who must have known of his whereabouts in those months was found to betray him. But all this, although splendid, heart-warming and heart-breaking, was not war nor politics. It all had to end, inevitably, either in tragedy or defeat. On 19 September 1746 Charles sailed away on a French ship from Scotland, from the selfsame Loch nan Uamh, never to return, despite that other nostalgic ballad:

> 'Will ye no' come back again?
> Better lo'ed ye couldna be. . . .'

Then, too late by a fortnight, the French gold had arrived at Arisaig – 40,000 gold *louis d'ors*, enough to have revived the entire campaign. This vast sum, unheard-of wealth in a Scotland where money was always in short supply, the equivalent of many millions of pounds today, not only failed to help the cause it was sent for but in fact did enormous harm. For reaching the rump of the Jacobite leadership which Charles had just left behind, it immediately sowed dissention, envy, greed and plotting amongst them. Consider the situation. These men, mainly Highland chieftains, had sacrificed security and position for the cause, had undergone great hardships and danger. Now their lives were forfeit if they were caught. And here, suddenly, were riches beyond the dreams of avarice, and nothing to spend it on, their forces dispersed, the Prince's cause abandoned, and these leaders left to extricate themselves as best they could. Is it any wonder that many of them felt that some at least of the money should be shared up amongst them, to help compensate for dire losses and to aid their escape overseas? They would scarcely have been human otherwise. But this led to suspicion, deceit, bad blood, sheer corruption. The band of brothers dissolved into venality, rapacity, and these chieftains and officers who would sooner have died than sell their Prince for the £30,000 offered, now schemed and plotted how to grab a share of the 40,000 *louis d'ors*. Not all, of course; some were for hiding the gold away, in the hope of the Jacobite cause being revived one day. Some of the money was indeed hidden somewhere on the shore of Loch Arkaig, where it presumably lies to this day, becoming in time known as the Loch Arkaig Treasure – although much had disappeared by that time, like those who purloined it. The names of Murray of Broughton, the Prince's secretary, Simon Fraser, Lord Lovat and Major James Mor MacGregor, a son of Rob Roy, were amongst those linked thereafter with the missing wealth; but details, by the nature of things, remained uncertain. What was certain was that it all effectively ended any possibility of a united effort on the part of the Jacobite leadership to keep the flame of revolt alight. It makes a sad but fascinating story.

For the rest, the aftermath of the rising was sheerest tragedy and shame. The London authorities had had the most almighty fright and now made up for it – and certainly chose the right man for the display of spleen and hatred. William Augustus well earned his by-name of Butcher Cumberland. His utter inhumanity and ferocity is almost beyond belief, extraordinary in the brother of the monarch towards subjects of the King. For instance, after the battle, triumphantly surveying the stricken field, he stalked past a gravely wounded young Jacobite lieutenant-colonel, Fraser of Inverallochie, who painfully raised himself on an elbow to eye the conqueror. The Duke turned to his aide, Captain Wolfe, later to be famous at Quebec, and cried, 'Wolfe – shoot me this Highland scoundrel who dares look on us with so insolent a stare!' Wolfe replied, saying that his commission was at His Royal Highness's disposal, but he was not an executioner. Furiously Cumberland turned to others of his entourage, but none would do the deed. But he insisted, and ordered a private solider to blow out Inverallochie's brains, in cold blood, there before all their eyes. This was no isolated case. The ducal orders were for no mercy to be shown towards wounded or prisoners. Everywhere casualties were shot, bayoneted or clubbed to death, the government soldiery, many of them foreign mercenaries, so crazed with slaughter that they sprinkled each other with the blood of their victims. And it was not all done in the heat of battle. Next day parties were sent to scour the country, every house and cottage of a wide area searched for hiding wounded, and these, when discovered, were clubbed to death – and typical reprisals taken on their shelterers. Nineteen wounded officers were found in a plantation on Drummossie Moor itself, and these were dragged out, thrown into carts, taken to the park-wall of Culloden House and there shot down and their skulls beaten in with musket-butts. One man, thought to be dead, survived, with smashed jaws, to tell the tale. Another party of forty were found lying wounded in a thatch-roofed hovel. On them the door was barred and the thatch set alight so that they all burned. And when the Provost of Inverness, no Jacobite, went to plead for some medical treatment for prisoners awaiting their fate, he was literally kicked head-over-heels down stairs. Duncan Forbes of Culloden himself, Lord President of the Court Session and a confirmed Hanoverian, protested to the Duke that the laws of the country should be observed, to which Cumberland replied: 'The laws of the country, my lord? I'll make a brigade give the laws, by God!'

All this was terrible enough. But it pales into almost insignificance in scale, beside the horrific treatment of the entire Highland area which followed on Cumberland's orders, a reign of terror indeed which even Edward, Hammer of the Scots, 500 years before, could not have exceeded. Scotland was to be taught that never again was the Stewart cause to be supported, nor any other which ran counter to London's interests.

This William Augustus, Duke of Cumberland, returned to that London, to be feted in a hero's welcome, proclaimed the saviour of the country, thanked by both houses of Parliament and an addition of £25,000 a year voted to his income by the grateful Commons.

Let us end this summary repeating that song still sung with romantic fervour wherever Scots gather:

> 'Will ye no' come back again?
> Will ye no' come back again?
> Better lo'ed ye couldna be. . . .'

That plea was for Prince Charles Edward Stewart. It surely tells something and more than one thing, about the Scots, both for themselves and others to think on.

Chapter 19

ENLIGHTENMENT

The long term effects on the Rising of 1745 were felt for fully a century after Cumberland's brutalities, through government policy – the Highlands bearing the brunt of it, but all Scotland suffering to some extent. A sustained and comprehensive programme was instituted to put down all manifestations of national spirit, and the clan spirit in especial. The Disarming Act was enforced drastically now, not as General Wade had applied it, so that no more than a single blunt-tipped eating-knife was permitted for any Highlander. Under a new provision of the Act, the wearing of the tartan and Highland dress was forbidden, on pain of transportation. The estates of the Jacobite chiefs were forfeited, Lowland lairds' also, of course. A shrewd blow was struck, in 1747, by the Heritable Jurisdictions Act, which at a stroke of the government pen abolished the hereditary privileges of the Scots ruling classes, their extensive baronial rights in law, the right to impose semi-military service – which did away with the lords' 'tails' of retainers, and the clan armies – although this was utilised by those in favour with the authorities to gain notable financial compensation, a sum of £152,000 being disbursed. It could be argued that this was no bad thing, for many of these jurisdictions were disgraceful, although latterly not apt to be exercised to the full. Nevertheless, as late as 1692, the Laird of Grant had sentenced three persons to be 'hangit' for horse-stealing; and the same year, a lad whom the laird convicted of stealing 'the socks of a plough', was sentenced 'to be nailit be the lug with ane irene naile to ane post, and to stand there for the spaice of ane hour without motione, and to be allowit to break the griss nailed without drawing of the nail.' It is salutory to note that in 1707 the Town Council of Perth applied to the Earl of Perth for the loan of his hangman, as being more expert than theirs at the business. For all that, this Act certainly aided in the repression of the Scots sense of nationhood.

A further development arose out of the government's ever-increasing need for soldiers, for India, Burma, Ceylon, the conquest of Canada and other spheres of colonial expansion, for the American War of Independence, and later still the Napoleonic wars. It was recollected what excellent natural fighting material the Scots made, especially the Highlanders, and since they were 'expendable' anyway, and 'idle' according to the authorities, here was a wonderful way of turning a distinct liability into an asset. So the forfeited and disgraced Highland chiefs, who had been lying low at home or abroad, were suddenly allowed to buy themselves back into government favour by raising clan or district regiments to serve in the vastly expanding British Army. Thus were formed the components of those celebrated military units whose names were to ring round the world for gallantry and fighting spirit, the Seaforth, Cameron, Gordon, Argyll, Sutherland and other Highlanders. Strange indeed that so soon after they had been so fiercely fighting the British Army, these same clansmen, under their chiefs and tacksmen, or lesser lairds, as officers, became the pride of the said British Army. The scale of this development is often scarcely realised, so many regiments were formed, usually to coalesce in time into battalions of the aforementioned famous units – Fraser's Highlanders (1757); Keith's Highlanders (1759); Campbell's (1759); MacDonald's (1777); Lord MacLeod's (1777); Atholl's (1778); Argyll's (1778); Seaforth's (1778); Cameron's (1739); Gordon's (1794); Sutherland's (1800); and so on. The casualties suffered by these regiments over the years, needless to say, hardly bears contemplation. But, as even Cumberland's Captain Wolfe, now a general, said at the Siège of Quebec, where so many Highlanders died: 'No great matter if they fall. How can you better employ a secret enemy than by making his end conducive to the common good?'

Some indication of the scale of this solution of the Highland problem is given by the fact that Skye alone, between the years 1747 and 1783, furnished the British Army with 21 lieutenant-generals and major-generals, 45 lieutenant-colonels, 600 majors, captains lieutenants and ensigns, 10,000 foot soldiers and 120 pipers – that for an island 45 miles long by 15 broad.

To encourage the recruitment of the clansmen to these new regiments, the government was persuaded to relax the provisions of the Disarming Act relative to wearing the tartan and kilt – but only so far as military service was concerned. All Highlanders on their return home, even on leave, were required to take off their kilts and tartan and leave them under lock-and-key on the edge of their home districts, to be donned again only on their return to military duty outwith the Highlands. It may be interesting to note that at Clachan Seil on one of the larger inshore Argyll islands south of Oban, where the well-known bridge connects with the mainland, known as the Bridge over the Atlantic, the old ferry inn is now known as the Tigh-an-Truish Hotel, the House of Trousers. This was where the proud Highland soldiers of this area had to change from kilts to trousers before they could visit their families. When visitors today wonder at the few kilts they are apt to see worn in the Highlands by the natives, as distinct from the incomers, let them ponder this enactment. The astonishing thing is that the said Highlanders were able to preserve their pride and carriage in these circumstances. That they did, on more than the battlefield, is revealed in the account of Sir Robert Munro, one of their officers, who when King George expressed the desire to see one of these curious if barbaric soldiers he had heard about, brought three privates, named MacGregor, Campbell and Grant, to be presented to the King, and to demonstrate their expertise with their weapons, at St James's Palace. Much impressed, the monarch gave each of them a guinea – which these privates of the Black Watch handed to the porter at the palace gate as they passed out.

At last and at least, London had found a use for the Highlands. The Lowlands too were involved in this exploitation of the martial spirit, although never on the same scale.

It is rather extraordinary that, contemporaneously with this period of national declension of the political front, and the drawing away of man-power on military adventures and empire-building, there should have developed, in Edinburgh and the Lowlands, a galaxy of intellectual and artistic talent such as had never before been seen in Scotland. Some will argue that this was a direct result of the Union of 1707; and there could be a certain amount of truth in that, for with no borders to defend, no battles to be fought, on British soil at least, and politics being effectively removed to 400 miles away, there was time, opportunity and inclination to indulge in social and cultural pursuits. But there was more to it than that. I would suggest that the fading of religious fanaticism, bigotry and argument had much to do with it, and this was happening all over Christendom. The Scots, the Lowlanders in especial, had always been intensely concerned with religion, theology and metaphysics, in hair-splitting enthusiasm. Consider how most of Scotland's internal upheavals for two centuries had been over such matters. With the decline of this sphere, the Scot's need for philosophical and dialectic dispute had to turn elsewhere, and found expression in the arts, humanities, sciences and the rest. Intellectually, the Golden Age had dawned.

Certainly a wonderful flowering of talent and brilliance blossomed from Scotland's hitherto not particularly aesthetically-productive soil. Just consider these – David Hume, Tobias Smollett, Adam Smith, Jupiter Carlyle, Henry Mackenzie (the Man of Feeling), Allan Ramsay, Robert Burns, Sir Henry Raeburn, Robert Fergusson, Sir Walter Scott, James Hogg (the Ettrick Shepherd), the Lords Jeffrey, Hailes, Cockburn and Kames, and so many more. It all seemed to display an astonishing transformation; and Edinburgh for a time became one of the most exciting and intellectually influential capitals of the world. London was presently to cream off a large proportion of Scotland's talent, in this respect as in others, so that Samuel Johnson could make his famous remark that the Scotchman's favourite prospect was the high road to London; but that was not quite yet.

Admittedly the Augustan Age, as the period of the early Georges is sometimes called, produced a somewhat similar

233

cultured harvest in England, throwing up such men as Gibbon, Samuel Johnson, Byron, Cowper, Coleridge, Keats, Shelley and Wordsworth. Other nations could show a like display, for it was a time of artistic ferment. But nothing can detract from the brilliance which this small nation, of only one-tenth of England's population, produced in the second-half of the eighteenth and the early nineteenth centuries.

Yet it was by no means all wit, wisdom and wonder, for trade was stifled, poverty was widespread, there were famines, exploitation and unrest amongst the common people – the Golden Age was far from golden for them. The French Revolution had its repercussions in Scotland, Burns extolling it in his verse – it is not always realised that he did more than extol it, for he actually sent four muskets to the French revolutionaries which he, as an excisemen, had extracted from a captured smuggling vessel. Something new began to develop in the Lowlands, class-warfare or the genesis of it, an attitude hitherto but little known in Scotland, whose class barriers were much less pronounced than in England. An idealistic concern for the conditions of the poor, and reform of the government structure, met with short shrift at the hands of the authorities – which at this period meant in effect Henry Dundas Viscount Melville, who was the current uncrowned king in Scotland, and another rapacious and unscrupulous example of the genus; it was said that in those days the northern kingdom was really one great rotten burgh in the pocket of Dundas, and that anyone who desired not only a seat in Parliament but any government post whatsoever could only get it through the good offices of this man. He was, of course, a friend of William Pitt, the Prime Minister, and as well as ruling Scotland, after his fashion, was at one time or another Home Secretary, Treasurer of the Navy, President of the India Office, and Secretary for War. He it is whose statue stands on top of the lofty column in the centre of St Andrew Square, Edinburgh, surveying that haunt of big business – one of the most successful rogues even Scotland has ever thrown up. Less successful if more admirable was Thomas Muir, a young Edinburgh advocate, who championed the cause of reform and concern for the common folk, chief founder the 'The Friends of the People', who advocated extending the voting franchise from the few land-holders and other privileged people to all citizens, and that elections for Parliament should be held more frequently and fairly. This was held by Dundas and his friends to be as good as sedition, and Muir was arrested, charged and condemned, by the notorious Lord Braxfield, to transportation to Botany Bay for fourteen years. So great was the sense of panic aroused in the establishment by such stirrings amongst the people, that the story was put about that the wife of a certain suspect advocate in Edinburgh was guillotining her hens in the back garden, in practice for the day when she could behead the rulers of Scotland.

Then, arising out of the same French Revolution, came Napoleon Bonaparte. It is hard to overestimate the impact of this little Corsican on the Europe of the day, and far beyond, his limitless ambition allied to military genius and driving-power. Interesting to speculate, too, what might have been the position for Scotland had she not been attached to England by the Union, and with the traditional Auld Alliance with France still functioning. As an ally of Napoleon instead of part of the opposition, what might have transpired? Once again, all history might have been different. As it was, Napoleon's activities and campaigns affected Scotland more directly than might have been expected for a small country not likely to be a target; partly as indicated, owing to the ever-increasing demand for Scots soldiers, but almost more directly still, out of a new attitude towards the Highlands.

Napoleon's blockade of the British Isles is sometimes overlooked as to importance, in preoccupation with his great land campaigns and victories; but it came near to success and bringing Britain to her knees, as well as causing widespread and all but hysterical fear of foreign invasion, something these islands had not had to contemplate for many years. Everywhere elaborate and often rather ridiculous preparations were made to repel the French, somewhat similar to the situation in 1940–1 when the Home Guard, concrete tank-traps, blockhouses and trenches were devised to try to keep out Hitler's hordes. At the beginning of the nineteenth century it was martello towers, warning-beacons on hilltops, shoreline patrols and the setting up of innumerable volunteer yeomanry regiments all over two kingdoms, into which people like Walter Scott and even Robert Burns flocked, lame as Scott was. The volunteers' maneouvres and playing-at-soldiers make rather laughable reading today.

But there was nothing laughable about the impact on the Highlands. The blockade meant that England in especial grew short of food; also of imported wool to make uniforms for her new armies. It was realised that sheep, which produced both, would flourish on the Highland hills. So here was something more that the Highlands could contribute, as well as soldiers – sheep in vast numbers. All landowners, therefore, were encouraged to turn their estates and glens into great sheep-runs – and clearly huge profits were to be made. Hitherto the Highlands had had little to do with sheep, only a few being kept to produce wool for homespun clothing; cattle were the mainstay of the Highland folk. And cattle and sheep do not run well together, one spoiling the pasture for the other. So the clansmen's cattle had to go, and since the clansfolk could not live on sheep, which are not a population-sustaining crop, the clansfolk had to go too. And so started the Highland Clearances.

There have been many shameful episodes in Scotland's story, as these pages I fear have made all too clear; but this surely was one of the worst, in the widespread misery it caused, the heartless way it was carried out, and the permanent emptying of a vast area of the country – however much it may, in the long run, have aided in the development of overseas territories where the Highlanders were forced to go, especially Canada. That these evictions were taking place at the same time as so many of the young men were away from their homes fighting in the Napoleonic wars made the proceedings the more disgraceful.

Although these evictions are often referred to as the Sutherland Clearances, this is a misnomer. Those on the vast Sutherland estates, comprising almost the whole of that county, were probably on the largest scale and have received the most publicity, thanks to their especial brutality; but they were not the first. Indeed they started only in 1810 when others had been going on for years. It must be remembered that even after the Rising of 1715, estates of many of the chiefs involved were forfeited, handed over by government to a semi-official exploiting body named the York Buildings Company, and then sold by them to whomsoever would pay for them. This policy was much extended after the Forty-Five. So there were a great many non-Highland proprietors by the 1750s, many of them English, including Cumbrian and Yorkshire squires used to sheep-rearing on their fells; and these were amongst the first to perceive the possibilities of the Highlands, if the cattle and the people could be got rid of. When the blockade made this the more desirable and profitable, there was no lack of entrepreneurs. Moreover, sadly, quite a number of the chiefs who had managed to hang on to their clan lands saw the opportunity to become rich and followed suit, to their shame. It is to be noted, in this connection, that these lands were not in fact the chief's own property but the clan's. From time immemorial they had been the homelands of the various clans and septs, although no individuals, whether chiefs, tacksmen or ordinary clansmen, held any papers or charters to prove it. Of course southern, especially English, law accepted no recognition of such unwritten and patriarchal tenure, being feudal in conception; and in that law therefore the lands had to belong to individuals or families – and naturally these were assumed to be the chief's. So the chief could be dispossessed of or sell the clan's land under this dispensation, and this is what happened on a vast scale.

Probably the first to be turned over to sheep were the great Drummond lands in Strathearn, forfeited by that most Jacobite and Catholic of houses even before the Napoleonic era. But once the crisis developed, the thing spread swiftly.

In theory, the government itself was not involved; it was left to individual landowners. But these could rely on backing from the government from sheriffs, officers and troops where necessary, where opposition developed. Grievously too, it must be admitted, to a large extent from the Kirk, which, at the behest of the authorities, made a practice of sending up to Highland parishes Lowland non-Gaelic-speaking ministers who could not really be close to their Gaelic parishoners and whose whole attitude was inimical to the Highland way of life. Their normal teaching, in English or in Braid Scots, was apt to be that the people should bow to lawful authority, go quietly when evicted, and recognise that it was God's judgment on them for their sins of rebellion and idleness. So two kinds of shepherds descended upon the Highlands, those to scatter and disperse their human flocks and those to introduce and spread their animal ones. The new masters of the emptied glens were largely North Country English sheep-farmers.

There can have been few such wholesale land-clearances in the history of supposedly civilised nations since the Normans cleared whole areas of England to turn into their hunting preserves, such as William Rufus's New Forest; but these were on a comparatively tiny scale. It has been asked, time and again, why the Highlanders suffered it, these people whose sons made the finest fighting material of the European armies. Part of the answer lies in that very fact, of course – the Highlands were being bled white of their menfolk for the wars. Also the clans had lost their natural leaders, their structure, much of the pride in their identity, even their national dress. Likewise, the effects of the post-Culloden atrocities and repressions must not be forgotten. There *was* resistance, to be sure, in a large number of cases; but it was sporadic, individual, not co-ordinated. There was no leader, and by their very nature the clans, even under their chiefs, were not used to co-operation. So, on the whole, the evictors had it their own way. The folk were driven out of their homes, their cattle slaughtered, and if they refused to go, their thatches were burned over their heads, causing unnumbered casualties amongst the old and feeble. Then they were driven down to the nearest sea-shore and there left to survive as best they might, in hastily-erected shelters where they could not find caves, gathering shellfish and berries to eat, and suffering appallingly in winter weather. Not unnaturally soon, starving and hopeless, large numbers elected, as urged by the authorities, to go off in the overcrowded emigrant ships to the new colonies, especially Canada and Nova Scotia, which their sons were at the time helping to take over from the French – which explains why there are today many times the number of Gaelic-speakers in Canada than there are in Scotland.

If the scale of these Highland Clearances is ever doubted, remember that 16,000 were evicted from the Sutherland estates alone between 1810 and 1820 by the Marquis of Stafford, the English husband of the Countess of Sutherland, in the name of land-improvement. He was rewarded by being created Duke in 1833.

Yet, while all this was going on, the Golden Age was flourishing in Edinburgh. Surely the Scots must be one of the strangest peoples in God's creation.

The irony of it all was highlighted in 1822 when, at the urging of Sir Walter Scott, who had become immensely popular in England with his romantic Scots novels, George IV, the former Prince Regent actually paid a visit to his northern kingdom, the first monarch to do so since the Restoration – and not only came, but actually donned High-land dress for the occasion, a tartan kilt, albeit with pink tights for decency's sake. So much for the power of the novel.

If this episode has its ridiculous side, it should not detract from the services Scott performed for his native land for these were important and may be forgotten. He, in fact, made Scotland 'respectable' to the English, something unknown hitherto, with it being seen as a barbarous, backward and hostile land, a sort of prevailing nuisance to the north. This respectability, however humiliating the conception, was necessary if Scotland as a whole, not merely the Edinburgh intelligentsia, was to win back her self-respect and to resume any sort of national status after the disasters of the eighteenth century. It is strange that it should have been so largely imaginative writings which achieved this. Whatever his fail-ings and mistakes – and Scott was no more perfect that the rest of us – he was a patriot, who was ambitious for his country as well as for himself and his status. As well as influencing so many to see Scotland in a new light, he was largely responsible for the restoration of the Scottish Regalia, the crown, sceptre and sword of state, to proud keeping and public display.

The tale of these, the Honours Three as they were known, is fascinating and somehow typical of Scotland's own story. At Cromwell's invasion, the Three Estates, anxious that the Scots Regalia should not suffer the fate of the English Crown

Jewels, commanded the Earl Marischal to convey them to his strong castle of Dunnottar near Stonehaven, one of the securest holds in the land. But there the Cromwellians followed and besieged the stronghold. The garrison of forty were not provisioned to hold out for long, and it was clear that the Honours were going to be lost. Then the minister's wife of nearby Kinneff, concocted a scheme. She was in the habit of visiting the wife of the castle's governor, and the English soldiers permitted the lady to pass through the lines to do so. The plan was for the Honours to be smuggled out before the castle had to surrender. The sword and sceptre were to be taken out of the casket and disguised as a distaff on which Mrs Grainger's maid was spinning flax; and the crown itself was concealed under the lady's clothing, on her lap as she rode her pony. It is recorded that the ruse was almost discovered when the English commander courteously came to assist the minister's wife to mount her horse, but noted nothing amiss – perhaps he thought that she was pregnant – and the Honours were conveyed thus to Kinneff Church. There the Reverend Mr Grainger that night buried them in a hole he dug in the floor of the kirk, just before the pulpit, and sent word of what was done to the Countess Marischal. There they remained until the Restoration, when they were recovered. The son of the Countess was made Earl of Kintore, although he had played no part in the rescue, and a baronetcy was given to the governor of Dunnottar, Sir George Ogilvie. The Honours were put in a great chest and placed in a strong room in Edinburgh Castle for safe-keeping. Oddly, or perhaps typically, they were then forgotten, William and Mary, and then Anne and the Hanoverians having no interest in their Scottish crown, and succeeding generations lost all trace of these symbols of Scotland's sovereignty until Walter Scott and his romantic gift came along, got King George to give him authority to make search for them – the authority of a Royal Commission no less – searched the castle's cells and cellars, and at length discovered the chest with the missing regalia. Thereafter, cleaned and refurbished, they were put on show in what is now called the Crown Room of Edinburgh Castle, where they are still the most popular objective of visitors.

Also concerned with the castle, Scott was instrumental in obtaining the return of the famous cannon, Mons Meg, which had been removed to the Tower of London for some extra-ordinary reason in 1754; and it too still remains, although recently it has had to be placed under cover owing to deterioration caused by exposure to the weather. Sir Walter was also involved in the preservation of many items of historic interest in the city which otherwise would have perished at the hands of municipal vandals, a type which seems always to have flourished on our soil. Minor matters these, you may say – but significant as foreshadowing a change in Scottish attitudes and national consciousness, the first stirrings of reaction to the North British mentality which had succeeded the Union and the Jacobite disasters. Robert Burns was exemplifying a parallel if somewhat different Scottishness and patriotic spirit on the other side of the country. It is noteworthy that it was writers who led in this revival of identity and self-respect, not the natural leadership of the nation, the politicians, the aristocracy, the Kirk or the merchant classes.

It was as well that such revival came when it did, for there were to be new contrary pressures ahead which would mightily tax the sorely-tried Scots identity and its very existence as a nation.

Chapter 20

WHITHER SCOTLAND?

The Industrial Revolution of the mid-nineteenth century has been variously described – as the end of the old order; the commencement of the era of the common man; the victory of human ingenuity and industry over entrenched privilege; the triumph of machine over muscles; the opening up of the world's natural resources for the benefit of mankind; and so on. Likewise, of course, it could be said to be the beginning of the new slavery of man to machine, of work-force to master; the dominance of town over countryside; the era of extreme wealth and extreme poverty; the elevation of the profit-motive above all else. There is no lack of conflicting judgments on the matter. But one verdict is surely certain – it was no aid to the preservation and maintenance of national spirit and identity, especially for a small nation attached to a large one which moved into the forefront of industrialisation.

Not that Scotland was herself backward in developing the new ideas and skills; indeed in some aspects she led the way – for instance in coal-mining, where pits had been established at Culross, as James VI found out, and at Tranent in East Lothian, the latter well before the Reformation, and with the early shameful exploitation of female and child labour which was to be an ominous foreshadowing of things to come, in this nineteenth century. In iron and steel making Scotland was also well to the fore, sufficiently so for the cannon which Wellington used to defeat Napoleon at Waterloo to be forged at Carron Ironworks, near Falkirk, these indeed being known as carronades. It is interesting to note, in passing, that the other industrial development, the strike, was foreshadowed here near Carron also, at the so-called 'Battle of Bonnymuir' in 1820, when labourers, protesting at grievous working conditions, long hours and low wages, clashed with the military. Three were killed in the struggle and three more later executed.

Yet, although Lowland Scots were anything but backward in embracing the challenge of the Industrial Revolution, it scarcely assisted in national regeneration. Great fortunes were made by the few, in tobacco, jute, textiles and ship-building, as well as coal and iron, and Scots inventiveness was notable, as became an individualistic people; but somehow the benefits were apt to elude Scotland as a whole, with the profits, like so many of the inventors, tending to be channelled southwards towards the seat of government, privilege and social and commercial advancement. James Watt serves as a good example of this trend.

Watt, an ancestor of the present author, was born at Greenock in 1736, the son of a prosperous merchant and magistrate. He was well-educated, and trained as a mathematical instrument maker, but later developed into a civil engineer, designing canals and harbours just a few years before another West Country Scot, Thomas Telford, was to do likewise. But from an early age Watt perceived the possibilities of steam-power, and at Boness, in West Lothian, he built his first steam-engine in 1765. Watt did not *invent* the steam engine – this had been conceived as a possibility long years before – but he perfected the idea and turned it into a practical proposition, making an immense step forward, one of the very keys to the Industrial Revolution. It might have been expected that this would have given Scotland a head-start in this new era, especially as Watt was at Boness because of his links with Dr Roebuck, who had founded the Carron Ironworks nearby, and who encouraged Watt to make his engine, with a view to its mass manufacture at Carron. But Roebuck got into financial difficulties and the project had to be postponed and thereafter Watt went south to Birmingham with his invention, and went into partnership with Matthew Boulton of the Soho Foundry. Boulton, Watt & Company exploited and developed the steam-engine in England. Few were to realise that it was a Scottish invention.

Other problems created by industrialisation included an emptying of the countryside into the towns to feed the new factories and mills, with consequent overcrowding and vast spreading of city housing – usually of the poorest quality – for the influx, the beginning of the slums. Naturally a large proportion of the incomers were the dispossessed Highlanders, to Glasgow and its environs in especial, so that that hitherto quite modest and notably ecclesiastical and university city suddenly grew into the huge, shapeless sprawl of modern times, quite upsetting the population balance of the country, a situation which has never been rectified. To make this aspect of the matter worse, the demand for almost unlimited cheap labour coinciding with famines in Ireland resulted in a great and continuing importation of Irish immigrants into the West of Scotland, desperate for work and subsistence. These were fellow-Celts and ought not to have posed major problems of integration; but they were practically all Roman Catholics, and the south-west of Scotland was the most strongly Protestant area of all, as the Covenanters had shown. Moreover, since the Irish were so much in need, they were prepared to accept still lower wages, poorer working conditions and more wretched housing, which the new masters of industry were quick to exploit. So enmity grew between the indigenous Scots and the newcomers, there were confrontations, riots, and the Irish tended to be herded into ghettos, classed even by the Scottish poor as second-class citizens. Glasgow and what is now called Strathclyde, with much of north Lanarkshire and Renfrewshire, has never entirely got over this problem.

It was not all negative, to be sure. There was a great increase of material wealth, even if only in a few pockets, and benefit from this was bound to rub off on others than the new manufacturers. These wanted fine houses, in town and country, and roads thereto, large numbers of servants, tradesmen to cater for their requirements; also better communications between factory areas and for the transport of supplies and goods, better port facilities and so on. So there was a ferment of construction in the land; but it was very much a material ferment, with the ancient spirit of the country at a low ebb.

Two causes did arise out of it all to seek improvement on the non-material front, one political, one religious – the Reform Bill agitation and the evangelical revival, which helped to lead to the Disruption of 1843. These movements were not specifically Scottish, indeed they both started in England and were a natural reaction to the new pressures. But the Scots manifestations had their own aspects and character. The Reform Bill rose out of the crying need to improve the parliamentary representation, which was still, as far as Scotland was concerned, the same as it had been at the Union of 1707, and was appallingly inadequate. The agitation was to get rid of the rotten burghs which were in the pockets of a few important people, who nominated the members to suit themselves; to increase the number of seats at Westminster; to greatly broaden the franchise – for many constituencies still had electorates of less than one hundred, these mainly landowners – and to improve local government and town-councils. Something was achieved, in the face of stubborn opposition from the authorities, and at a cost of much sacrifice. The Scots representation in the Commons was increased from 45 to 53, these 8 new seats to go to the burghs; and voting rights were extended from land-holders to lease-holders in the country constituencies, and to house-holders with a £10 qualification in the towns – not an earth-shattering improvement, but at least a step in the right direction. Politically the day of the common man was still only a vision.

The evangelical movement was concerned with church-government almost as much as with evangelism, especially in Scotland. In England the Established Church worship badly required a shake-up, having become formalised and class-ridden to a degree. In Scotland it was much less so, the Kirk nearer to the folk, less thirled to the upper classes – who, indeed tended to be quite largely Episcopalian or Catholic. But there was a grievous stumbling-block for many, the matter of patronage. This was a relic of the ancient pre-Reformation Church, when the livings of hundreds of parishes were vested in abbeys, priories and monasteries, whose heads had the right of appointment of the parish clergy. This had been stubbornly retained by the new Protestant gainers of the vast Church lands, for mainly financial and disciplinary reasons, and still remained in force, so that lords and lairds could appoint their own nominees to vacant kirk parishes, even when these superiors were Episcopal or Catholic adherents; and where they were not, it was common-place to appoint their own younger sons or kinsfolk, irrespective of quality or ability, by no means always to the advancement of the Christian message or pastoral care. Moreover there was the matter of the Oath of Abjuration. This was an oath which every parish minister was required to take, by law, on penalty of a fine of £500 for refusal, declaring that the sovereign ought to be a member of the Church of England, an utterly preposterous assertion for a Church of Scotland minister. Similarly a demand was issued from London that each Sunday the ministers must pray for King George IV and all the royal family – but specifically not for Queen Caroline, with whom George was at odds. This sort of folly aroused the ire of the Scots clergy, not unnaturally, and the evangelical or reform party were in the majority in the General Assembly.

In 1834 things came to a head. In Auchterarder parish, in Strathearn, a new minister was presented by the patron, who was objected to by a majority of the heads of families in the parish. The patron insisted, and when the Presbytery supported the parish, took the issue to the Court of Session – which found against the Presbytery. The brave Strathearn folk, many of them Drummonds, appealed to the House of Lords, who also took the part of the landowner and insisted on the new minister being installed. Meantime, another parish, Strathbogie in Aberdeenshire, the Gordon centre, had done the same; but when faced with the Lords' decision, that local Presbytery got cold feet and climbed down, and when no fewer than seven of its parish ministers protested, they were actually suspended by the Presbytery. Appeal was made against this suspension to the General Assembly of that year, 1841, but the Assembly leaders, left in no doubt of government and legal reaction, weakly toed the line and actually dismissed the seven clergymen from their ministry. This was just too much for many and, led by Dr Thomas Chalmers, over 400 parish ministers marched out of the

Assembly in 1843, left the Established Church altogether and formed the Free Church of Scotland. This was known as the Disruption and, in a country like Scotland where things spiritual and metaphysical had always been important, it had a profound effect. It was no mere gesture on the part of the protesting clergy, for it entailed very great sacrifice, the giving up of churches, stipends and manses. Many of the charges remained vacant and unfilled for years, the patrons and heritors often quietly pocketing the stipends.

George IV had died in 1830 and was succeeded by his brother William IV, an honest, quiet man very different from his flamboyant predecessor, a professional sailor, whose short reign was personally unspectacular and unremarkable, although major improvements were effected by his governments, for it was in his name that the Reform Acts were passed, the Poor Law legislation enacted, and slavery was abolished in the British colonies. William never came to Scotland and in his seven years' reign made little impact on his northern kingdom. He died in 1837, leaving no lawful issue by his German Queen Adelaide – but a swarm of ten offspring by his actress mistress Mrs Jordan. He was succeeded by his brother the Duke of Kent's eighteen year-old daughter, Victoria.

The Victorian era has a well-established popular image, sufficiently near in time to be a familiar concept for most of us. Yet so much of that image, of empire-building, seemingly endless prosperity, stuffy and self-satisfied rectitude and so on, should not apply to the entire reign. After all, Victoria was Queen for 63 years, longer than any other monarch before or since, and they were years of enormous change. The first third of the reign was very different from the second, and the second from the third. It was certainly not all peace and prosperity. There were Bread Riots and Chartist Riots and the Corn Laws had to be repealed – these had banned the import of foreign grain – and famine in Scotland in the years 1847–50 resulted in major emigration. There was insurrection in Ireland, and Canada was in a state of revolt. Whig and Tory governments rose and fell with alarming rapidity.

The extraordinary thing was that, in the midst of all this,

247

the newly-married young Queen should have fallen in love
with Scotland – although undoubtedly it had much to do
with her husband, Prince Albert of Saxe-Coburg-Gotha,
whom she had married in 1840. No doubt, before that, she
was, like her Uncle George, a devotee of the novels of Sir
Walter Scott, and their romantic and less-than-accurate
portrayal of the Scots was certainly reflected in the Queen's
subsequent attitude – for it must be recognised that Scott's
own view of his fellow-countrymen and their land was less
than realistic, as seen from the Edinburgh of the Enlighten-
ment, some interpretations, particularly of the Highlanders,
being almost laughable. The same could be said, of course,
of many of his talented, vocal contemporaries and successors.
So it is scarcely the Queen's fault if she developed a somewhat lop-sided and fanciful notion of her northern subjects.
At least it was a vast improvement on that of her predecessors
on the throne, even of George IV with his pink tights, kilt
and fortnight's visit. And her affection was genuine, and
significant in its results – for instance when her daughter the
Princess Louise became engaged to the Marquis of Lorne,
heir to MacCailean Mor, Duke of Argyll, Sir Henry
Ponsonby saw fit to congratulate the Queen on breaking the
tradition of always marrying off the royal family to foreigners,
and choosing an Englishman. Victoria answered: 'You speak
of him as a young Englishman, but he is *not*, he is a Scotsman
and a Highlander.' No monarch would have enunciated such
sentiments since Jamie the Saxt.

It is not always realised that it was Prince Albert who
bought the Balmoral estate on Deeside in 1852, not the
Queen herself. They had been renting the old castle of
Balmoral for four years, mainly for the deer-stalking – of
which more anon. Next year Albert began to build the great
Scottish Baronal palace which was to be the royal couple's
autumn home for so long – unfortunately they demolished
the genuine old Scots fortalice to do so, very typical of their
attitude. It was the Highlands and the Highlanders that the
Queen fell for, or a tartan-clad, romantic view of them, the
land of the mountain and the flood, and a noble and politely
respectful people, not too many of them, the source of her
splendid Highland regiments which were painting half the

world British Red for her. To be sure, this was a notable
change, after the proscription of the Highland dress, the
Disarming Acts and the behaviour of her great-great-uncle
Cumberland, added to the general English attitude that
Gaelic-speakers were barbarians and mountain scenery
'horrid'. It is worth remarking that the Queen never showed
a similar fondness for the Lowlands, and found her ancient
palace of Holyroodhouse, in Edinburgh, not to her taste, she
not being amused by the breweries which had sprung up
nearby. It is recounted that her disillusionment with Edinburgh was complete when, seeking a more salubrious resi-
dence than Holyrood, she took a fancy to the newly-erected
and magnificent building of Donaldson's Hospital, for poor
children and the deaf, set in its own grounds beyond Edinburgh's West End – and was refused it by its governors.
Victoria, as all the world was to learn, never forgot. Although
she spent so much of her time at Balmoral, and as a guest
at other Highland houses, her Scots capital saw little of her.

To revert to the deer-stalking. Albert, as a German princeling, was notably fond of the Germanic sport of shooting
deer, in his native forests; and it was Deeside's abundance
of red deer which took him and his wife to Balmoral in the
first place. It is interesting that this predilection, together
with the comparable sport of grouse-shooting, was to change
much of the economy and even the ecology of the Highland
area, affecting the way of life of its remaining people. For,
of course, what the royal family did, was soon to be copied,
not only by the aristocracy but by the large new wealthy
classes of the manufacturers, coal-masters, railway-builders,
contractors, India merchants and nabobs, and the rest, all
of whom must have deer-forests, grouse-moors and great
shooting-lodges at which to spend their autumns and entertain their guests. Now, deer and sheep no more go together
than do cattle and sheep. So, after a tenure of only a century,
the sheep had to go. These new landowners were not interested in making profits from their Highland properties, their
profits from industry and Empire were more than sufficient,
and the said empire seemed in no danger of blockade. The
Highlands were to be a picturesque recreation area for the
rich and important, even if only for six weeks in the year;

and the new folk of consequence in the glens and straths for the remaining forty-six weeks changed from sheep-farmers and shepherds to head-stalkers and gamekeepers. At least these tended to be Highlanders.

Thus Balmorality arrived, an odd change from the Clearances. The tartan was *de rigeur*, not for the Highlanders nor lower orders but for the 'toffs' as they were known, Scots ancestry had nothing to do with it, English Midlands manufacturers equally with London lords wearing kilts, plaids and long shaggy sporrans with great gusto if odd effect. Long-legged deer-hounds and wolf-hounds were the thing to own. Landseer, with his stags at eve and very still-life heaps of slain grouse, was the artist to patronise, and was duly knighted. And sham-castles and shooting-lodges sprouted up every glen and by every loch-side.

All this, of course, brought money and some people into the Highlands, and was certainly better than sheep, which needed so few to tend them. And by any standards we must take off our hats to the energy, initiative and sheer driving-force of those Victorian industrialists and others, who filled the empty glens with literally thousands of great houses. Consider the vastness of the conception, in a roadless, water-logged mountainous land. Today, to get even a mile of new road built demands much agitation, great financing, almost government involvement. But to erect mansion-houses and all their domestic appendages in remote areas required roads. So the Victorians built roads, out of their own pockets, by the thousand miles, and the necessary bridges, drainage-works, reservoirs and the rest, their energy and enthusiasm admirable indeed even if their taste was not always so. We tend to take it for granted that these large houses and imitation castles were always there; but before the mid-nineteenth century they were not. They tell us something vital about the Victorians.

The same spirit, of course, was sending these forefathers of ours out to the far corners of the earth, not only in colonising zeal and showing the flag, but in exploration, missionising, developing new lands. Nothing was too much for them to tackle, too great a challenge. Let us remember this when we talk slightingly of the Victorian age, as we are so apt to do. They achieved, they did what we would never contemplate doing or affording, and all without the advanced technology which is at our disposal.

Partly because conditions were not good at home, partly out of their natural individualism and personal enterprise, the Scots took a major share in this overseas exodus, far out of proportion to their numbers, ever in the forefront of empire-building, pioneering and pushing back the frontiers, so that more than any other small nation they left their names on the world-atlas, from the Mackenzie River to the Ross Sea, from Macquarie Island to the New Hebrides, from Livingstonia to Mount Mackinley; so that Scotland overseas became a synonym for adventure, courage, drive, organising ability, reliability. But at a price. In the 63 years of Victoria's reign, Scotland lost 1,400,000 of her best and most enterprising citizens by emigration, out of a total population of only 4 million, a percentage unequalled by any other people on earth. It was, no doubt, to the benefit of mankind in general, the newly-developing countries in particular, and in the main to the great advancement in living conditions, status and power of the emigrants themselves. But it left Scotland grievously weakened when strength was needed to assert and maintain her identity, especially with the continuing influx of the Irish. We are still paying for it all.

A word should be said about the 'overseas Scots', since it is computed that there are at least 20 million of them, four times as many as the present population of Scotland itself. They make quite a strange phenomenom, superficially almost more Scots than the indigenous variety, intensely proud of their roots, but few showing any desire to return, save on the occasional visit – and then often much disappointed in what they see. It is to be noted that, irrespective of background identity, their conception of Scottishness tends to be Highland rather than Lowland, with emphasis on the tartan, kilts, bagpipes, Highland Games and dancing, and of course nostalgic Jacobite songs. Clan, Caledonian and St Andrew societies and Burns clubs proliferate wherever even a few overseas Scots are to be found – which is all over the globe – the last perhaps seeming to clash rather with the Highland image, also with the prosperous leader-of-the-community character to which Scots seem to gravitate when outside their own country. For Burns was very much a Lowland peasant-farmer, with earthy attitudes. But perhaps the Highland link is there, after all. For, unsuspected by most, Robert Burns was almost certainly of Highland extraction – which would account for much in his life and temperament. I learned this from a doctor in Taynuilt, Argyll, many years ago. It seems that, in the late seventeenth century, an individual in the Taynuilt area, north of Oban, a Campbell like most others in that Campbell country, had the misfortune to kill a man in some unspecified affair, the sort of thing that could happen to any spirited Highlandman. Summoned before the sheriff – who naturally was also a Campbell – his judge found a certain amount of sympathy for the man's predicament, the victim obviously not being a Campbell; and after sentence, the sheriff had a quiet word with the malefactor. He indicated that the cell-door might well be left unlocked that night, and that if the condemned man was to slip quietly out and disappear thereafter to distant parts, never to show his face in the Campbell country again, he probably would be scarcely missed. Recognising good advice when he heard it, the murderer proved the cell-door theory to be accurate, and promptly disappeared eastwards into the night. He kept going eastwards until he could go no further, at the North sea coast near Stonehaven in Kincardineshire. And there he remained and put down new roots. Prudently, however, he changed his name from Campbell to an anglicisation of his home area of Taynuilt, which should really be Tigh-an-allt, the House on the Burn. So he called himself Burnhouse – and in the speech of the north-east this soon became Burness. Robert's father William Burness came south to the Lowlands of Ayrshire, but always retained that name. However, in the Ayrshire tongue it became Burns and thus his sons spelt it. So it looks as though the Bard was really a Campbell – a thought which, if generally accepted, might gravely affect the membership of certain Burns clubs. Tombstones and other memorials to the Burness family are still to be found in the Stonehaven and Montrose areas.

Some might say that the overseas Scot, to which might be added the London Scot, is in fact the more accurate personification of the true Scot than is his stay-at-home kindred, in that individualists of such intensity can never develop fully in the congestion of thousands of their own kind, with whom they are in continual disagreement inevitably. They cannot all be leaders, and consequently none are, and more united and less argumentative outsiders step in to lead them, whereas outwith Scotland, their natural energies and drive find scope amongst less combative folk, and they quickly rise to the top. It is a theory, at any rate.

Victoria did not die until 1901, and the final years of her long reign saw Scotland entering into modern times. By the end of it, the country's material position had improved undoubtedly, on many fronts, but whether in her spiritual and national state is open to question. The empire was still draining her man-power, the North-West Frontier of India and the Boer War typical of the calls on Scots soldiery. But at least parliamentary representation in the House of Commons had risen, in 1868 to 60 and in 1885 to 72, nearer the numerical proportion of the population, although English numbers increased also. And in 1885 the rule of the Lord Advocate, who had succeeded the old Secretaries of State as political king-pin for Scotland, and had resulted in great abuses, was ended and a more answerable Secretary for Scotland was instituted – it was not until 1926 that the Secretary was elevated to Cabinet rank and made Secretary of State once more. In that year too there was a small but significant improvement. Scots advocates appearing before the House of Lords, in appeal cases and so on, were required to wear the dress of English barristers. However a young Scots advocate protested and insisted on wearing the Scots dress, wig and gown, and reluctantly their lordships accepted the situation from then on.

In 1886, too, another reluctant response to long agitation in the Highlands and the activities of the Land League resulted in the Crofters Act legislation, a major advance for those coastal areas and the Hebrides, where the descendants of at least some of the dispossessed clans-folk of the Clearances had clung on, scratching difficult cultivation in patches of stony or sand-blown land, pasturing a few beasts and fishing the seas. Distant and unsympathetic landlords had borne heavily on even these crofters, and their numbers were falling each year, to the detriment of recruiting for the Highland regiments. The new legislation improved matters, under four main heads. Security of tenure was given, so that crofters could not be evicted at the whim of the landowner. Compensation was to be paid to outgoing crofters for their improvement of the land, stone-clearance, drainage and so on, and the erection of their own houses, hitherto unconsidered. A fair rent was to be fixed, consonant with what the land was worth, and in the event of dispute, the final decision would be made by a statutory Commission, later called the Land Court, and of its three members one was to be a Gaelic-speaker and one an experienced member of the Scots bar. That such provisions were necessary was in itself significant.

So Scotland faced the twentieth century still, despite all contrary influences, an identifiable nation, and that something of a miracle. But – what sort of a nation?

Looking back over these pages, it might seem as though the country's long story was little more than a series of disasters, betrayals, mistakes and follies. It was not, of course. There were good times, great advances, heroic periods and progress. But as, today, most of what the media serves up as news is bad, since good and normal improvement is not news, so quiet advancement and non-events do not make history.

There is a moral here somewhere.

POSTSCRIPT

The author's remit was to tell something of the story of Scotland's history, however inadequately, sketchily and summarily, with no intention of dealing with modern times. To deal with recent history would have demanded a very different approach and treatment, and one in which the writer would be all too apt to take sides – even though, in all the foregoing the discerning reader might just possibly imagine that he or she has detected some slight side-taking, and storytellers must have feelings or they would tell no stories.

So the story ends with the start of the twentieth century, dire and eventful, fateful as that was to be for Scotland along with the rest of mankind. As well to finish there, for the prospect of any coherent pattern-tracing would be daunting indeed, with emigration continuing – 630,000 no less leaving the country between 1911 and 1921 – two great world wars, the eclipse of empire, the rise of political socialism, of trade unions, of the lessened impact of religion and the consequent lowering of standards of behaviour – this to so large an extent leaving a vacuum in the basic Scots outlook – the explosion of technology, the increase of material wealth, leisure, taxation and higher education, and the grievous dominance of centralising influences – which means London – in the mass government, mass media, mass advertising, mass entertainment, mass everything; all of this affecting Scotland relentlessly and tending inevitably towards the elimination of national identity and consciousness. If it was a miracle that Scotland survived as a nation until the end of the nineteenth century, it is infinitely more so that she still does so today.

Can it continue? I am an optimist and believe that it can, and should, if the rest of mankind can survive its follies. The world has a real need of the Scots nation and what it has to offer, now perhaps more than ever; and that is said in no vaunting tone. I think that so characterful and individualistic a people *cannot* change its nature. Whether it is good or otherwise – it is certainly not indifferent or mediocre – is not the point. It is *different*. And that difference, having survived untold centuries, is unlikely to evaporate now, even under the pressures of modern conditions and centralisation. Somehow, as has always happened in the past, the Scots will resist the levelling process and bureaucratic control. Reading through this story, time and time again it seemed like the end; but the obstinate, awkward identity always overcame and survived. The Creator surely never made anything so odd, difficult, contrary, intriguing and unlikely as the Scot ever to let it fizzle out? One day the same Scots are going to reach out and take their destiny into their own hands again – and that will be the day!

INDEX

257

Index

Index